Journeys to Professional Excellence

Journeys to Professional Excellence

Stories of Courage, Innovation, and Risk-Taking in the Lives of Noted Psychologists and Counselors

Edited by

Frederic P. Bemak
George Mason University, Fairfax, Virginia

Robert K. Conyne
Professor Emeritus, University of Cincinnati

Los Angeles | London | New Delhi
Singapore | Washington DC | Melbourne

FOR INFORMATION:

SAGE Publications, Inc.
2455 Teller Road
Thousand Oaks, California 91320
E-mail: order@sagepub.com

SAGE Publications Ltd.
1 Oliver's Yard
55 City Road
London EC1Y 1SP
United Kingdom

SAGE Publications India Pvt. Ltd.
B 1/I 1 Mohan Cooperative Industrial Area
Mathura Road, New Delhi 110 044
India

SAGE Publications Asia-Pacific Pte. Ltd.
3 Church Street
#10-04 Samsung Hub
Singapore 049483

Copyright © 2018 by SAGE Publications, Inc.

Printed in the United States of America

ISBN (pbk): 978-1-5063-3714-2

Library of Congress Control Number: 2017942489

This book is printed on acid-free paper.

Acquisitions Editor: Abbie Rickard
Editorial Assistant: Alissa Nance
Production Editor: Kimaya Khashnobish
Copy Editor: Tina Hardy
Typesetter: C&M Digitals (P) Ltd.
Proofreader: Ellen Howard
Cover Designer: Scott Van Atta
Marketing Manager: Jenna Retana

SUSTAINABLE FORESTRY INITIATIVE   Certified Sourcing   www.sfiprogram.org   SFI-01075

17 18 19 20 21 10 9 8 7 6 5 4 3 2 1

Contents

Acknowledgments

Fred Bemak wishes to recognize individuals who have pursued social justice, equity, harmony, and a more humane world through their acts of courage, innovation, and originality that have enabled them to take chances and break new ground. I am especially grateful to those psychologists and counselors who have contributed the chapters in this book and have taken their valuable time to share their extraordinary stories and pass on words of wisdom to others in the mental health field. I offer my deepest gratitude to my coauthor, Bob Conyne—as always, it is good to work with the best. And finally, to my amazing wife and children, who are each making the world a better place with their work and passion, which inspire me to continue to march forward, I thank you.

Bob Conyne recognizes and honors all psychologists and counselors who have made a positive difference in the lives of people and society and expresses gratitude to his partner, Fred Bemak, in compiling the exceptional stories contained in this book.

We would also like to thank the following reviewers:

Mary Olufunmilayo Adekson
St. Bonaventure University

E. Anne Andrews
Thomas Nelson Community College

Anna A. Berardi
George Fox University

Andrew M. Byrne
Ohio University

Rochelle Cade
University of Mary Hardin–Baylor

Lynne Carroll
University of North Florida

Rita Chi-Ying Chung
George Mason University

Maria Cuddy-Casey
Immaculata University

Kathy DeOrnellas
Texas Woman's University

Amanda M. Evans
Auburn University

Kerrie R. Fineran
Indiana University–Purdue University Fort Wayne

Helen M. Garinger

Kristopher M. Goodrich
The University of New Mexico

Teresa J. Haase
Eastern Mennonite University

JoAnne Holbert-Quince
Wayne State University

Allison M. Hrovat
The College of Saint Rose

Enobong J. Inyang
Texas A&M University–Texarkana

Veronica I. Johnson
University of Montana

LaVerne K. Jordan
Colorado Christian University

Douglas Knutson
Oklahoma State University

Julie M. Koch
Oklahoma State University

Kurt L. Kraus
Shippensburg University of Pennsylvania

Aneneosa A. G. Okocha
University of Wisconsin–Whitewater

Angie C. Smith
North Carolina State University

Ingrid M. Tiegel
Carthage College

Renee Blocker Turner
University of Mary Hardin-Baylor

Felicia E. Ward
Texas A&M University–Commerce

1

Courage, Innovation, and Risk-Taking in Professional Journeys

By Robert K. Conyne and Frederic P. Bemak

Professional Journeys

We all are all living our lives with the richness of our experiences and personal journeys, sometimes by happenstance and sometimes with focused intentionality. This book is about life journeys and examines the "professional journeys" of notable psychologists, counselors, and academics. It describes each of their stories and the lessons we might learn from them to help illuminate our own journeys. One way to think of a professional journey is as "a work trek: a more-or-less focused wandering, full of highs and lows, ups and downs, as the Beatles said, 'a long and winding road' for many. But, if we are mindful, we can take away the obstructions to reflect and find the meaning that's there; to locate some magic in the ordinary" (Conyne, 2014, p. 15).

Through the lessons that emerge from the first-person accounts of the professional journeys contained in this book, we hope to highlight aspects of courage, innovation, and risk-taking. We believe these behaviors will be needed ever more within academia and the helping professions as people and the larger society confront significant challenges to psychological well-being, such as poverty, injustice, racism, homophobia, sexism, oppression, discrimination, civil and religious conflict, and powerlessness.

Courage

We have asked well-known psychology and counseling professionals to describe their successful professional lives and discuss how courage, innovation, and risk-taking influenced their professional careers. Our goal is to provide you with inspiration and support to continue—or, perhaps, to begin—injecting your own careers with these elements. We also seek to encourage faculty, educators, and practitioners to infuse training programs and practice with clear attention to these domains.

Along with wisdom, courage is considered to be a universal virtue (Snyder & Lopez, 2007), prized across cultures around the globe. In fact, Winston Churchill is credited with stressing that "courage is rightly esteemed the first of human qualities . . . because it is the quality which guarantees all others" (*Maxims*, 1949).

Courage is a multidimensional construct. Within the *Values in Action* classification system in positive psychology (Peterson & Seligman, 2004), courage is identified as one of six key character domains. It is considered to embody those emotional strengths that emphasize accomplishing goals in spite of strong internal or external opposition. These strengths include bravery, where a person steps forward and defines his or her behavior based on convictions about what is right and just for everyone, even if this is seen as unpopular in the eyes of others. Persistence is part of having courage so that despite barriers and obstacles to impede courageous actions, individuals persevere for the good of others. Thus courage would include having emotional strength, personal integrity, and an enthusiasm and zest for life and life's situations in order to speak the truth despite resistance and a lack of support by others.

The work examining courage has led to the classification of four broad types of courage (O'Byrne, Lopez, & Petersen, 2000). The first type is *physical* courage, which occurs when someone takes physical steps to help others in dangerous or perilous situations. This can be seen when someone rushes into a fire to save another person in a burning house, or intervenes with a group of bullies who are taunting and threatening an individual, or dives into shark-infested waters to rescue an individual who is being attacked by a shark. The second type of courage is classified as *moral* courage, which is shown when someone stands up for what is right and moral despite strong disapproval and the threat of rejection and social isolation.

Moral courage does not necessarily involve physical courage, since it is an action that demonstrates and makes a statement about a moral position. For example, Rosa Parks, who refused to move from her seat on the bus, which made a statement that established a tone for the entire civil rights movement, and the man who stood in front of the column of tanks that were there to suppress the demonstrations in Tiananmen Square in China, are examples of individuals displaying moral courage. The third type of courage is classified as *vital* courage. Vital courage relates to perseverance when despite personal and sometimes immutable obstacles, one continues to act and promote actions and activities that help oneself and others reach their goals, which improves lives and life's conditions. For example, Lauren Hill, who continued to play college basketball while terminally ill as she sought to draw attention and funding to prevent her disease from inflicting others in the future, and Magic Johnson, who publicly announced that he had contracted the HIV virus in order to promote treatment and research for HIV/AIDS, are illustrations of vital courage. The fourth type of courage is *psychological* courage, which is demonstrated when a person shows strength while confronting personal challenges, threats, destructive habits, or behavioral dysfunctions. Every day, untold numbers of people are buffeted by intense stressors, destructive relationships, unpredictable calamities, and consequences of their own negative behaviors. Coping with these difficult life events requires a psychological courage for which there is relatively little training available (Putnam, 1997).

Courage provides a primary bulwark that supports and drives many other attitudes and actions. Two of the main characteristics that we see as an essential link with courage are innovation and risk-taking. Given the prominence of these two virtues, we asked the contributing authors in this book to consider these two additional domains in their life reviews. For example, many of us are familiar with the courageous, innovative, and risk-taking life of Jackie Robinson, who confronted and withstood incessant racist insults and attacks when he entered professional baseball as the first African American to ever play in the major leagues. Thus in 1947 (and beyond), when he steadfastly broke the "color line" in the major leagues, despite persistent bigotry and racism from teammates, fans, and the public, his courage opened up formerly closed opportunities in many other areas beyond professional baseball for African Americans and other oppressed minorities in the United States. It has been said, when comparing the legacy of Jackie with that of the iconic baseball star, Babe Ruth, that "Ruth changed the way baseball was played; Jackie Robinson changed the way Americans thought" (Swain, 2006). Closer to home, the ordinary work lives of psychologists, counselors, and university faculty members often contain instances of inestimable courage. These professionals assist clients and students (or take action directly themselves) to challenge oppressive administrators and institutions that stifle creativity and good work, confront substance abuse, take on discrimination, find creative ways to continue the daily struggle of supporting and caring for a partner with depression, and far more. In many ways, we see courage as an umbrella term that covers and serves to motivate other related and important expressions of human thought and output.

Why are we according courage such a prominent place within the work of psychologists and counseling professionals? As we touched on earlier, it is important to realize that courage contributes substantially to the ability of people to more effectively cope on a daily basis with life's never-ending stressors and demands and enhance the quality of life for oneself and others. Seeing one's way through the desiderata of life, with ongoing challenges connected with managing work, relationships, finances, family, and life's demands, takes what might be called "ordinary courage." From the world of therapy, more particularly, it takes courage to do the right thing ethically in difficult situations or, with reference to prevention and social justice in mental health, to "swim upstream" against the strong tides of conventional practices. It requires courage to take on new professional roles, such as moving from what may have become a comfortable faculty role to a new one, such as a dean. It takes courage to become a client who challenges one's own ineffective or damaging attitudes and behaviors and who takes the risk to change.

Moreover, we hold biases that connect with courage. Dire life conditions, such as poverty or oppression, are lived by far too many people across the world and need desperately to be changed for the better, and there are civil conflicts and wars causing millions of people to flee their homes throughout the globe. Psychologists and counselors can make more significant contributions to help people in these types of situations than we are making at present. In order to become more effective in promoting needed change, practitioners and faculty must become increasingly aware of what we value, assertively act on those values, become engaged in innovative and creative practice and training, be willing to take appropriate risks, and—yes—be motivated by courage to challenge the status quo and challenge people and systems that may be blocking the growth and development of all people. We salute all those in psychology and counseling, both the "famous" (such as Viktor Frankl, who found meaning through his concentration camp experience and went on to develop the system of logotherapy), and those practitioners who have not achieved fame or glory but who stand courageously day after day with clients or students experiencing the incessant challenges of life and who challenge systems that create barriers for their client's growth and development. Courage as a psychologist, counselor, or faculty member requires more than just "doing one's job"; it necessitates going "above and beyond," with an aim for the improvement of psychological, social, and ecological health.

Courage, Innovation, and Risk-Taking: The Pathway to Personal and Systems Change

Helping others through counseling and psychotherapy is a good and noble thing, indeed. It brings relief and benefit to clients every day. Yet, dominant psychology and counseling practice and training models tend to place practitioners in responsive, if not passive, modes. Conyne (1987) labeled this traditional orientation the "counseling services paradigm," defining the focus on three dimensions that include targeting individuals one at a time, tackling already existing problems for remedial interventions, and delivering direct services face-to-face.

Certainly, courage, innovation, and risk-taking are involved when the traditional counseling services paradigm is invoked. It is satisfying and rewarding but not easy work. Listening and responding to clients who may present complex and high-risk situations, such as being abused, depressed, or suicidal, requires practitioners to possess not only expertise but also strength and courage. However, it is our contention—and bias—that it also is necessary for psychologists and counseling professionals to supplement this traditional way of working by seeking to influence changes in the conditions and systems that bring clients to their offices in the first place, that is, to exert a preventive effect that advocates for personal and social justice and to embed these concepts in training so they become part of one's work in psychology and counseling (Chung & Bemak, 2012; Conyne, 2015).

Engaging in change efforts of this kind requires many professionals to adopt what may be unfamiliar, unique, and sometimes uncomfortable approaches to practice and training. Changes in the way one is working as a practitioner or teacher may involve becoming more assertive, considering larger systems that impact clients and training, moving beyond one's office to become engaged in neighborhoods and communities, expanding one's network to collaborate and consult with others who may also be from different professional backgrounds, at times confronting power brokers and leaders in an organization or system, working toward social and environmental rather than limiting one's scope to personal change, adopting innovation and sometimes riskier strategies for promoting transformation, and being open to exploring new opportunities and methodologies.

In taking on these new behaviors and directions, practitioners and university faculty can build on their fundamental competencies and perspectives to expand traditional practice and training. Adopting innovation, courage, and risk-taking provides an expansion beyond the conventional way of working as a psychologist, counselor, or professor, embracing qualities such as collaborating, creating, consulting, confronting, challenging, asserting, and advocating. It certainly takes courage to move in these newer and riskier directions, kind of like swimming upstream against the tide. Bemak and Chung (2008) identified the "nice counselor syndrome," characterizing professional counselors (and psychologists) as placing greater emphasis on collegiality and professional coherence at the expense of advocating for systems change that will improve conditions for clientele and training. "In short, it is important to maintain courage in the face of resistance and have the bravery to take a stand for one's convictions and beliefs by understanding the historical tradition and successes upon which the future of multicultural/social justice advocacy is based" (Bemak & Chung, 2008, p. 380). We believe that larger numbers of courageous, innovative, and risk-taking practitioners are needed, more like those who are featured in this book. This outcome, though, will not be attained through individual efforts alone. It must be supported by training programs and related credentialing bodies: accreditation, licensure, and continuing education. Training and credentialing standards need to support future practitioners who are authentically caring and competent while taking risks to improve training and practice. It is our belief that in order to promote and embrace psychologists and counselors who move beyond convention, they will need support both to learn prevention and social advocacy theory and process and to nurture the courage, innovation, and risk-taking that are required to make these intentions possible.

The Stories

The 12 stories you will read are written by exceptional professionals in psychology and counseling. They write about experiencing the challenges and joys related to ethnic identity, moving from poverty, finding significance, dealing with immigrant status, exploring public policy, challenging the status quo, experiencing serendipity and exploring one's way, moving into new professional roles, and taking risks personally and professionally. These noted authors, with their chapter titles, are as follows:

Jean Maria Arrigo, "Peace to Our Ghosts"

Sharon L. Bowman, "Taking the Scenic Route: A Professional Journey"

Jean Lau Chin, "Journey to the West"

Y. Barry Chung, "My Journey as a Chinese Immigrant Counseling Psychologist"

Patrick H. DeLeon and Omni Cassidy, "Public Policy's Highly Personalized Nature"

Dorothy L. Espelage, "A Journey From a Single-Wide Trailer to the White House"

Cheryl Holcomb-McCoy, "Journey to Advance Equity: A Never-Ending Road"

Arthur M. Horne, "Prepared Serendipity Mixed With Naïve but Eager Curiosity"

Anthony J. Marsella, "Travels With a Contrarian Person, Psychologist, Activist: Becoming 'Radicalized' by Injustice, Violence, and Stasis"

Isaac Prilleltensky, "The Road to Mattering: Challenging the Status Quo, Promoting Wellness and Fairness"

Edil Torres-Rivera, "Buscando Mi Propio Camino: A Journey of Professional Identity and Honesty"

Melba J. T. Vasquez, "My Professional Journey"

How to Examine the Stories You Will Read

The stories contained in this book range across the fields of psychology and counseling. Authors have sought to trace their professional journeys, giving particular attention to courage, risk-taking, and innovation. How can you, the reader, approach these stories to derive personal meaning?

We suggest two ways. The first is to read intentionally, guided by the "road map" we have prepared, which follows. In short, this map will ask you to think of each author's professional journey in terms of historical influences, how the authors experienced their professional lives, any connection with courage and risk-taking and innovation, multicultural linkages, styles of working, future directions the authors envision, and specific advice they may have offered. While not every question will apply in each case, we think you will find applying this template to be generally helpful in facilitating your appreciation of the upcoming stories.

Professional Journeys "Road Map"

A. Past Influences of the Journey
  - How did the journey take this author to the psychology/counseling field?
  - Were there any significant life events that led the author to psychology/counseling?
  - Were there any significant life events that led the author to gain courage and become a risk taker?

- Were there any significant life events that led the author to become innovative in his or her professional career?
- What values or family influences contributed to the authors becoming courageous, a risk taker, and innovative?

B. Experiencing the Professional Journey

- How does it seem the journey has been for the author?
- What seem to be the most fulfilling moments?
- What may have been the most difficult moments?
- Were there any scary times when the author took a courageous stand or risk professionally?
- How did the author acquire confidence in his or her work?
- What does it seem the author has most valued over the years?
- What appears to have been most burdensome for the author?
- How has the author seemed to have "kept focus" and maintained courage in the midst of daily events and challenges?
- What does it seem were his or her biggest challenges?
- From what sources does it appear the author has gathered strength and support?
- How does it appear the author has been able to balance work and personal life?

C. Connection Between Professional Life, Courage, Risk-Taking, and Innovation

- What does it seem the author believes about people and change (e.g., the philosophy that is the foundation for his or her work in the psychology/counseling field)? How do courage, innovation, and risk-taking fit into these beliefs?
- What advice does the author provide for newcomers to the field related to risk-taking, courage, and innovation?
- What advice does the author give for people who are at a midcareer point in a psychology/counseling field related to risk-taking, courage, and innovation?

D. Development as a Multicultural Psychologist/Counselor

- When did the author seem to learn about or become aware of cultural diversity?
- How did the author learn about cultural diversity?
- Were there any key moments in the author's life that heightened his or her awareness and sensitivity, beyond his or her own culture?
- What significant personal and/or professional experiences did the author have that helped integrate cultural diversity into his or her work?
- What advice or suggestions does the author offer up-and-coming colleagues in the field regarding the development of multiculturalism as a line of research, practice, and/or service?
- What importance does the author suggest that innovation, risk-taking, and courage play in doing cross-cultural work?

E. Viewing the Author's Work Style and Accomplishments

- What is the author's work style?
- How does the author infuse creativity into his or her work style?
- Given the author's accomplishments, how has he or she approached taking risks professionally?
- What does the author seem to consider his or her biggest accomplishments and how was he or she able to do these things?
- What were some of the author's biggest challenges?
- What does it seem is the "secret" of the author's success?
- Where does the author get new ideas from?
- Does it seem it was difficult for the author to be courageous?
- In looking back, what does it seem the author learned?

F. What Does the Author Say About His or Her Future Journey?

- What more does the author seem to want to do?
- What does the author see as realistically coming next?
- Where does the author see the profession going?

G. What Advice Does the Author Give Younger Professionals?

- What's the author's advice for how graduate students can best prepare for becoming a courageous and innovative faculty member and/or future professional?
- How does the author see graduate training programs more fully supporting these directions?
- What "tips" does the author give to younger faculty members or practitioners for infusing courage, risk-taking, and innovation into their work?

A second way to gain from each professional journey story is to consciously address the following five questions and, in fact, to discuss them with another reader of these accounts.

Chapter Discussion Questions

1. Overall, identify three lessons you can take from this author's professional journey.

2. What seems to be a "key" factor supporting the author's progress toward becoming courageous?

3. How did this author's professional journey include courage, risk-taking, or innovation—or all three?

4. Indicate any connections between your journey so far and that of this author.

5. Suppose you were to meet with this author. What would you most like to ask him or her?

Our Intent: Inform and Challenge

We think you will find the chapters engrossing and enlightening. Our purpose in organizing and presenting them to you is both to inform you of how well-established and notable psychologists and counselors have taken risks, found courage, and been innovative, and to challenge all of us to be better professionals while making our professional lives significantly richer and more meaningful. We wish you happy and meaningful reading.

References

Bemak, F., & Chung, R. C.-Y. (2008). New professional roles and advocacy strategies for school counselors: A multicultural/social justice perspective to move beyond the nice counselor syndrome. *Journal of Counseling & Development, 86,* 372–381.

Chung, R. C.-Y., & Bemak, F. (2012). *Social justice counseling: The next steps beyond multiculturalism.* Thousand Oaks, CA: Sage.

Conyne, R. (1987). *Primary preventive counseling: Empowering people and systems.* Muncie, IN: Accelerated Development.

Conyne, R. (2014, Summer). On a long and winding road. In K. Smaalders (Ed.), *The banner* (p. 15). Seattle, WA: Seattle University.

Conyne, R. (2015). *Counseling for wellness and prevention: Helping people become empowered in systems and settings* (3rd ed.). New York, NY: Routledge.

Maxims and reflections of the Rt. Hon. Winston S. Churchill. (1949). Boston, MA: Houghton Mifflin. Retrieved from http://izquotes.com/quote/37150

O'Byrne, K., Lopez, S., & Petersen, S. (2000, August). *Building a theory of courage: A precursor to change?* Paper presented at the 108th Convention of the American Psychological Association, Washington, DC.

Peterson, C., & Seligman, M. (Eds.). (2004). *Character strengths and virtues: A handbook and classification.* New York, NY: Oxford University Press/American Psychological Association.

Putnam, D. (1997). Psychological courage. *Philosophy, Psychiatry, & Psychology, 4,* 1–11.

Snyder, C. R., & Lopez, S. (Eds.). (2007). *Positive psychology: The scientific and practical explorations of human strengths.* Thousand Oaks, CA: Sage.

Swain, R. (2006). Jackie Robinson. Retrieved from http://www.sabr.org/bioproj/person/bb9e2490

2

The Road to Mattering

Challenging the Status Quo, Promoting Wellness and Fairness

By Isaac Prilleltensky

N o PhD student had ever written a theoretical or philosophical dissertation in the Department of Psychology at the University of Manitoba until 1989. Empirical studies were the norm. A combination of chutzpah, innocence, courage, and a mild degree of stupidity propelled me to challenge convention in the very traditional department. Supported by my PhD advisor, Freddy Marcuse, I proposed to write a theoretical and philosophical critique of the conservative ideology of mainstream psychology. The dissertation would be called *Psychology and the Status Quo*. My main argument was that psychological theories and practices tended to redefine social problems into intrapsychic maladies. As a result, instead of focusing on social injustice, psychology helped society focus on personal inadequacies.

Growing up in Argentina during a dictatorship, I developed a precocious distrust of authorities, including the authority of scientific discourse. I had witnessed how the press and social science were used to suppress dissent. As a member of a youth movement opposing the military dictatorship, I was exposed to social critique early in life. From the age of about 12 to 16, I attended regular discussions of social issues, such as injustice, oppression, and dictatorships. They took place in a Zionist youth movement that aimed to promote peace and collectivist ideas in Israel and around the world. The movement was called Amos, after the prophet.

In the early and mid-1970s, many Jewish kids like me joined social movements in Argentina to fight fascism. In 1976, the situation was so dangerous that a group of us decided to leave the country and make aliyah, which means to ascend, or migrate, to Israel. Friends and family members opposing the regime would disappear or be killed in broad daylight in Argentina. My sister was a political prisoner there and was subsequently sent to exile in Paraguay, a cooperating regime. It took us seven years to reconnect with her.

The youth movement placed a lot of emphasis on what we might call today critical thinking. We critiqued articles, books, and political propaganda. We dissected popular culture and its ideology. This was a form of discourse analysis aimed at understanding how culture and politics reproduce the societal status quo. A famous book we read at the time was *Para leer al Pato Donald* (Dorfman & Mattelart, 1971), which was later translated into English as *How to Read Donald Duck* (Dorfman & Mattelart, 1975). The subtitle of the book was *Imperialist Ideology in the Disney Comic*.

The involvement of the CIA in toppling the democratically elected government of Salvador Allende in Chile in the early 1970s hit close to home (Dinges, 2004). Ariel Dorfman, the author of our guide to imperialism, was born in Buenos Aires, to Jewish parents from Odessa and Kishinev, the same part of the world where my ancestors came from. Dorfman lived in Argentina, Chile, and the United States. His counterculture *How to Read Donald Duck* (Dorfman & Mattelart, 1975) resonated very much with all of us who were struggling against fascism.

In Israel, I finished high school and my first two degrees. I lost my parents in a car accident when I was 8 years old, an experience that led me to psychology. I thought I could use my life experience to help others. While working on my master's degree in the Clinical Child Psychology program at Tel Aviv University, I was exposed mostly to psychoanalytic approaches. I read, on my own, the works of Erich Fromm, who was the most socially minded psychoanalyst I knew at the time. I loved his work, and I devoured all of his books. There was a bookstore in Tel Aviv where I remember finding a treasure trove of his works in Hebrew. Luckily, the books were used, so I could afford them.

When my wife and I moved to Canada in 1984, I wanted to pursue a doctorate in psychology. Since we were place bound, I applied only to the University of Manitoba and got accepted into the PhD program. I wanted to get into the clinical program, but I was not accepted. Instead, I was offered a spot in the Personality program, which I gladly took. There I met my wonderful advisor, Freddy Marcuse, who shared my worldview. Freddy was a cousin of Hebert Marcuse, who was one of the famous members of the Frankfurt School, along with Erich Fromm.

As a licensed school psychologist, I worked at the Child Guidance Clinic of Winnipeg during my doctoral studies. Working with kids from disadvantaged families solidified my desire to understand psychological problems in light of social problems. Working with clinicians who ignored social problems strengthened my interest in exploring how psychology masked social injustice. My own observations of how school psychology was being used to deflect social injustice, along with my early readings of Dorfman, Erich Fromm, and other critical thinkers, catalyzed my dissertation project.

Once I conceptualized the project, I had to convince the department to approve my proposal. With support from Freddy, we put together a committee that consisted of four psychology professors, one philosopher, and one professor of English who specialized in Marxist theory. I had six full professors on my committee, and they all approved the idea of a philosophical critique of psychology, but the department had a policy of giving the proposal to a "shadow" reviewer, who was not part of the committee. That "shadow" professor rejected the project.

It took some courage and determination to stand up to the rather conservative Department of Psychology and insist that, first, a theoretical dissertation was warranted; and second, I was capable of writing one. After a few agonizing weeks of back-and-forth among myself, my advisor, and the department chair, my proposal was approved. My dissertation was a critical review of major schools of thought in psychology, including psychoanalysis, behaviorism, cognitivism, and humanism. The dissertation also critiqued applied fields, such as clinical, school, and industrial/organizational psychology. The main thrust of my argument was that social context was missing from all of these fields of theory and practice. Consequently, psychology was handmaiden to society. If all of our problems are psychological in nature, there is no need to reform social structures (Prilleltensky, 1989, 1994).

The first battle, to get departmental approval for the project, was won, but I still needed to prove that my research was worthy of publication, the standard by which dissertations were measured. Determined to prove to my committee that my work was publishable, I decided to submit a summary of my argument for publication, before I completed the dissertation. I submitted it to the *American Psychologist,* and it was published there a few weeks before my defense (Prilleltensky, 1989). The timing could not be better.

Proposal, check. Committee, check. Publication, check. Now I had to convince an external examiner, outside of the University of Manitoba, that my work was original, relevant, scholarly, and important. I submitted names of three distinguished psychologists who could act as reviewers of my dissertation: George Albee, Ed Sampson, and Seymour Sarason. The department chose to send it to George Albee, who had been president of the American Psychological Association and was an outspoken critic of the psychology establishment. Albee wrote a glorious review of my dissertation, which helped.

Over the years, I got to know Albee and Sarason pretty well, and I met Sampson at conferences. The three of them were role models for me, and I owe them much gratitude for their mentorship and inspiration. As a young scholar challenging the establishment, it was vital to find role models. Albee and Sarason, with whom I developed a close relationship over the years, were absolutely wonderful to me. Albee wrote for me several letters of recommendation for jobs, and Sarason wrote a review for *Contemporary Psychology* (now called *PsycCRITIQUES*) of my first book, *The Morals and Politics of Psychology: Psychological Discourse and the Status Quo* (Prilleltensky, 1994), which was an outgrowth of my dissertation.

Throughout the dissertation process I felt pretty lonely, especially because I had chosen an unusual route and my topic was not mainstream. Neither the methods nor the contents were conventional. Reading the work of Sarason, Albee, and Sampson was very inspirational. The three of them were well-established psychologists who challenged the discipline to pay more attention to social context and social justice. Reaching out to them required a bit of courage, as I was just a young academic, but they responded in very caring and warm ways. It was wonderful to experience affirmation from distinguished and admired colleagues.

At the University of Manitoba, I felt like an outsider. Being an immigrant, choosing an unconventional topic for my research, and working at the Child Guidance Clinic—sometimes ful-time—during my studies prevented me from integrating fully into the life of the department. I hadn't imagined pursuing an academic career until the very end of my degree, at which point I started publishing. Following the publication of the *American Psychologist* paper, my advisor urged me to consider an academic career. I was thrilled to have published a paper in a very prestigious journal. Soon after publication, I started getting very positive feedback. I had tasted the forbidden fruit of publishing, and there was no going back.

Upon completion of the doctoral program, I continued working at the Child Guidance Clinic. However, I reduced my load to part time to devote time to writing. I used material from my dissertation to publish several papers that would help me land an academic job. I got two job interviews and was very lucky to get a position in the Community Psychology program at Wilfrid Laurier University in Waterloo, Ontario, Canada. I found there an intellectual home, and a wonderful mentor, my dearest friend and colleague Geoff Nelson. Nelson is one of the best psychologists I've ever met. He is a leading figure in community psychology and a wonderful researcher, scholar, teacher, and social justice activist. He introduced me to colleagues and helped in myriad ways.

At Wilfrid Laurier I remained a *sui generis* professor. I got tenure on the basis of mostly theoretical and philosophical writings. Although I had begun publishing some of my community-based research, it was the strength of my theoretical, moral, and political writings that helped me get tenure. Building on my dissertation work, I participated in the development of the critical psychology movement (Fox, Prilleltensky, & Austin, 2009; Prilleltensky, 1994). While my publication career was going well, it took a second paper in the *American Psychologist* in 1997 to bring some attention to my scholarship (Prilleltensky, 1997).

That paper required some courage and determination. The article dealt with values, assumptions, and practices in major fields of psychology and proposed an emancipatory-communitarian approach to well-being. The paper was sent back to me by the editor of the *American Psychologist* without review. There was a form letter attached to the note from the editor. The form listed several possible reasons why the paper was not being sent for review. Most of the reasons had to do with the paper not being perceived as relevant to a wide audience of psychologists. In response, I sent a polite but assertive letter to the editor contesting his decision not to send the paper for review. The editor ultimately sent the paper to several reviewers and it was eventually published. This 1997 paper got a lot of attention from a variety of quarters in psychology.

At that point, publishing had become not only an intellectual outlet but a social one as well. I met wonderful colleagues who first wrote to me about my papers and with whom I developed lasting friendships, like Dennis Fox. With Fox, I edited the first edition of *Critical Psychology: An Introduction* (Fox & Prilleltensky, 2009). Until I met Fox, I thought I knew how to write, but working with him made me very humble and a much better writer. He taught me how to write succinctly. He is one of the best writers I know and from whom I had the privilege of learning the craft of good prose. It was good to know though that there were folks more obsessive than me when it came to publishing, and I thank him.

By the mid-1990s, community psychology had become my professional home. I felt very welcome and appreciated in this wonderful field. Through the American Psychological Association Division of Community Psychology and the Society for Community Research and Action, I met inspiring colleagues doing important work at the intersection of what I came to call *wellness and fairness* (Prilleltensky, 2012).

I could not have maintained my convictions without the support of critical and community psychologists around the world. Herein lies my strongest recommendation for young scholars: Reach out to role models and enlist their support.

While the fields of critical and community psychology posited valid critiques of the status quo, within psychology and within society, they were not without limitations. I admonished critical psychology for its lack of social action (Davidson et al., 2006) and community psychology for its lack of attention to structural power (Prilleltensky, 2003, 2008). I needed to find a vocabulary to raise the commitment of both critical and community psychology to social transformation. I developed a new construct: *psychopolitical validity*. Hitherto, the concept of validity in psychology had been restricted to empirical methodologies. I introduced the notions of *epistemic* and *transformative psychopolitical* validity to bring attention to psychological and political power to understand and change society, respectively.

Following approximately a decade of research dealing with the moral dimensions of psychology, I turned my attention to the promotion of well-being in applied settings. I wanted to translate theory into practice. I published a few books striving to integrate psychological with social change (Nelson & Prilleltensky, 2010; Prilleltensky & Nelson, 2002; Prilleltensky, Nelson, & Peirson, 2001; Prilleltensky & Prilleltensky, 2006).

To integrate my emerging insights about well-being into a concise paradigm, I developed an approach called *SPEC,* which stands for *S*trengths, *P*revention, *E*mpowerment, and *C*ommunity change (Prilleltensky, 2005). Based on work with social services and community-based organizations, I realized that most efforts to improve well-being were flawed on four counts. The dominant models of help were (a) *D*eficit-oriented, (b) *R*eactive, (c) *A*lienating, and (d) *I*ndividualistic (the *DRAIN* approach).

The SPEC model was innovative in its synthesis of helping modalities into several continua. The time and place of help intersect into what I call the *contextual field*. Help can be proactive or reactive (time continuum), individualistic or collective (place of help continuum). The focus on participation and competencies intersect into what I labelled the *affirmation field*. Help can focus on strengths or deficits (capability continuum), and helpers can include citizens or alienate them in the process of help (participation continuum).

This model guided my community-based work for several years (Evans et al., 2011). It was clear to me that unless we radically changed how we address psychosocial problems, professional helpers were doomed to reproduce the societal status quo. My critique of the helping professions argued that most approaches followed the DRAIN approach. They were deficit oriented, reactive, and alienating of the people they wanted to help, and by and large they blamed the victims. This is largely a vestige of the medical model, which is highly reactive, expert driven, and arrogant. The SPEC model builds on people's strengths and assets. This is the only way to accord people the dignity they deserve. Moreover, people who struggle with psychosocial problems must be included in crafting solutions to their problems as opposed to the infantilization embodied in the medical model. Finally, the SPEC approach addresses structural injustice, as opposed to individual inadequacies.

A consistent theme throughout my career has been the integration of psychological with social well-being. I came to call this dual concern *wellness as fairness* (Prilleltensky, 2012). Without social fairness there cannot be personal wellness. Furthermore, to develop a sense of mattering, that our lives count, we require wellness as fairness. Mattering depends on recognition and impact (Prilleltensky, 2014). To feel recognized, valued, and appreciated, we need to experience wellness as fairness. These are social attributes. The recognition we gain from others, that we are valued, accepted, and welcomed, derives from psychological nourishment and from interpersonal and communal justice. To make an impact, in turn, we must experience both self-efficacy and opportunities in life. Without equal opportunity, or fair opportunities, it is difficult to experience impact.

The question of impact has concerned me for a long time. I realized that in order to move the needle on wellness as fairness, psychologists must find innovative ways to reach large audiences. The public at large needs to be educated on the connections between mental health and social health, personal suffering and inequality, family well-being and community conditions (Marmot, 2015). This concern led me to find new ways to spread the word about wellness as fairness. First, I started writing serious newspaper articles. Initially, I wrote a few articles for the *Kitchener-Waterloo Record,* my local paper in Ontario. Then I published a couple of pieces in the *Toronto Star* and *Maclean's,* Canada's leading weekly. With time, I found a more engaging way to talk about social issues: humor. In the last three years, I've been using satire to discuss topics related to personal and community well-being through my blog, *Going Wellnuts* (http://prilleltensky.blogspot.com), and newspaper columns in the *Miami Herald* and *Miami Today.*

To deliver a message that could be heard by many people, without eliciting defensive responses, I framed issues of well-being in terms of six dimensions: Interpersonal, Community, Occupational, Physical, Psychological, and Economic (I COPPE, pronounced *I cope*). Domains such as community, occupational, and economic well-being touch on justice and fairness and their impact on quality of life, happiness, and personal satisfaction (Prilleltensky et al., 2015). In my humor writings, I use the I COPPE framework to illuminate the connections between wellness as fairness.

Humor turned out to be not just an effective tool of mass communication but also a very enjoyable one. In the summer of 2015, I received an award from the National Newspaper Association for second best humor column. Encouraged by positive feedback and popular resonance, I wrote a humor book on well-being, *The Laughing Guide to Well-Being: Using Humor and Science to Become Happier and Healthier* (Prilleltensky, 2016).

Trying to get a humor book published required not so much courage and innovation as perseverance. Since I was not very well-known as a humor writer, it took a while to convince a publisher that I could combine humor with science to deliver an engaging message. I found it much more difficult to publish a popular book than an academic book.

My pursuit of engaging modalities took me from humor to technology. Given the ubiquitous nature of mobile devices and computers, I decided to develop a platform with games, videos, and coaching sessions online. Together with an amazing team of colleagues, including a software engineer, professors, and producers from the School of Communication at the University of Miami, and psychologists, methodologists, educators, and PhD students at the School of Education and Human Development at the University of Miami, we developed *Fun For Wellness*. This is an online program designed to teach essential skills for well-being. Built around vignettes with real actors, we introduce skills related to seven drivers of change: *B*ehaviors, *E*motions, *T*houghts, *I*nteractions, *C*ontext, *A*wareness, and *N*ext steps (BET I CAN). My wife, Dr. Ora Prilleltensky, wrote most of the contents of the program, while the rest of the team helped with the creation of games and interactive features of the platform. Adam McMahon, our software engineer, single-handedly created an amazing online program full of engaging activities.

To evaluate the effectiveness of *Fun For Wellness,* we conducted a randomized controlled trial with close to 500 participants. The results are very encouraging. Compared to the control group, people in the experimental condition report improvements in self-efficacy and in most I COPPE domains of well-being (Myers et al., 2017). This intervention has the potential to reach thousands of people in cost-effective and engaging ways.

This exciting project required not only innovation but a great deal of perseverance as well. Since we did not have major funding for it, we could not hire a team of software developers or subcontract the technical aspects to a software company. We also had to write and produce 36 videos, which required hiring professional actors, producing, and editing about two hours of work, which is more than a regular feature film. We had to be both patient and creative to produce a low-cost, high-quality psychoeducational intervention online.

When I reflect back on several projects I was involved in—from writing my dissertation, to promoting critical psychology, to publishing humor, to developing online interventions—a common factor emerges: delay of gratification.

A sense of mattering derives from multiple ways to have impact. Writing scholarly and humor pieces is a form of impact. Developing online interventions is another. Leadership is a form of impact that I had not yet tried in any formal way until 10 years ago. At that time, I decided to pursue a leadership role in academia. I became dean of the School of Education and Human Development at the University of Miami in 2006. Delay of gratification would also serve me well in the deanship.

One of my major goals as dean was to synergize three departments that dealt with different aspects of well-being. Teaching and Learning dealt mostly with educational development, Exercise and Sport Science with physical well-being, and Educational and Psychological Studies with psychological well-being. To unify the school, we created a new vision statement: "To be a center of excellence in the study, promotion, and integration of psychological, physical, and educational well-being in multicultural communities." It required some ingenuity to create a common purpose that would build on the strengths of different strands of the school. To further the cause of unity, we needed to change the name of the school from School of Education to something that would resonate with all members of our faculty. Following several rounds of conversations and consensus building, we changed the name of the school to School of Education and Human Development. Consensus building, patience, faculty participation, and a great dose of delay of gratification helped me achieve an important goal for the school.

To sharpen the focus on community well-being, we developed a series of new programs. We built an undergraduate program in Human and Social Development, a master's program in Community and Social Change, and a doctoral program in Community Well-Being. We also built a master's program in Education and Social Change. These new programs train hundreds of students in theories and practices that blend wellness with fairness. Creating new programs is a form of impact.

I believe that impact, creativity, and innovation derive from diversity of experiences. I grew up in Argentina and lived in Israel, Canada, Australia, and the United States. In addition to my three fluent languages (Spanish, Hebrew, and English), I study Italian and Portuguese. Being exposed to different cultures and social policies enriches your reservoir of ideas. Reading from a variety of fields also helps. In my case, I always had an interest in moral and political philosophy, public health, social policy, and more recently, humor. Collecting emotional, cultural, and intellectual experiences is the first step in innovation. The next step is doing something with these experiences. I like to incubate ideas. Before I commit to writing a paper or a proposal I draw diagrams, write words on pieces of paper, make connections among seemingly disparate ideas, and eventually create a meaningful and coherent concept. Since I've been asked by the editors to offer advice about working habits, here it is: Do not write anything before you have a clear outline of what you're going to write. Scholarly writing is like architecture. You wouldn't dream of constructing the kitchen before knowing exactly the dimensions of the living room and bedrooms. Academic writing is the same. You have to have a clear blueprint of your argument before you produce a single sentence.

Humor writing is totally different. That's why I like it so much. After years of thinking very analytically about ideas, humor affords me complete freedom and creativity with the sole purpose of generating laughter. Fusing my academic knowledge with my interest in humor has been a lot of fun. In humor, as in scholarly work, creativity emerges from connecting seemingly unrelated topics. It is all about making connections, logical ones in research, and illogical ones in humor.

The editors have asked me to reflect also on risk-taking. I've moved countries four times. Sometimes, I knew exactly what I was getting into, but sometimes I didn't. For example, moving to the southern part of the United States was a complete shock to us. We were living in Melbourne, Australia, when I was offered a job at Vanderbilt University. I was excited to work with wonderful colleagues at Vanderbilt in Peabody's College of Education and Human Development, a wonderful school. I had some reservations, however, about living in a rather conservative part of the country. We took a risk as a family, for which I have to thank my incredible wife Ora and our amazing son Matan, who have been willing participants in our family adventures. As it turned out, we loved Vanderbilt but could not easily get used to Nashville.

Moving to Australia was also a bit of a risk. I had a very good position at Wilfrid Laurier University in Canada, with wonderful and supportive colleagues. I was about to pursue full professorship in Canada when we started exploring Australia. I was invited to be a keynote speaker at the first International Conference in Critical Psychology in Sydney. I nearly rejected the invitation because I had done quite a bit of travel that year and did not have any funding. When the conference organizers offered to pay for half of my trip, I was convinced. I landed in Sydney in April 1999 to attend two conferences back-to-back: the International Society for Theoretical Psychology and the Millennium Conference in Critical Psychology. A few hours after I landed in Sydney I called Ora, my wife, and told her that we should move to Australia. She thought I was crazy. Back in North America I attended the Biennial Conference of the Division of Community Psychology at Yale University, where my colleague from Melbourne, Adrian Fisher, told me that they were looking for a research chair in his department at Victoria University. To make a long story short, I got the job, and in December 1999, we moved to Australia, six months after I first visited Sydney. Other than Fisher, we did not know anybody in Melbourne, so we took a risk as a family. In addition, I did not know much about Victoria University or higher education in general there. It was a risk worth taking, however. Our family loved living in Australia for three years. We met incredible people and enjoyed learning about the culture.

If you've read thus far and haven't fallen asleep, I wonder about your mental state. To make it up to you, let me end by offering some completely unproven advice:

1. If you think that writing an extensive outline is a waste of time, try submitting a paper without one.

2. Becoming an academic administrator is a wonderful thing. It's like having a colonoscopy in the woods. Historically, it makes the inquisition look like a piece of cake.

3. If you ever doubted that psychologists can engage in unethical behavior, read the Hoffman Report.

4. Try not to lose your parents at the age of 8. There are easier motivators to becoming a psychologist.

5. Some people's theories may make you laugh, but never confuse humor with academic writing.

6. If you are going to change the world one client at a time, take good care of your health. Based on current epidemiological data and longevity studies, it will take you 23,778,934 years. Most importantly, become a vegan like me and hit the treadmill.

7. If you didn't have a psychiatric disability before you read the new *DSM,* you will surely have one by the time you're done.

References

Davidson, H., Evans, S., Ganote, C., Henrickson, J., Jacobs-Priebe, L., Jones, D., . . . Riemer, M. (2006). Interdisciplinary critical scholarship on power and action: Implications for community psychology. *American Journal of Community Psychology, 38*(1–2), 35–49.

Dinges, J. (2004). *The condor years: How Pinochet and his allies brought terrorism to three continents.* New York, NY: New Press.

Dorfman, A., & Mattelart, A. (1971). *Para leer al Pato Donald* [How to read Donald Duck]. Valparaiso, Chile: Ediciones Universitarias de Valparaiso.

Dorfman, A., & Mattelart, A. (1975). *How to read Donald Duck.* Amsterdam, The Netherlands: International General.

Evans, S., Prilleltensky, O., McKenzie, A., Prilleltensky, I., Nogueras, D., Huggins, C., & Mescia, N. (2011). Promoting strengths, prevention, empowerment, and community change through organizational development: Lessons for research, theory, and practice. *Journal of Prevention and Intervention in the Community,* *39,* 50–64.

Fox, D., & Prilleltensky, I. (Eds.). (2009). *Critical psychology: An introduction.* London, UK: Sage.

Fox, D., Prilleltensky, I., & Austin, S. (Eds.). (2009). *Critical psychology: An introduction* (2nd ed.). London, UK: Sage.

Marmot, M. (2015). *The health gap: The challenge of an unequal world.* New York, NY: Bloomsbury.

Myers, N., Prilleltensky, I., Prilleltensky, O., McMahon, A., Dietz, S., & Rubenstein, C. (2017). *Fun for wellness: Results of a randomized controlled trial to promote well-being through an online platform with videos and games.* Manuscript in preparation.

Nelson, G., & Prilleltensky, I. (Eds.). (2010). *Community psychology: In pursuit of liberation and well-being* (2nd ed.). New York, NY: Palgrave/Macmillan.

Prilleltensky, I. (1989). Psychology and the status quo. *American Psychologist, 44,* 795–802.

Prilleltensky, I. (1994). *The morals and politics of psychology: Psychological discourse and the status quo.* Albany: State University of New York Press.

Prilleltensky, I. (1997). Values, assumptions, and practices: Assessing the moral implications of psychological discourse and action. *American Psychologist, 52,* 517–535.

Prilleltensky, I. (2003). Understanding and overcoming oppression: Towards psycho-political validity. *American Journal of Community Psychology, 31,* 195–202.

Prilleltensky, I. (2005). Promoting well-being: Time for a paradigm shift in health and human services. *Scandinavian Journal of Public Health, 33,* 53–60.

Prilleltensky, I. (2008). The role of power in wellness, oppression, and liberation: The promise of psychopolitical validity. *Journal of Community Psychology, 36,* 116–136.

Prilleltensky, I. (2012). Wellness as fairness. *American Journal of Community Psychology, 49,* 1–21. doi:10.1007/s10464-011-9448-8

Prilleltensky, I. (2014). Meaning-making, mattering, and thriving in community psychology: From co-optation to amelioration and transformation. *Psychosocial Intervention, 23,* 151–154.

Prilleltensky, I. (2016). *The laughing guide to well-being: Using humor and science to become happier and healthier.* New York, NY: Rowman & Littlefield.

Prilleltensky, I., Dietz, S., Prilleltensky, O., Myers, N., Rubenstein, C., Jin, Y., & McMahon, A. (2015). Assessing multidimensional well-being: Development and validation of the I COPPE scale. *Journal of Community Psychology, 43,* 199–226.

Prilleltensky, I., & Nelson, G. (2002). *Doing psychology critically: Making a difference in diverse settings.* New York, NY: Palgrave/Macmillan.

Prilleltensky, I., Nelson, G., & Peirson, L. (Eds.). (2001). *Promoting family wellness and preventing child maltreatment: Fundamentals for thinking and action.* Toronto, Ontario, Canada: University of Toronto Press.

Prilleltensky, I., & Prilleltensky, O. (2006). *Promoting well-being: Linking personal, organizational, and community change.* Hoboken, NJ: Wiley.

3

Peace to Our Ghosts

By Jean Maria Arrigo

The American Psychological Association (APA) Psychological Ethics and National Security (PENS) debacle over psychologists' roles in the War on Terror has commandeered my efforts since 2005. But I am driven by a different matter of conscience that overlapped the APA PENS course for a decade, an individual mission in the area of ethics of weapons development on human subjects. Others on mission may perhaps find useful methods or warnings in my "professional journey," or a sense of solidarity.

The Road Not Taken

Carl Jung's (1971) theory of personality types was all I knew of the field of psychology until my mid-40s. By this typology I am easily pegged as an introverted, intuitive, thinking type. At age 71, waking early today to frame this essay, I grieve for unfulfilled ventures in my natural domains.

I graduated Phi Beta Kappa in mathematics at the University of California (UC), Berkeley, in 1966, but left a doctoral program a year or so past the master's degree. Much later, amusing myself with a booklet of recreational IQ tests, I found I could not beat 106. It was my consistent failure at timed anagrams (e.g., EONCA —> OCEAN) that created the ceiling. Subsequent clinical cognitive testing revealed deficits in my visual processing and in my recall of uncontextualized information. I traced these deficits to a brain injury at age 9. This morning I pause to envision another life, in the flow of mathematics, still at the point of wonder in first apprehension of orders of infinity.

Entertainment as a Social Psychologist

I took my first psychology course in 1989 at age 45, by correspondence from the University of Colorado. I had been living alone for nine years after my first marriage to the most honorable man in my universe. On five acres of chaparral and boulders in the lap of Gaskill Peak in Alpine, California, I built a one-room cabin. It was my woodstove, carry-water, latrine-ditch hermitage. Twice a week I drove an hour west into San Diego to teach service courses at local colleges, mostly calculus for engineers and mathematics for prospective school teachers. Otherwise, visibly, I backpacked in the desert with a Sierra Club leader, took lessons in improvisational dance, and wrote stories for my informal storytelling troupe. Invisibly, I meditated, with no teachers but high-desert brush and stone. I think it was in my second summer of meditating three hours a day when I had a vision that has never lost its authority over me: A yard-thick brick wall blocked my way forward. A certainty arose in me then that I had to take social responsibility for what I *knew* before I could pass through that wall.

A quarter century earlier, at UC Berkeley, during the Free Speech Movement of 1965, I one day walked into an empty Ancient Near Eastern Literature classroom. My classmates, graduate theology students, were protesting the Vietnam War. How did skipping class oppose war? I "woke up" around 1985 when President Ronald Reagan proposed to invade Nicaragua. I spent two winter weeks with the Central American March for Peace and then returned in summer 1986—at the bottom of my bank account—with Peace Brigades International as a human shield for a Guatemalan human rights leader. I am haunted by the perennially barefoot Guatemalan child who begged to come home with me. She would be 40 now. From interviews, I wrote *Who Defies the Death Squads? A Storytelling of the Moral Development of Jesus Alfredo Campos, Former Salvadoran Judge and Professor of Political Science* (Arrigo & Campos, 1989). With friends, I performed it widely in San Diego County. But I sensed I had to apply myself *up* the chain of power, to the source of atrocities, not downward to the victims.

The seeds of that revelation were planted much earlier. In my youth I had provided operational support to anthropologists in U.S. military weapons development experiments on human subjects. That account is archived for a future context of believability, when the silencers have disappeared into their own safe silences. It was my direct knowledge of particular historical operations, albeit from a lowly perspective, for which I had to take social responsibility, sometime, somewhere, somehow.

Without a plan, I found myself attending local conferences on topics tangentially related to the weapons of concern: the anthropology of consciousness, dissociative disorders, and paranormal psychology. I heard social psychologist Ervin Staub (1989) theorize about the social process of mass killing during the Holocaust. There was an uproar in the International Society for Traumatic Stress Studies from audience members who believed that to explain is to excuse. But I *heard* Staub: To explain is to discern the means of transformation.

At a loss for direction, I turned to psychology, about which I knew nothing. Psychology, at least, was science, I consoled myself, having spent my first two years in UC Berkeley's College of Chemistry. And, curious about human extremes, I had deliberately engaged with people in prisons, insane asylums, and a nursing home. Maybe that would help.

On a maximum scholarship, I enrolled at Claremont Graduate University (CGU), three hours north of my cabin—adjacent to the 80-acre Rancho Santa Ana Botanic Garden of native plants where I walked every day. My mother, Nellie Gephardt Amondson, supported my project as her own. From CGU I sent her serial cartoon postcards, with regular news of Chicago park bum Uncle Beebee, the dogs for whom he interpreted, and his little niece Alice who accompanied me to classes. Passionate though I was in my psychology coursework, mental reservations about details of free will, causation, nomenclature, discarded outliers, and deception drove me into the Philosophy Department for courses in philosophy of science, epistemology, and ethics.

First Epiphany as a Psychologist

My graduate course in Roger Barker's (1968) ecological psychology required me to observe and describe a local "behavior setting," where persons act in fixed roles in a known program of activity, in a specific time and place. I leaned on the gated fence that enclosed a toddlers' playground, taking notes on parents and children at the bucket swings, the sliding boards, and the hemispheric jungle gym. At the swings parents were like gods, strapping in the toddlers and swinging them at will. Playful parents ran under swings or caught the bucket seats and paused midsweep to surprise their captives. By contrast, the hemispheric jungle gym, with small openings through triangular metal bars, left the parents helpless, with useless exhortations, once the toddlers climbed inside. "Jimmy, Jimmy, don't drop!" Jimmy lets go and thuds on the sand.

Thus I began to review the behavior settings through which I had passed in various roles. I considered monastic settings where I spent three-month retreats—focused sitting and walking meditation from 5 a.m. to 10 p.m., daily lectures by teachers, an occasional interview, ideologically perfect meals, no reading, no writing, no talking. I noted the hierarchy and clarity of social roles, the routinization of action, the minimalization of interpersonal engagement. I scrutinized the "ecological validity" of monastic spiritual practice. Why had I assumed that peace, compassion, and acuity of mind developed there would transfer, like a hospital hernia repair, to other, worldly settings? The fourth- and fifth-century Christian Desert Fathers whose sayings I contemplated; the sermon on detachment by the 13th-century mystic Meister Eckhart that I memorized in German; my Hindu teacher in my 20s, Eknath Easwaran; my Buddhist teachers in my 30s, Christopher Titmus and Jack Kornfield—I came to regard my spiritual teachers as specialists in metaphysical domains and social environments that did not accommodate my mission.

The Consense Reality as a Locus for Social Action

The goal of Solomon Asch's (1951) classic conformity experiment was to study the conditions that induce individuals to conform in the special case where the individual finds the group perception *obviously contrary to fact*. For each trial, the subject had to state aloud which of three comparison lines was the same length as the target line. But the subject followed seven confederates who all named the same incorrect comparison line. With no influence of confederates, fewer than 1% of subjects made errors. But, following the confederates, only a quarter of subjects never conformed. Fully conforming subjects even transferred the culture of error to newcomers in subsequent trials. More than simple conformity, it struck me as an exhibit of the social construction of the consensus reality.

The constellation of the consensus reality had mystified me. In grammar school I was a popular child, but I recall bewilderment at the omnipresent competitive games. How could anyone care who "won"? For relief, I designed a diagonal pathway of noncommercial properties across the Monopoly board and proposed erratic Parcheesi tokens. In junior high, I complied with tribal requirements of self-presentation, even as cheerleader, but never felt intrinsic motivation. In high school and college I deliberately tested many norms, retreating just before censure. The psychedelic era of UC Berkeley culture passed me by. My own explorations were enough: sitting in the dark, staring long into mirrors. I took advanced classes in topics of no evident advantage to me—Søren Kierkegaard, Seed Plant Taxonomy, Latin IV. I was always searching for something *more*.

In my wilderness cabin, two decades later, my search came to its source. During a summer of high-risk meditation, I devised techniques of exploration. Extrapolating from mindfulness meditation, I tracked distress, not peacefulness. Extrapolating from my improvisational dance class, I moved until arrested by postures of felt significance, which I held and experienced intently. Three weeks of outdoors movement meditation concluded each day with a hand held high, gripping air. Then it came to me: In that pose I was an infant holding the hand of my grandfather, Robert S. Gephardt (1894–1985). Two years ago, cleaning my mother's garage, I found a photograph: my arm held high, my hand disappearing in his, me at age 1, Grandpa at age 50. He was my primary caretaker until age 3 while my mother worked a weather-station night shift. Then we moved to join my father, home late from the war, in Fort Lee, Virginia. A CGU course in children's autobiographical memory grounded my homemade techniques in cognitive science.

Grandpa was a self-taught Theosophist, from age 15 on the Great Plains in a sod house. In the late 1800s, western travelers to the east returned with an amalgam of Eastern religions called Theosophy. It circulated among intellectuals, such as William Butler Yeats. After retirement from the weather bureau, Grandpa spent his final years in Theosophical Society facilities. I pieced together the story, with episodes from my mother, aunts, and cousins. Grandpa had tried to train me from birth, his first grandchild, as a spiritual adept. With an intuitive grasp of infant brain plasticity, he visited most of his 19 subsequent grandchildren soon after birth. By Grandpa's reckoning, we were his associates from former lives, reborn with *karmic* opportunity for his early training of us.

Through a concatenation of discoveries, I came to understand the consensus reality as a mental locale for social action, which my mission would require. This understanding inadvertently rendered me a sort of informal counseling psychologist for a dozen isolated government whistle-blowers, "throwaway" covert operatives, and victims of bizarre weapons development experiments. Through my later role in the APA PENS debacle, I have also come to mentor a few young psychologists. Where social advocacy generates opposition, the activist must navigate with a durable public persona.

The Study of Weapons
Development on Human Subjects

For my dissertation study, I thought I had a clever idea. I would interview military members of the National Association of Radiation Survivors (NARS) who were both *victims* of the atomic tests and *facilitators*. From their integration of these conflicting perspectives, I intended to create a model for victim-perpetrator moral deliberations in the ethics of weapons development. However, when my interviewees spoke of facilitation, they used only military schemas. When they spoke of their own travails, they used only victim schemas. When I pressed hard for integration of facilitator and victim perspectives, the interviewees became irrational, nihilistic, or numb. What I found was fierce dissociation, not integration, in the facilitator-victim conflict.

In a CGU human rights course, I understood why study of the victims was not the tactic for me. Every kind of weapon—mustard gas, radiation, psychoactive drugs—generates a different world of tragic circumstances for victims. But the motivations of weapons developers are unrelated to the long-term miseries of victims. Focus on these miseries misses their ideological-political-military-institutional causes. I had to touch the causes.

So instead of moral discourse between facilitators and victims, I aimed for discourse among intelligence professionals, scientists, and ethicists. With former intelligence analysts and operatives, some from NARS, I developed six basic premises for an epistemology of intelligence from which other principles could be deduced. For example, the premise that "The goal of knowledge is preparation for action" necessitates, when urgent, action with incomplete justification. Similarly, I developed five premises for *as-is,* not ideal, ethics of intelligence. For example, "There is no ultimate recourse to third-party adjudication to defend the good against the evil" implies that those who defend the Constitution at times cannot adhere to it. In this framework, then, tractable moral problems resulting from incompetence, corruption, and power plays are distinguished from intractable moral problems resulting from epistemic method. The sciences, too, are fraught with such intractable moral problems, as arise in randomized double-blind medical trials and social psychology deception experiments.

Early in the course of my interviews, a postwar operative showed me a forbidden film of a psychiatric experiment. I came under months of harassment, as my interviewee had warned. It began with a telephone call to my department from someone posing as a disgruntled interviewee. I obtained informal affidavits from all my interviewees to clear my research. Then a man, unknown to the operative, approached me with accurate details from a conversation between the operative and me; there was a break-in at my apartment without theft; and related events accumulated. My department resorted to denial. I kept my bearings in monthly examinations of conscience, continuing to this day, with bioethicist James Dwyer. Years before, we had made a pact to prepare ourselves for the moment of death. To anyone on mission, I would recommend an agent of accountability outside the domain of one's engagement.

At the end, my dissertation committee consisted of only environmental psychologist Stuart Oskamp from my department. Four intrepid outsiders were moral philosopher Charles Young and social sciences philosopher Alfred Louch at CGU, professor of strategy and diplomacy Harold William Rood (a former Army intelligence officer) at nearby Claremont McKenna College, and, in Houston, retired social psychologist Paul Secord (1976), famous advocate in the 1970s for a taxonomy of contexts for human behavior. They still reside as modules of intellectual resources in my mind. And I note that a wide network of resolute supporters is good insurance for controversial studies.

I finished *Sins and Salvations in Clandestine Scientific Research: A Social Psychological and Epistemological Inquiry* (Arrigo, 1999) at age 53. In the process, I shifted from the traditional "name, blame, and shame" approach in human rights work to insider moral action with intelligence professionals of conscience.

The Obdurate Financial Reality

From fieldwork across many societies, anthropologist Alan Fiske (1992) proposed a typology of Four Elementary Forms of Human Relations: Market Pricing, as in commercial transactions between strangers; Authority Ranking, as in unequal exchanges between role players in hierarchical institutions; Equality Matching, as in reciprocal exchanges between friends; and Communal Sharing, as in uncalculated sharing in nuclear families. This reductionist schema startled me, because I saw a black hole in my first quadrant, Market Pricing—owing to Grandpa's ministrations in infancy, I suppose. It had never occurred to me at UC Berkeley that education should result in a job. Although a star student at CGU, upon graduation in 1999 I submitted an application for one impossible position. Sensible classmates submitted 40 applications for possible positions.

In 2000, at the end of a short contract to write ethical guidelines for a College of Pharmacy, an SUV traveling 45 mph (by police report) struck my stopped Honda from behind. A shearing of my corpus callosum disrupted right-brain, left-brain communications. Daily yoga classes—"cross your right knee over your left and look right"—sort of reconnected me again, although with lingering losses. By evidence of my curriculum vitae, I was somewhat productive, as in a previously arranged, spring 2001, Rockefeller Fellowship on Violence and Culture at the University of Virginia. There I best recall walking along a train track, listening to the whistle, but not thinking "train" until an engine appeared around the bend and I leapt out of the way. Three or four years were hazy.

While at CGU I remarried, to John Crigler, whom I met at a Zen retreat. He was a mischievous person with a degree in music composition, five guitars, and a financial services business. Around 2004, his latent hepatitis C advanced. Debilitating clinical trials drew me into his business, at each stage just enough to keep things going. With five harrowing financial examinations behind me now, I am licensed as an insurance agent, stockbroker, and financial advisor. Limited by software frustrations (the visual processing deficit again), I have been of some use with customer, partner, and broker dealer relations; regulations and compliance; reconnaissance of products and services; and written presentations. But without that elementary form of human relations called Market Pricing, I sell nothing.

For a psychologist with an unauthorizable mission, I recommend attention to funding, perhaps from another domain. With a time machine I would persuade myself retroactively.

Giving Voice to "Intelligence Professionals of Conscience"

As I nevertheless continued my oral histories, I came to conceive of my work as assisting insider personnel in the development of ethics of operations research and covert operations. Intelligence professionals I interviewed had moral experiences at the extremes, some so unusual that right conduct was difficult to discern. Their experiences and reflections had no venue for discussion in their agencies. As a low-keyed approach, I archived their oral histories, along with interview commentaries from relevant experts for accountability. I envisioned a future when these documents could enter the moral discourse for national security personnel. My *Oral History Series on Ethics of Intelligence and Weapons Development* (Arrigo, 2004a) is in Bancroft Library at UC Berkeley. My *Intelligence Ethics Collection* (Arrigo, 2005) is in Hoover Institution Archives at Stanford, with items such as the 1994 court martial records of antitorture whistle-blower Lawrence Rockwood (2003).

As interviewees aged, I preserved critical documents for some, such as Harry Wagner (2013), Psychological Operations Officer for the U.S. Embassy in Saigon (1966–1968). When the NARS (2010) folded, I arranged for its medical and association records to go to UC Berkeley. I also supervised oral histories and archival deposits by others, such as "The Papers and Oral History of Elizabeth Rauscher, PhD" (Rauscher, 2012), a maverick physicist who conducted classified paranormal research for the government.

For a half dozen "intelligence professionals of conscience," I arranged extensive speaking tours. One was Tashi Namgyal (2000), the Dalai Lama's head of security from 1998 to 1999. Especially when asked to speak on the APA PENS debacle, I invited intelligence professionals to accompany me as copresenters, for instance, retired Army counterintelligence operative David DeBatto (2008) to Universidade de São Paulo. In the Iraq War, DeBatto had worked extensively with psychologists.

In a failed attempt at continuity, I initiated the Intelligence Ethics Section at the Joint Services Conference on Professional Ethics (JSCOPE) in 2004 and then the International Intelligence Ethics Association (IIEA) in 2005. In 2006 (Shane, 2006) and 2007, we put on two-day conferences, back-to-back, with JSCOPE. On return from the 2007 conference, my doctor's office called to say routine blood tests indicated I had chronic kidney disease, Stage 3, despite the absence of known risk factors. Misinformation from a kidney specialist led me to suppose that in a year I would need dialysis. I withdrew from the IIEA board to put my affairs in order. The move of JSCOPE to the West Coast and the recession of 2008 eventually sank the IIEA. Annual blood tests detect no change in my kidney function. But I keenly feel the press of time. And I lost the IIEA.

Most fruitful, I think, were the closed seminars that built community and resulted in action. In 2000, moral philosopher Charles Young gathered fellow philosophers, and I gathered operatives, for a closed ethics workshop. Young argued that no consistent moral theory could be created to encompass all levels of conduct from individuals to groups to government. I reported on this intense workshop to JSCOPE (Arrigo, 2001).

The philosophers-operatives workshop included a poet and my husband with a guitar, in an attempt to ponder ethics without divisive political reflexes. In our nonprofit Project on Ethics and Art in Testimony, John and I pursued this path for several years. One performance was *Redemption from Black Operations* (Arrigo, Koepfinger, Crigler, Ely, & Gemini Theater, 2001) at Carnegie Mellon University, with actors and singers from Gemini Theater, and retired Soviet technical intelligence analyst Herb Ely. Thus interviewees became coactors.

With the descent of the United States into torture interrogation of War on Terror detainees, I consulted earlier interviewees to write a comprehensive argument against torture interrogation (Arrigo, 2004b). It covered historical background and alleged psychological mechanisms for the efficacy of torture, societal implications, and the global military experience of degradation of chain of command. When some officers thanked me at JSCOPE for explaining "why we don't need to torture," I felt the strength of social psychology.

Beginning with the high-minded, existentialist interrogator Ray Bennett, a dozen, mostly retired, intelligence professionals contacted me, seeking outsider help to end the abuses and the shame. Colleagues and I organized three product-oriented weekend seminars: *Seminar for Psychologists and Interrogators on Rethinking the Psychology of Torture* (Arrigo & Wagner, 2007); *Psychology and Military Intelligence Casebook on Ethics of Interrogation, Training, Treatment, and Research* (Arrigo, Bennett, & Soldz, 2008); and *The Ethics of Operational Psychology Workshop* (Soldz, Arrigo, & Olson, 2015).

My mother, now frail and slow at age 94, still picks up neighborhood trash when she goes out with her walker. My work is like hers: many impediments, much effort, little to show, but inexorable. I feel that preparation for failure is essential in order to continue.

The 2005 APA Pens Task Force

For me personally, Stanley Milgram's (1974) survey of 39 psychiatrists was the most illuminating psychological study. Milgram asked psychiatrists to estimate the percentage of participants in his basic obedience experiments who, in the role of "teacher," would follow the researcher's instructions to shock the confederate "learner" in response to memory errors, to the meter level of "Danger—Severe Shock." In spite of psychiatry's predilection for the dark side of human nature, the survey respondents' estimate of 0.01% fell far short of the actual 66% (Milgram, 1974). The survey taught me that my own reports of weapons development experiments on human subjects could never be credible (except to a few operatives I know). But Milgram's survey teaches us all it was an easy exercise for elements of the Department of Defense to obscure psychologists' facilitation of potentially abusive interrogations and detentions in the War on Terror.

My "moral bad luck" (in ethicists' jargon) was an unsought appointment to the 2005 APA Presidential Task Force on PENS. Our ostensible task was to write guidelines for psychologists as consultants to interrogations (Arrigo,

2006). The worst day for me was the first, when I walked into an APA boardroom scenario that Asch himself might have planned. For 2½ days, 14 or so confederates and a previously vetted conformist provided a setting to induce conformity in two unwitting subjects, psychologist Michael Wessells and myself. Name cards sat us on the same side of the table, each flanked by staunch confederates, in a configuration preventing eye contact between us. No agenda was presented, and no writing materials were on the table. There was silence when a military member in uniform told me not to take notes. There was silence when the APA president-elect said I should have stayed home if I wanted APA to recommend investigation of psychologists' conduct in interrogations. Complete confidentiality was imposed in the guise of a spontaneous vote. I voted "no" but was bound just the same.

Like Asch's anxious, compliant subjects, my sense of reality wavered that day. At night I called home to my husband, who had broker's experience with corporate boards. He told me to stick out the meeting and learn what I could, that outside forces likely governed events in the room. In retrospect, I recognize intimations from APA authorities that things could go well for me professionally if I cooperated, but, blind to Market Pricing, I was unaffected.

Two years later, revelation of task force conflicts of interest broke my promise to secrecy. My counterintelligence contacts, David DeBatto and Lawrence Rockwood, reviewed my list of disclosed and undisclosed task force participants. They quickly declared the PENS Task Force "a social legitimization of a decision made at a higher level" of government (DeBatto, 2007). And that is what I reported, naming all undisclosed participants, to the APA Mini-Convention on Ethics and Interrogations in August 2007—a talk unexpectedly posted online by *Democracy Now!* (Arrigo & Goodman, 2007).

In 2015, a cache of revelatory emails from deceased CIA contractor Scott Gerwehr provided the "smoking gun" to prove intelligence agency control of the task force (Soldz, Raymond, & Reisner, 2015). An independent review by former federal prosecutor David Hoffman (2015) found that collusion between APA staff and Department of Defense representatives provided cover for psychologists in abusive interrogations. One after another, APA staff and elected officials exonerated themselves, saying they had been fooled. Like Milgram's psychiatrists, I think, what they did not know was their own capacity for harmful compliant behavior.

To any reformers I want to say, borrowing from Barker and Asch, that institutional settings are naturally populated with confederates of the authorities, or the settings could not accomplish their stated programs of activity. An isolated truth, like my 2007 exposé to the APA board, can be futile. The savvy, deep-research, swift-response team of the Coalition for an Ethical Psychology is what it took for my piece of the truth to penetrate at all the consensus reality of APA governance. The coalition consists of psychologists Trudy Bond, Yosuf Brody, Roy Eidelson, Brad Olson, Steven Reisner, Stephen Soldz, Bryant Welch, and me—networked with such membership organizations as Psychologists for Social Responsibility and Physicians for Human Rights, other dissident factions such as WithholdAPAdues, Harvard Law School Human Rights Clinic, and other attorneys, ethicists, journalists, and especially military and intelligence professionals. Because of them, some moral progress may evolve from the APA PENS debacle. Otherwise, there is just an APA scandal and then a return to business as usual.

Peace to Our Ghosts

I find myself with a faith in the historical truth to bring peace to the ghosts of the APA PENS tragedy. To this end, archivist Bruce Montgomery and I established the APA PENS Debate Collection (Arrigo, Montgomery, & Parker, 2010), with its dozens of photos and videos, hundreds of blogs, tens of thousands of LISTSERV communications, many series of private correspondence, a bewilderment of official documents, and paraphernalia from protests, with some items temporarily restricted. And my own ghosts of weapons development may come to peace in the record of human subjects experiments I preserve in the *Jean Maria Arrigo Papers* (Arrigo, in press), searchable under this name and available in 2030.

Acknowledgments

Roy Eidelson contributed to the intelligibility of this account, John Crigler to the specificity, and Jack O'Brien to the immediacy.

References

Arrigo, J. M. (1999). *Sins and salvations in clandestine scientific research: A social psychological and epistemological inquiry* (Unpublished doctoral dissertation). Claremont Graduate University, Claremont, CA.

Arrigo, J. M. (2001, January 25). *A pilot workshop on the ethics of political and military intelligence for insiders and outsiders.* Paper presented to the Joint Services Conference on Professional Ethics, Springfield, VA. Retrieved from http://isme.tamu.edu/JSCOPE01/Arrigo01.html

Arrigo, J. M. (2004a). *Oral history series on ethics of intelligence and weapons development*. Berkeley: Regional Oral History Office, Bancroft Library, University of California.

Arrigo, J. M. (2004b). A utilitarian argument against torture interrogation of terrorists. *Science and Engineering Ethics, 10,* 543–572.

Arrigo, J. M. (2005). *Intelligence ethics collection*. Stanford, CA: Hoover Institution Archives, Hoover Institution on War, Revolution, and Peace, Stanford University.

Arrigo, J. M. (2006). *Unofficial records of the APA PENS Task Force*. Intelligence Ethics Collection. Stanford, CA: Hoover Institution Archives, Stanford University.

Arrigo, J. M. (in press). *Jean Maria Arrigo papers*. Boulder: Norlin Library, University of Colorado; Durham, NC: Human Rights Archive, Duke University.

Arrigo, J. M., Bennett, R., & Soldz, S. (2008). *Psychology and military intelligence casebook on ethics of interrogation meeting*. Retrieved from http://www.pmicasebook .com/PMI_Casebook/Origins.html

Arrigo, J. M., & Campos, J. A. (1989). *Who defies the death squads? A storytelling of the moral development of Jesus Alfredo Campos, former Salvadoran judge and professor of political science*. Durham, NC: Human Rights Archive, Duke University.

Arrigo, J. M., & Goodman, A. (2007, August 20). APA interrogation task force member Dr. Jean Maria Arrigo exposes group's ties to military. *Democracy Now!* Retrieved from http://www.democracynow.org/2007/8/20/apa_interrogation_ task_force_member_dr

Arrigo, J. M., Koepfinger, C., Crigler, J., Ely, H., & Gemini Theater. (2001, October 29). *Redemption from black operations*. The University Lecture Series. Pittsburgh, PA: Carnegie Mellon University.

Arrigo, J. M., Montgomery, B. P., & Parker, R. E. (2010). *The APA PENS debate collection*. Durham, NC: Human Rights Archive, Duke University.

Arrigo, J. M., & Wagner, R. V. (2007). Psychologists and military interrogators rethink the psychology of torture. *Peace and Conflict, 13,* 393–398.

Asch, S. E. (1951). Effects of group pressure upon the modification and distortion of judgments. In H. Guetzkow (Ed.), *Groups, leadership, and men* (pp. 222–236). Pittsburgh, PA: Carnegie Mellon University Press.

Barker, R. G. (1968). *Ecological psychology*. Stanford, CA: Stanford University Press.

DeBatto, D. (2007, June 10). *A counterintelligence perspective on the APA PENS Task Force—David DeBatto* [Telephone interview]. Records of the APA PENS Debate. Intelligence Ethics Collection. Stanford, CA: Hoover Institution Archives, Stanford University.

DeBatto, D. (2008, June 17). *A counterintelligence operative reflects on psychologists as clinicians in the Iraq War. Interviewed by J. M. Arrigo*. Intelligence Ethics Collection. Stanford, CA: Hoover Institution Archives, Stanford University.

Fiske, A. P. (1992). The four elementary forms of sociality. *Psychological Review, 99,* 689–723.

Hoffman, D. H. (2015). *Independent review relating to APA ethics guidelines, national security interrogations, and torture*. Retrieved from http://www.apa .org/independent-review/revised-report.pdf

Jung, C. G. (1971). *Psychological types*. Princeton, NJ: Princeton University Press.

Milgram, S. (1974). *Obedience to authority*. New York, NY: Harper & Row.

Namgyal, T. (2000, January 15–16). *The security-sanctity dilemma of the Tibetan government-in-exile. Interviewed by J. M. Arrigo*. Ethics of Intelligence and Weapons Development Oral History Collection. Berkeley: Bancroft Library, Regional Oral History Office, University of California.

National Association of Radiation Survivors (NARS). (2010). National Association of Radiation Survivors Collection. Berkeley: Bancroft Library, Regional Oral History Office, University of California.

Rauscher, E. (2012). *Papers and oral history of Elizabeth Rauscher, PhD*. Berkeley: Bancroft Library, Regional Oral History Office, University of California.

Rockwood, L. (2003, November 18). *Moral and spiritual initiative by a U.S. Army counterintelligence officer. Interviewed by J. M. Arrigo*. Intelligence Ethics Collection. Stanford, CA: Hoover Institution Archives, Stanford University.

Secord, P. F. (1976). Social psychology in search of a paradigm. *Personality and Social Psychology Bulletin, 3*, 41–50.

Shane, S. (2006, January 28). An exotic tool for espionage: Moral compass. *The New York Times*. Retrieved from http://www.nytimes.com/2006/01/28/politics/28ethics.html?pagewanted=all&_r=0

Soldz, S., Arrigo, J. M., & Olson, B. (2015, September 20). *The Brookline principles on the ethical practice of operational psychology*. Retrieved from http://psychintegrity.org/wp-content/uploads/2015/10/Brookline-Principles-of-Ethics-of-Op-Psych.pdf

Soldz, S., Raymond, N., & Reisner, S. (2015, April). All the president's psychologists. *International New York Times*. Retrieved from http://www.scra27.org/files/9614/3777/1227/Soldz_Raymond_and_Resiner_All_the_Presidents_Psychologists.pdf

Staub, E. (1989). *The roots of evil: The origins of genocide and other group violence*. New York, NY: Cambridge University Press.

Wagner, H. (2013). *Papers of Harry Wagner, psychological operations officer for the US Embassy in Saigon, 1966–1968*. Lubbock: Vietnam Archive, Texas Tech University.

4

Taking the Scenic Route

A Professional Journey

By Sharon L. Bowman

There is something both freeing and scary about reflecting on one's professional journey. Doing this act requires that I really focus on my history, but to a great extent I also must focus on my future. As an academic in a graduate program, I often challenge my students to think about their own journey, reflecting on the messages they want to share with others along the way. Thus, the decision to discuss my own path in this chapter is a natural progression in my own developmental process.

To help frame my story, I should first share my worldview, which governs how I teach, conduct therapy, run meetings, provide supervision—basically how I walk through the world on a daily basis. At its foundation, my perspective is cognitive-humanistic (Glasser, 1999; Hayes, 2012; Wampold, 2007). In short, I operate on the assumption that the people I meet are traveling along their path (the more humanistic piece of my thinking). My role is to travel beside them, seeing what they see, and highlighting areas along the path that are ignored or avoided. For example, if the individual is focusing only on the trees, I will point out the gravel and the flowers, or vice versa. If the individual is 30 feet off the self-defined path, I will highlight that fact as we try to establish which is the desired path. I don't need to define someone else's path; I just need to understand how it works and where the individual is going before I can learn what to do to assist. The cognitive piece of this perspective stems primarily from reality therapy (Glasser, 1999; Wubholding, 2000). My focus becomes the here-and-now consequences of our travels. When we come to a fork in the road, that is, when a decision must be made, I help the individual delineate the possible paths and the consequences for each. It is the individual's responsibility to choose the preferred path. The overarching goal for me, then, is facilitating the individual's progress a little farther along the path than he or she was before.

There is also a diversity foundation to my worldview. I cannot look at the individual without considering the influence of her or his background, for example, age, ethnicity, disability, socioeconomic status (SES), nationality, and sexual identity. I was long ago influenced by ideas from Linda James Myers's (1993) concept of optimal psychology ("I Am because You Are") in shaping a collective perspective. More recently, I became intrigued by the concepts of cultural psychology (Kitayama & Cohen, 2010) and the influence of cultural practices on psychological health. And, while I don't consciously identify as a feminist, I have also been influenced by the work of both feminist and multiculturalist perspectives as addressed in Enns and Williams's (2013) *The Oxford Handbook of Feminist Multicultural Counseling Psychology.*

In late 2014, I developed my professional self-study as part of my application for board certification in counseling psychology. I was gratified to realize my worldview remains fairly congruent with how I actually present myself to the world. I have overtly identified myself as cognitive/humanistic since 1988. However, while formulating my self-study, I realized that the cultural perspective to my worldview had never been discussed. I consider it integral to my work, but somehow I had not verbalized that until I wrote the self-study. Further examination led me to cultural psychology, and now my professional self-concept seems complete. With these brief paragraphs as foundational to understanding my history, I can describe my journey.

Past Influences on My Professional Journey

I often tell students the "story" of my path to counseling psychology. I was raised in Columbus, Ohio, the oldest of three children, and only daughter, to an African American mail carrier from Columbus and an African American housewife from a small town in Georgia. Our neighborhood was overwhelmingly African American and working class, filled with stay-at-home moms and working dads who wanted a better life for their kids. We lived across the street from the neighborhood elementary school. I was a "watcher," an observer of people at an early age. I was content to sit quietly in the background and not necessarily draw attention to myself. I would, however, come out of the corner to defend the underdog at every opportunity, even in first grade.

Over the years, I have recognized that I am a composite of my parents' personalities and sensibilities. My mother taught me to listen to the ramblings of others, smile and nod, but not necessarily share of myself without a very good reason. She was a Southern woman, raised to fully understand the need to be silent in order to remain safe. She avoided trouble as much as she could, and she wanted her children to do the same. Strangers never truly knew what she was thinking, as she seemed to believe that sharing her thoughts could easily backfire and come back on her. I reflect that aspect in my own life on a daily basis. I can be quite enigmatic, and the inability to fully "read" my expression often stirs a sense of anxiety in other people.

My father, on the other hand, was raised in the Northern United States. He, too, understood issues of safety, but he did not believe in reticence or backing down from a fight. His opinion was always obvious, if not always appreciated by others. He took leadership when required, and he wanted his children to do the same. Being the leader and taking charge, my father reasoned, reduced the likelihood of following someone else's lead into trouble. Further, he pressed us to be pioneers, to try new things, even if no one "who looked like us" was doing it. If we waited for someone else to first "discover" the activity, we could be waiting forever; nothing should be prohibited to us just because we are African American. My father's words often come to mind when I am faced with a new opportunity. I've accepted countless personal and professional experiences, and leadership roles, because I took the risk instead of waiting for someone else to go first.

My sixth-grade teacher, a White man (in a predominantly Black school, no less), told my parents that I was "college material." From that point on, my parents made it clear that I would be going to college, and I understood that I needed to choose a major. I eventually opted for social work, but my father vetoed it because social workers didn't make enough money.

Through the magic of some vocational flash cards in the guidance office, I learned about "psychologist" as a career option and settled on it almost immediately. Early on, I understood only that meant being a psychologist in private practice. Near the end of high school, I visited a residential treatment institution of some nature; I remember only that the residents/patients had very severe issues. By the end of that day, I had equated "severe patient" with "clinical psychologist" and quickly decided I wanted to be a counseling psychologist. I always assumed I would be in a practice position at the end of my training, shifting location with each subsequent degree: from undergraduate degree (psychology; private practice) to master's degree (counseling psychology; community mental health or corrections) and doctoral degree (counseling psychology; university counseling center). I did not expect to be where I am today: an academic and administrator with a private practice on the side. As an aside, being a psychologist is who I am, not only what I do; my psychological understanding of the world operates constantly, even during my avocational pursuits.

Graduate School Experiences

There were a number of surprises and fortuitous links along the way to earning those degrees and becoming licensed as a psychologist. The first surprise came in my junior year of college when I suddenly realized that I would have to go to graduate school to achieve my dreams (never mind that I had been the graduate assistant for social psychology doctoral students and thus KNEW about graduate school). I was really unhappy in college and wanted to quickly end a difficult experience; the idea of even more schooling was horrible. That was the closest I ever came to dropping my major in favor of something more practical, like nursing (which, in retrospect, I am certain I would have hated). Fairly quickly I realized that nothing else would satisfy my curiosity about people's motivations and stressors or allow me to assist them with resolutions. Obviously, I kept on the original path to finish that first degree.

The second surprise came in my master's program, as I increased my awareness of being the "other." During that period, all of the master's students were White American, except for two international students and myself. I was the only American ethnic minority student in the master's program; I had no family nearby, and I did not know the community well. Thus, my support system, in relation to ethnicity, was not strong. I had to decide how to manage this feeling of "otherness" and not allow it to keep me from achieving my goals. Those two years helped me begin to frame my identity, though I did not begin to fully embrace my identity until the latter years of my doctoral program.

The next surprise came in my doctoral program, where people continued to assert their perspectives about who I should be as an ethnic minority student. In my experience, my undergraduate education was about what we did in the classroom, while my master's training incorporated other experiences (e.g., practicum, research training). My doctoral training, though, was really less about what happened in class and much more about personal and professional growth via mentors, practicum training, peers, and professional networking. Self-reflection was crucial to my development, as I needed time to incorporate varying experiences into my perspective. In particular, several of my professors, all of them men, expressed strong opinions about who I was or should be as a psychologist (a woman, a minority, a minority woman). As they become more insistent, I saw that I would need to form my own definition. In other words, their definition of a Black psychologist, or a woman psychologist, revealed some fairly tight, stereotypical perspectives on those roles. Those stereotypes did not adequately describe me; instead, I was pushed into forming my own understanding of an African American female counseling psychologist.

The introvert in me gave way to the extrovert; I found my voice in those four years of school. I spoke up when a faculty member insisted that ethnic minority students commonly struggle with understanding statistics (this occurred in conversation with another African American graduate student who was, in fact, struggling in statistics). The faculty member tried to use me as an example in support of his contention. Instead, I noted that I did not have this "universal" problem with statistics, as I had been consistently successful in several statistics courses. The faculty member expressed his bias regarding ethnic minority students' struggles at other times during my training; I eventually accepted that there was little I could say or do that would deter him from that belief. The best I could do was continue to disavow those assumptions, lest I appear complicit in them.

Becoming an Academician

During my doctoral program, I learned that I could be an effective instructor. As an introvert, standing in front of a classroom is not fun for me. I had to find something to say to those expectant faces in front of me or at least some way to entertain them. The day my advisor first suggested I should become an academic, I thought he was crazy, and probably said it aloud. He persisted, however, and the idea was planted in my head. Each semester that I taught, I weighed my future vocational path based on whether the class went well; I reasoned that an unsuccessful semester was a sign that I should not become a professor. Conversely, if a class *did* go well in a particular semester, I did not consider it the definitive sign that I should be an academic; thus, the cards were always stacked against me to enjoy my teaching experience. Funny enough, I recall having only one "bad" class; it was an early morning, summer course, and the students were singularly unmotivated to be there. I consciously put that class aside as an aberration and assessed their feedback as irrelevant to my own decision-making process. Even then, I did not openly embrace the academic path until internship, as I began applying for jobs (academic positions are generally advertised before clinical ones). I surmised I could always land a clinical position if the academic ones did not pan out. As it turned out, my second job interview was for a Ball State University (BSU) position; I have been here ever since.

My Professional Journey

Development as a Multicultural Psychologist/Counselor

I have referenced my awakening to diversity throughout this chapter, but I'll make some more explicit statements here. I am an African American, heterosexual woman with a doctoral degree, teaching at a predominantly White university in a small, conservative, primarily White community. I am constantly aware of my individual diversity and the cultural diversity of my department and community. When I was initially elected as department chair over 20 years ago, I became the first African American department chair at BSU and was one of probably seven women chairs. Among approximately 900 faculty members, maybe 14 identified as African American then (today's numbers are not very different). I am aware of my uniqueness in nearly every professional meeting on campus. Texts such as that by Benjamin (1997) remind me that an African American female faculty member's experience can be a lonely one but that her existence also has a significant purpose, whether on an historically Black campus or a predominantly White one.

Over 20 years ago, I attended the Winter Roundtable in New York City, a long-running conference devoted to cultural issues in psychology and education organized by faculty in Teachers College at Columbia University. While there, I had the opportunity to chat with pioneering counseling psychologist and African American woman, Janet Helms, and another newly minted African American female counseling psychology professor, Suzette Speight. We began a tally of the number of African American women teaching in American Psychological Association (APA)-accredited doctoral counseling psychology programs. Between us, we could name maybe 14. It was sobering to realize that we needed only three hands to count our sisters. While there are certainly more of us now, I have never forgotten the importance of my role in diversifying the academic arena, and I always take it quite seriously, especially when it comes to mentoring students to find their own voices and move forward as social change agents (Gormley, 2013).

As I noted earlier, I became aware of cultural difference as a child when a White child spit at my mother and me as we passed his parked car. As I grew older, I was usually pretty aware of the ethnicity of people around me and how it seemed to influence experiences. It was most noticeable when I was in junior high school, where the student body was diverse. In consultation with my parents, I made a conscious decision to attend a predominantly White high school instead of a predominantly Black one since I knew, even then, which one would have a more positive impact on my future college plans. My high school friends were a culturally diverse group and the smartest kids in the school; my parents did not raise a fool, so I knew that friendship with this cohort influenced my own standing in the school. This high school was 20 minutes from my house but may well have been in another county in relation to the SES differences among us. Even if I wanted to ignore ethnicity, I was confronted by the difference when my school friends were not allowed to visit my neighborhood (though I was more or less welcome to visit theirs). To their credit, my friends were appalled by the admonitions of our teachers and their parents and did not let those reactions affect our friendships. I walked in two different worlds, that of my White, Asian, and biracial friends in high school, and my African American friends and neighbors in my home community. Being bicultural had become second nature to me.

On a professional level, my cultural development was put to the test in my first semester as a faculty member, when I taught both our undergraduate and graduate diversity courses. Most of us who teach diversity courses will concur that such courses challenge our self-assumptions; if taught in a way that challenges the students, the teaching evaluations will likely be low. It is not a course for the faint of heart; and new, untenured professors may want to have a frank discussion with their department chairs about potential backlash before they tackle the class.

In my case, my most significant challenge came from an African American male student who was quite distanced from me (according to him, our only similarity was ethnicity). Every week, he complained about comments made by other students or by me; other students were angry at him but generally remained silent. Near midsemester, we experienced the inevitable blowup (or what I now can see as inevitable), in which the student exploded in anger and then left in the middle of class. The rest of the students, mostly White, deflected their frustrations with him onto me—to wit, I must have agreed with his anti-White diatribe because I did not immediately refute his statements. It was so hard to sit still through the students' expressions of anger before they could vocalize their fears. It was even harder to navigate my own reactions to the whole experience and not take it personally. Over that semester, other faculty members regularly discussed my class, igniting a wave of reactions throughout the department. In three months, I had a crash course in class management, while my students got a real-life experience in diversity dialogues.

In the years since, I have offered the following advice to neophyte instructors of diversity courses. First, consider how you are going to teach the class. If your goal is to encourage students' skills in self-reflection, be prepared for backlash as they take things personally. Second, be prepared for all manner of personal reaction to the content and process of the semester. While you may be sensitive to your own development on this topic, students have a way of inadvertently pushing "buttons" you didn't know existed. Many capable instructors for my department's undergraduate and graduate diversity courses have walked away in tears, frustration, or both, after a class session. Third, accept that not every student is going to develop a more enlightened attitude. Some will become more sensitive to diversity issues, others will remain on a plateau, while a small third group may regress. Much like conducting therapy, an instructor has to have faith in the process because the true effects may not be obvious until well after the semester ends. Fourth, be flexible, be flexible, be flexible. When you challenge a student's assumptions or push buttons to encourage growth, you have to know that different players will hear the message in a variety of ways. Think about multiple ways to get your message across to different groups of students. Finally, be courageous. I can't reiterate enough that teaching this class is a challenge. I am not suggesting that instructors should constantly look for a fight, but I am saying that one must be strong and confident. Looking and sounding fearful is, in this instance, a guarantee that the class will get out of control quickly.

Work Style: How to Keep Going Every Day

There is a running joke among my students and faculty that I never sleep (sadly, it is closer to the truth than I care to admit). Trying to sneak a message past me in the wee hours, thinking I won't see it until much later, can backfire on the sender; it is not uncommon for me to send a 3:00 a.m. missive simply because I happen to wake up at that time. I am also heavily connected to my electronic devices (laptop, tablet, phone), so I am rarely far from one or more of them. In reality, while I do check my email regularly, it is because I get 100-plus emails a day. If I don't keep on top of it, things will quickly get out of hand.

People are often surprised by what I do outside of my psychology world. I have a pretty large creative streak; I make art quilts, do other handcrafts, and bake often. I am fortunate enough to have a large blank wall in my office where I hang a different quilt every few months. I regularly bake breads, cookies, or other items; I love the feel of dough in my hands. Both my academic and private practice offices benefit from my floured hands, as

I usually bake much more than we can consume at home. In short, I MAKE things, crafting tangible products that use a different section of my brain and keep my hands busy. The opportunity to do these things allows the "always-spinning" psychology wheel to continue processing problems in the back of my mind. I also crave the low-tech experience of writing with fountain pens and other writing implements. I may live by electronic devices, but I decompress with slow, old-school techniques. As an introvert by nature, these extracurricular activities allow me to relax.

I challenge my students and my clients to step outside of their boxes, too. Whether that means reading for leisure, taking a mental health day when needed, or picking up a new hobby, I encourage others to give themselves a break. The same is true when it comes to balancing work, school, and family issues. We do not live in a vacuum; life keeps going when we aren't looking. Sometimes we have to give attention to our partners, children, and pets, both for their sanity and for our own. It is easier to point this out to others, of course, than to live by my own rules, but sometimes I get reminded that my husband, my dog, and my extended family need my attention, too. When I least think I have time to take a break is when I most need to do it. I agree with the adage that no one ever died wishing for one more day of work.

Where Am I Going Next, and How Would I Advise Someone Else?

I have accomplished many things since graduation, although I did not have a long-term plan in mind. In most cases, I never seriously considered the next opportunity until someone else suggested it. At those points, I would take the suggestion under advisement, consult with trusted advisors, and then decide whether to accept the opportunity. Early on, I rarely proactively sought out an opportunity, but I've gotten better about that over the years. One of my best experiences came as president of the Society of Counseling Psychology (APA's Division 17); more recently, I had an unsuccessful run for APA president. In my professional circle, I suppose it doesn't get much higher than those elected positions.

That begs the question, what am I going to do next? It is time for a new professional challenge, and it appears to be coming in my academic job, as my department is poised for a significant transition from our long-time home in Teachers College to a newly formed College of Health. One thing I have learned (finally!) is to try to manage only one huge change at once. In our new college, we will work in conjunction with other health and mental health professionals in training to highlight the importance of integrated health care. This academic overhaul will need to supersede almost anything else I might consider for the next year or so.

Preparing for the Future

I am a cautionary tale; students should do what I say, not necessarily try to follow my path. I made a last-minute decision to apply to doctoral programs and was fortunate to be accepted into one of the top programs in the country. That is NOT how potential students should make such an important decision about their training. Graduate education is not easy; the leap from undergraduate education to graduate school is bigger than the leap from high school to college. As professionals in training, students must think about the big picture; classroom learning alone will not make them marketable after graduation. Graduate school does not work if students arrive without a plan of action. It is okay if the plan changes in the middle of training, but they must have a reasonable plan on which to build the foundation for their graduate school experience.

I also believe that students must find their "voice," or learn to speak up and speak out when faced with an ethical dilemma, social justice issue, or a potentially difficult dialogue. I've learned that students often hold two mindsets. First, they seem to fervently believe that psychologists and counselors should be generally nice people; that niceness, however, deters them from voicing a complaint or dissenting opinion, or confronting a problem. The second mindset they tend to hold is that speaking one's mind is dangerous in some way, possibly leading to a bad reputation with the academic department or the new job. When I point out the double standard this reticence to speak poses for their work (i.e., it seems unfair to challenge their clients to be assertive if the therapists aren't willing to challenge themselves), students begin to reconsider their position. It is essential that students learn to speak up when it is professionally and/or ethically indicated. Speaking out serves as a model for clients and younger peers. They may also find it safer to practice their professional assertiveness while they still have the support and guidance of the faculty. Through their advisors, they often become aware that the worst thing that could happen in response to one of their questions is that someone will say no. We won't kick them out of their program for raising a question; to the contrary, they may ignite something that changes the program.

As trainers, if we want to create innovative professionals we need to introduce the students and new professionals to opportunities to share their perspectives, even if the comments are not uniformly positive. As senior professionals, we can respectfully ask questions of our junior colleagues and students about the climate of the department—then listen to what is said and try to effect change. Constantly and consistently encourage dialogue, and facilitate implementing new ideas when feasible.

A program/department that models the opportunity to speak up and speak out is more likely to facilitate that behavior in its trainees. For example, perhaps the program could get involved in a social justice situation happening on campus or in the local community. New professionals might present the minority opinion on some issue occurring within the department or within the college. When the department chair supports those conversations, the message is clear to everyone that those voices are valued. When a difficult dialogue is needed, the department should facilitate its occurrence. Doing this does not mean the person presenting a minority view is always automatically correct. Instead, it shows that the department is willing to facilitate such dialogue for all concerned. Departments should also encourage new professionals to try for grants, technology, conferences, or other experiences that bring innovation.

Conclusion

To sign off on my musings, I am led back to a concept that I referenced in my Division 17 (Society of Counseling Psychology) presidential address (Bowman, 2015). Dudley (2010) eloquently discussed what he calls "lollipop moments," when two people have an interaction that seems insignificant to one person but turns out to be profound to the other. When I ask people to reminisce about such a moment in their lives, I am struck by how rarely they have shared the lollipop with the other person. Each time I reflect on my life, I recall yet another lollipop moment that significantly shaped my path. When possible, I try to thank the other participant for the push, tug, or kind word. If reading this chapter reminds you of a lollipop moment, I hope you will revisit that experience with the person who initiated it. Let that person know how things turned out.

References

Benjamin, L. (Ed.). (1997). *Black women in the Academy: Promises and perils.* Gainesville: University Press of Florida.

Bowman, S. L. (2015). Conversations and collaborations: What has really changed? *The Counseling Psychologist, 43,* 127–137.

Dudley, D. (2010, September). Everyday leadership. *TED Talk*. Podcast retrieved from http://www.ted.com/talks/drew_dudley_everyday_leadership

Enns, C. Z., & Williams, E. N. (Eds.). (2013). *The Oxford handbook of feminist multicultural counseling psychology*. New York, NY: Oxford University Press.

Glasser, W. (1999). *Choice theory: A new psychology of personal freedom*. New York, NY: HarperCollins.

Gormley, B. (2013). Feminist multicultural mentoring in counseling psychology. In C. Z. Enns & E. N. Williams (Eds.), *The Oxford handbook of feminist multicultural counseling psychology* (pp. 451–464). New York, NY: Oxford University Press.

Hayes, S. C. (2012). Humanistic psychology and contextual behavioral perspectives. *Psychotherapy, 49*, 455–460.

Kitayama, S., & Cohen, E. D. (Eds.). (2010). *Handbook of cultural psychology*. New York, NY: Guilford.

Myers, L. J. (1993). *Understanding an Afrocentric world view: Introduction to optimal psychology*. Dubuque, IA: Kendall/Hunt.

Wampold, B. E. (2007). Psychotherapy: The humanistic (and effective) treatment. *American Psychologist, 62*, 857–873.

Wubholding, R. (2000). *Reality therapy for the 21st century*. Philadelphia, PA: Taylor & Francis.

5

Travels With a Contrarian Person, Psychologist, Activist

Becoming "Radicalized" by Injustice, Violence, and Stasis

By Anthony J. Marsella

Introduction

I must begin my journey's account by acknowledging my gratitude to the editors for selecting me as a notable psychology and counseling professional, deserving inclusion in their compendium of stories of courage, innovation, and risk. I am humbled by their decision. I am also humbled by the fact that there are many people in the world living daily lives of courage, innovation, and risk, struggling for survival amid traumatic circumstances of war, violence, abuse, oppression, and deprivation.

Consider what is required of Syrian refugees, Somali displaced persons, Yemeni bombing victims, Palestinian Gaza sufferers, and Afghans caught in a 14-year war in which death has become welcome in the absence of hope. This is courage of a different type, a courage demanding world recognition and support for the extraordinary demands imposed by an absence of basic human requirements of food, water, and shelter; and even when basics are present, there remain among the wretched of the earth struggles with meaning, faith, and dignity. Amid the madness of daily life, these courageous individuals continue to take yet another desperate breath, wipe tearing eyes, and walk the next step toward an unknown path to sustain life and lives.

That is courage. It demonstrates uncommon valor, bravery, and heroism. I can only pray my humble journey of courage and risk, lived amid the struggles for justice of a different sort, can contribute in some way to the tapestry of efforts, not only to survive but to advance human knowledge, wisdom, and dignity. My inclusion, if deserved, is because I did not hesitate for most of my life to condemn injustice, to denounce war, and to be a voice for the voiceless. All of this was happening as I entered power platforms of academia, professions, and citizenry, only to find myself contending with them. Was I bold, confident, and/or foolish as I pursued different visions? Yes. I was scared out of my mind by my actions, wondering what would befall me as those in power suggested I be ignored, then dismissed me as an irritant, and subsequently considered me a risk to conventional thought and society.

When I delivered, in 1998, a "radical" challenge to the American Psychological Association (APA) to become "a psychology for a global community" (Marsella, 1998), I was toasted by some as a liberator but by others as a danger to their comfort and canon. I was, after all, calling for an internationalization of psychology, and this would mean recognition of relativity in Western assumptions. And then there was the querulous contention: "All psychologies were indigenous to the origins." When I delivered and published a paper titled "The United States of America: A Culture of War" (Marsella, 2011), the die was cast. One courageous person used a Hebrew word, *Dayenu*, to thank me. *Dayenu* means, *"If you never do anything more, this would be sufficient."* When I argued that the psychology of terrorism must be understood historically and contextually, that states could be terrorists, and that terrorism and terrorists were relative to the abuses of the situation and powerlessness to change them, I was called by some, "An enemy of the State and a person of interest." What state? What interest? I would learn, with difficult consequences, that my contentions were essentially challenges to power, and challenging power always has consequences. Disagreements, criticisms, creative options, and alternatives are considered by those in power to be deserving of a score of pejorative labels: radical, extremist, militant, activist, revolutionary, or even terrorist. I am grateful here to Anthony Judge, one of the most brilliant minds of our times, who captured the dilemma and risks of disagreement with convention and the ease with which labels are assigned to those who contend. Invoking John Keats, Judge (2016) quoted the word, from Wikipedia:

[Radicalism is] a capacity of those capable of creative process, a capacity that negates intellectual pursuit of answers. . . . It explains how human beings innovate and resist within confining social contexts, rigid social divisions and hierarchies, and to transcend and revise these contexts.

Ultimately, and not without struggle and failure, it was recognizing the fusion of my personal, professional, and civic lives that inspired and sustained me—nurturing the courage to accept the mantle of activism, to grasp my path that would challenge authorities and conventions and require that I shoulder the duties, responsibilities, and obligations of and for life. It is not chance after years of witnessing the abuses authorized by the destructive mantra, "God made mankind the master of all things," that I wrote and spoke ardently of "lifeism." Lifeism is a belief positioning humans as one form of life amid a cosmos of swirling visible life in the world and heavens. Lifeism is about connecting, transcending, bonding, and joining: Biblical admonitions, scientism, and popular culture statements masquerade as truth; they sponsor conformity, convention, and compliance, and in doing so, they limit grander visions. And as for psychology and counseling, there is now the possibility of an international stage—a global prophecy challenging simplistic and erroneous views.

The result is this: "Serve life, not death." "Protect and defend equality, justice, and beauty as natural expressions of life." "Accept life as your basic identity; this is above nation, ethnic group, gender, or any other status." I was an advocate for "Big History." And with this, my life became a part of billions of years of time and evolution and of the long history of life on earth. Academia and professional life demands remained present, but my life was cast into a larger narrative of events, often eluding my understanding but never eluding my awakened consciousness.

I advocated compassion, I taught the power of empathy, and I witnessed and walked the importance of accompanying. Above all, I became committed to documenting humanity's journey toward peace and the fulfillment of human potential, a commitment arising from lived experience amid torrents of confusing emotions and crystallized images. It was a journey. I was not born into it. But I am pleased I did not seek to evade life's mantle when called on by circumstance. Could I have done more? Yes. But I could *not* have done less.

Past Influences of My Journey

At what point in my life should I begin to weave my journey, to unfold a life in which I regret much and yet find forgiveness in contributions? In retrospect, each event—each setting—along the way is a starting point. If I must choose, however, I begin in my early infancy and childhood. I was born into a Sicilian immigrant family in 1940, in Cleveland, Ohio. Time, place, and circumstance still bewilder me as I seek insight and meaning in this particular beginning. Clearly, an immigrant family is immersed in a score of courageous efforts to survive the strange world to which family members have journeyed. And so I became a cultural carrier of immigrant survival efforts, testing them, using them, accepting and denying them, as I entered the world outside the family. I *was* the family. I was Sicilian tradition. I was a "defender."

While the world inside the immigrant family was well-defined, dominated by adherence to old-world traditions and customs, the world beyond my family was filled with an acute awareness of differences among language, appearance, dress, food, and assumptions about acceptable behavior. I attribute my eventual interest and passion for promoting diversity to the profound differences I was compelled to negotiate. What was sealed, however, was awareness that my family was different—poor, uneducated, unaware of the formalities and legalities of citizenship. Businesses, taxes, laws, regulations, banks, loans, and customs were frightening sources of confusion. They had to be learned. But the learning suppressed old-world approaches—handshakes, relationships, family ties, and personal and familial obligations sealed by head nods and smiles and something called "honor." Lose honor and you have nothing. It is better to accept indignities, to know their source, and to vow to never let them occur again. And above all, be alert to the many people and forces seeking to remove your honor, for it is your mantle of existence.

It was both an acceptance, a tolerance, and an understanding of early individual and community differences and contrasts, and also a recognition of the harsh abuses associated with a failure to acculturate, which, in my opinion, shaped a combination of personal qualities that carried me to my present-day status as a pioneer figure in clinical and cultural psychology, psychopathology, and psychotherapy. I learned from others: watching, measuring, weighing their actions and consequences. In many instances, awareness of others' positions enabled me to offer unconventional positions and methods with comfort. I could see the emphasis on their immediacy and their absence of vision. Here I must also acknowledge the enduring genetic sources of temperament: energy, determination, stamina, and social presence and dominance. This combination of opinion and style was the emerging crucible sustaining me.

I understood the construction reality via language, the strength and determination necessary to face biases and ridicule, the tenacity to endure and recover from failure, the courage to assert personal presence and pride. The Sicilian word *sopportare* is relevant here. It means to bear the burden and continue. But within the context of Sicilian life, embedded in a fatalism and cynicism from centuries of oppression, it becomes a support, a resilience for looking life in the eye, often with a jaundiced stare, muttering, spitting, and continuing. Sometimes an English word would be bastardized: *endura*. The meaning is always understood.

In so many ways, this is also the root of my concern for injustice. From my earliest days, I was aware of "fairness" and its abuses. I recognized and resented our poverty. Sunday drives in a packed car to view the wealthy houses in Shaker Heights left me questioning: "Aunt Rose, why don't we live here in these houses?" Laughter and hugs followed. "Oh, Babe, these are for the rich people. Eat your frozen ice before it melts." I did not understand. ("You mean we are not equal? We are considered lower class and have a low status? We are not respected? How can that be? Who did this?")

My questions—many and often—were never answered. What was registered at unconscious levels were issues of identity, insult, indignity, and anger and resentment. The struggle for me was the absence of knowledge and wisdom I could turn to for advice and counsel. "Aunt Jean, I want to be president of the United States. What do I have to do?" "Who in the hell knows, Babe. Go to school. They will tell you. Besides why would you want to be president? Just get a job!"

In my youth, growing up in the working-class and poverty-class areas of Southeast Cleveland, areas inhabited by Italians, Sicilians, Hungarians Bohemians, Slovenians, Poles, Irish, Blacks, and Jews, brought groups together, often with a silent sense of competition. It seemed natural—struggles for dominance, territoriality, presence, not unlike other evolutionary settings. Changing postwar neighborhoods became a cauldron for struggles, as Whites moved to the suburbs, while poor Black families entered White enclaves. Playground fights among boys from ethnic groups were not unusual: "I do not want to fight you, but I am not running away." For me, this was especially true in that most traumatic of ages—the adolescent years of 12 to 16.

Fighting was accepted in Sicilian culture, where manliness required being "tough." There were ethnic sections, and crossing these required a willingness to understand the differences. "They are not like us, Babe. And who could eat that stuff they cook? Polish weddings are good. I love the dancing—polkas." Differences, judgments, good and bad, right and wrong, constancy, and change: In many ways, I am still struggling with the issues of those days. What has changed is the recognition that "differences" are not only good but essential. "Life is diversity, death is uniformity," said Octavio Paz, the Mexican Nobel Prize winner.

I have often wondered about the absence of typical privileges I faced. My parents, both from immigrant Sicilian families, were divorced when I was 3. There were shouting, crying, arguments—the presence of pure, uninhibited, visible, emotional expression—as father and mother condemned and criticized each other, in my presence. Was I confused by these displays? Yes. They were never directed at me, but I was a silent witness. It was as if I was present to witness the anger, discontent, discord, and accusations, but only as an observer. I was not expected to enter the fray. If I was the cause, I did not know it. Later, of course, I wondered if my presence was part of the problem, and I wondered if my silent support for my mother added to the wars.

My sensitivity to prejudice, violence, conflict, and war was etched—inscribed permanently—in my mind and being during those years, awaiting only the opportunity to speak for them. I would have to work my way through the seemingly Byzantine pathways to recognition, reward, and the fruits of professional status. Does the world not recognize the rejections and insults it imposes on the poor and the marginalized Blacks, Hispanics, Asians, and Islamic youth of today are inscribed in their minds? The resentment, the anger, the determination to respond within and beyond the law, are all being forged in young minds, never to be erased—possibly channeled and sublimated, but never lost. Those with "majority" power are foolish to think they can defeat justice by force, including laws, regulations, corruption, cronyism, and control.

Each step along the way revealed the "secrets of status" to me—knowledge, achievements, earnestness, genuineness, empathy, and concern for others; responding to others' core identity, not to their problems; learning to be well-spoken, to recognize the culture of schools and cultural expressions present in people—to be smart, to be educated, to be ambitious, if only to please mother and family.

And so it was. In a large, inner-city, multiracial, multiethnic, multiclass high school, I was president of the senior class, president of the student council, a National Honor Society member, an athlete, and boyfriend to a beautiful and bright girlfriend. My inner demons—a sense of vulnerability, inferiority, and educational inadequacy; a fear of losing; financial poverty—were hidden. I knew them, but I could not let my mother know I was anything less than the son she prized for loyalty and love.

The seeds of courage, determination, endurance, and resiliency were sown amid awareness of how the world looked at us (me); the seeds were planted and would grow—especially as I and the world became of intellectual and personal talents, and I was given or seized opportunities. At some point, my concerns for peace and justice journeyed beyond my life, and the life of my family, and became located and positioned amid humanity—all humanity.

I entered college on prestigious scholarships as a chemistry major but soon changed to psychology. Psychology was about behavior! Psychology was about me! Psychology was about helping others, and psychology was about contesting injustice, promoting peace, and accepting nonviolence. But college was also the place where I betrayed values to which I aspired, as I sacrificed courage for acceptance and wallowed in confusion about morality and religion. College, for me, was a disappointment. I was pulled into the harsh world of conformity for acceptance, at the cost of self-loathing. I lost my prior identity, and I became a college guy!

I wanted to pledge a Black fraternity. I wanted to engage in intellectual discussions. I wanted to confront the social problems of the times and become a voice for the voiceless. Did I? No, I did not. I yielded to a White fraternity, drank beer and vomited, and got by in classes on memory—all of the time wondering: "What is life was about? What is my future?" I didn't like it, and I didn't like myself. I had betrayed myself and the personal state of grace I had earned in late adolescence because of my idealism, determination, struggles, and courage. I had become a member of the conventional culture and lifestyle of the time. Ugh! I later wrote a poem describing my regrets and my felt sense of betrayal of all I believed.

College, higher education, academia: I played the game, rising to a rank of vice president for academic affairs, hopeful I could join with others in building a university committed to peace and justice. But this was not to be. Access to this position revealed sources of abuse that were inherent in the institution and its control and dominance by power bases within and without the proverbial "ivy-covered" walls. Scores of networks linked to money, power, racism, cronyism, and national and international political interests created an elusive web of deceit hidden beneath a contrived veil of self-serving interests. "Hey, Tony, wake up! Realpolitik!"

As senior vice president, I took strength in the words of Yale University's distinguished president, A. Bartlett Giamatti, who, when called upon to announce Yale's purpose in lengthy administrative prose, simply stated, "Let evil be abolished and paradise restored." Giamatti was a Milton scholar and the prototype of the academic-administrator model so needed in universities but denied by the military-industrial-congressional-educational complex. But I was soon to learn universities are not controlled by faculty but by politicians with long-established power bases. There were kings and queens whose interest was protecting their status and insuring a false legacy. The United States was now engaged in destroying nation, people, and laws, and universities had become pawns. I endured some of the most vicious and punitive assaults on life and character from avaricious people seeking to perpetuate their political interests and to acquire control by empowering crony colleagues. Betrayal!

I resigned, but not before openly sharing my disdain, disappointment, and determination to endure. Some may call this courage. If so, it was a courage fueled in anger, resentment, and disillusion because of the staining of an institution supposedly committed to truth and other enduring human values. The university had fallen from grace, driven by external and internal interests for power. I would not fall from grace again. I would choose peace over war, voice over silence, respect over advantage, action over passivity, and justice over all.

Experiencing My Professional Journey

I am here today, approximately 60 years after the warm days in September when I moved into my undergraduate college's quarried stone dormitory across from a bell tower, chapel, and class buildings. How can I describe the changes in these years, these decades filled with a spectrum of personal and professional experiences, many still bewildering in their origin and consequences? I sit now before a computer blessed with word processing and auto correction. I smile at the changes from when knowing how to use a slide rule made you a geek. How many handwritten, pencil-erased, yellow pad pages capturing my thoughts have there been? How I longed for endless secretarial time to type drafts of my scribbled and margin-filled words.

I knew no restraint in writing and sharing my thoughts, submitting them to journals that rejected, suggested, approved, and modified my ideas, promising to publish them in next year's issue. The game, academia, acquire status from papers, books, grants, students, conventions—learn the culture! I found you must play well, but you must also learn to "selectively detach" yourself from the game. Could I become a voice for change, sometimes radical change, without being cast as radical, extremist, revolutionary, or terrorist, and thus be labeled and marginalized?

The editors of this volume asked me to share some examples of "courage" in the face of personal and professional risks and abuses. There are many! At times I find myself exhausted from the requirements of conscience, ethics, justice, duty, and responsibility. It has become for me a 24–7 lifestyle, but I would have it no other way. Some specific examples follow. Figure 5.1 offers a graphic display of arenas in which I faced risk by struggling for truth and justice amid a world dominated by homogenized visions supported by power connections.

Figure 5.1 Graphic Representation of Risk Events

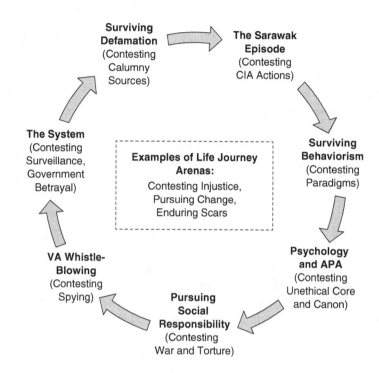

The Sarawak Episode. As a new clinical and cultural psychology PhD, I was recruited to become a field director for a psychiatric epidemiological project in the jungles of British colonial-controlled Sarawak (Malaya). The recruiters were government shills, and the project was funded by CIA money! The project was pioneering ethno-cultural epidemiology, identifying rates and patterns of mental disorder among Chinese, Malay, and Iban tribes through systematic personal interviews. I accepted, filled with visions of being able to find ethno-cultural variations. I reviewed and analyzed Chinese and Malay data and led excursions into the Sarawak jungles for Iban interviews. It was very *National Geographic,* until I became increasingly aware of what was occurring during the period from 1965 to 1970 in Southeast Asia.

I saw Chinese being kept in camps and prisons; I was told surreptitiously that the CIA had overthrown the Sukarno government and replaced it with Suharto, and more than 500,000 Chinese were killed, all in the name of fears Maoist China would become dominant in Southeast Asia. The Vietnam War was on! The United States was crazed with fears and lost all reason. And me—I was part of a project, unknowingly, funded by the CIA under the Foundations Fund for Research in Psychiatry at Yale University. I was to identify the names and residents of the subjects. In brief, I was participating in a secret project with nefarious purposes that would result in the death of the very subjects I was studying. How evil! To comply would mean I was complicit in the deaths of innocents.

I resigned and gave the data to the director in Kuching, Sarawak, who was a former self-reported German physician recruited via Project PaperClip to work for allied interests. I now understood the nefarious purposes of the epidemiological project; I had also come to see the psychiatric biases in instruments and assumptions, resulting in all Iban people being labeled as "psychotic." "Yes, doctor, we speak to trees and spirits; yes doctor, we are surrounded by evil spirits; yes, doctor, we are the clouds...." It was a double whammy: "Identify potential Chinese communists, and in the process, prove primitives are insane." My decision was to place myself in jeopardy from various political and military sources for the rest of my life. The struggle was on. I was a target. I endured but not without scars. "We will get even, Tony." And they have. There is a lesson here.

Behaviorism Domination. I accepted a position as an assistant professor in the Department of Psychology, University of Hawai'i, Honolulu, in 1970. I assumed I would teach courses and develop a cross-cultural research program under the protection of some senior professors critical of the war and upheaval in Southeast Asia and the Pacific. The Vietnam War revealed how ignorant we were of Asian cultures. In retrospect, I believe some principled people saw what happened to me in Sarawak and managed to convince the powers of the following: "He is a good person—idealistic, naïve, and unaware of the big picture struggles occurring, but he is bright, creative, and resilient. He could be a resource for the University of Hawai'i, psychology, and Hawaii."

Nevertheless, my assignment to the clinical field was a mismatch. The seven members of the clinical psychology program were committed behaviorists. I was a marginalized member, often subject to derisive comments and insults regarding my cross-cultural efforts. Behaviorism in the 1970s was a religion. The more I pointed out the paradigmatic relativity of behaviorism, the more I was ostracized and simply tolerated with an all-knowing shake of the head. As I endured, developing a strong academic record of publications, grants, and teaching, my dismissal became untenable. At one point, the sole trump card played by department bullies was the curriculum committee's open announcement in a faculty meeting: "We do not want you teaching our students this junk." Cross-cultural was for them—"junk!" I was being ostracized for speaking against the Western canon, replete with all of its limitations. I smiled with narrowed eyes. They wished to exclude student contact with both me and my content expertise. I was patient. I formed a new concentration area in the department—cultural and community psychology— recruiting faculty members who recognized the power game, and I developed courses soon required by APA for accreditation. Ironically, the bully who insulted me—angry because of my antiwar and critical U.S. Middle East political views—resigned and took a nonacademic position on the mainland.

You see, "cultural psychology" challenged ethnocentric, biased, and conventional teaching and research. Closed-minded faculty lived to perpetuate a status quo, under the mantle of pseudoscience. "The minorities were taking over, and he is encouraging this—look at his students!" Cultural psychology identified abuses in psychology's Western canon of knowing (i.e., epistemology, ontology, and praxeology), now institutionalized in the APA's emergence as a corporatized power for controlling psychology. How dare they do this? It was colonization of mind!

I was now involved in a deep struggle that extended far beyond myself. I was challenging Western psychology, the APA, and all of the hidden resources pushing for homogenization and hegemony. I had entered a new arena of struggle for justice, speaking for minority rights, pressing for indigenous psychologies and people, contesting political powers in Washington, D.C., and interfering with their "evil action agenda."

I kept writing, speaking, researching, and challenging the status quo around the world. I found great support and eventually a position as a pioneer figure. This does not mean I was free of abuse. Some of the worst came from ethnic and racial minority group members benefitting from the largess of government and professional associations. I had to learn the harsh lesson that among people of color, the poor, indigenous populations, and many oppressed gender and marginalized populations, the temptations of acceptance and reward by the system are hard to resist.

Psychologists for Social Responsibility. In 2004, I was asked by Richard Wagner to accept the presidency of Psychologists for Social Responsibility (PsySR), an activist group initially formed to address nuclear war issues but subsequently emerging as a voice challenging the APA. The concerns for human rights, antiwar activism, poverty, and other domestic and global social problems fit my beliefs. I assumed the presidency from 2005 to 2007. This was a time of U.S. invasions, and torture advocacy was becoming rampant. The APA members were complicit, and the APA was engaged in efforts to justify and participate—the infamous Psychological Ethics and National Security (PENS) report. PsySR was considered a thorn in APA's efforts to support military and intelligence activities. I worked hard to strengthen

PsySR, increasing membership, enhancing communications, raising funds, and stabilizing identity. What I soon discovered was that some members of PsySR were APA loyalists, actually working against PsySR. This was an old tactic: penetrate and undermine; the big boys will protect you. I spoke against their efforts, and PsySR today remains a bulwark against torture, ethic violations, and corporatized psychology.

The Mental Health Industrial-Professional Complex. I saw the mental health corporate-professional system (i.e., medicine, custodial hospitals, psychiatrists, pharmacological companies, staff hierarchies, diagnosis, and patient controls) as the problem. I began to criticize the mental health system, raising ethical, conceptual, and practice issues. I soon found the "system" could be vindictive. Manuscripts were rejected. Publication is reserved for those who agree with the canon, and the canon is the power structure. I struggled, taking advantage of every invitation to speak or to write a book chapter to raise criticisms of what we were doing. Think about it: "What is this thing called mental health?" It is an anachronism, in conflict with everything we know about body-mind-spirit relations. I was on the outside, so I decided to form my own publishing company. I could then publish anything I wished without the constraints of convention. Yes, I know the risks of this approach. But there was so much I wanted to say in an effort to change and reform the system (see, e.g., Marsella, in press).

Connections Among Professional Life, Accomplishments, Future, and Advice to Young Professionals

You cannot be anything other than your unique self. Know it and treasure it. Your uniqueness is your gift and your burden. "Know thyself," said Socrates. You can't be anything other than yourself without sensing discomfort and betrayal. Our professions are cultures, and they call on members to accept the conventions (rules) for participation; there is often little room for personal latitude. We have fads in theories (e.g., psychoanalysis, behaviorism, humanism) and therapies (e.g., cognitive behavioral therapy). If you disagree, you can run afoul of the "thought police," especially as they are guided by the APA, the American Counseling Association, and other subgroups. There are cries for following "evidence-based approaches," but evidence-based approaches are flawed in assumptions, design, and conclusions. Understanding "culture," not as external artifacts or products but as internal constructions of reality, with thousands of diverse spectacles for viewing and negotiating reality across generations, liberated my mind. So much more was relative and a function of power rather than accuracy.

The current emphasis on using cognitive behavior therapies for all problems, for all people, by all therapists and counselors, is sheer madness, for so many reasons. The gospel is taught, but it does not acknowledge variations. Here is my equation: Healing = F (V1) Client Characteristics (V1) × Disorders (V2) × Therapist/Counselor Characteristics (V3) × Methods (V4) × Time (V5) × Costs (V6) × Extraneous Life Factors (V7). It is essential we recognize that there are scores of healing methods (e.g., abreaction, advice, catharsis, confession, forgiveness, information, insight, practice, empathic acceptance, courage).

Why are we forced to rely on one method governed by one principle (e.g., reason), when the challenges are so much more complex? Becoming a cultural psychologist liberated me from accepting one worldview. Diversity is life, and homogenization is destructive. I was now free to study and address numerous problems, especially as I saw Western psychology limited by its narrow assumptions (e.g., empiricism, objectivity, individuality, reductionism, scientism).

Some Suggestions

Clinical psychology and counseling psychology are professional service specialties. Contrary to belief, the intellectual foundations of both are limited; they are too often confined to skill-set acquisitions and restricted professional guidelines. Missing are substantive emphases in training on knowledge in the humanities, social sciences, and physical sciences, resulting in a limited range of knowledge and interventions in services. Technician mentalities arise in which the professionals seek specific knowledge for specific problems, frequently bolstered by professional workshops offering certificates confirming competencies. The result is that practice is limited to accepted conventions, often devoid of critical, intellectual, and wise traditions.

We must not mistake good intentions and eagerness to serve with the ability to serve well. Professionals and students must ask whether they knowingly accept limitations in offering services to specific problems and whether they are aware of the importance of using skills and talents consistent with personal values and temperament. It takes courage to acknowledge one's professional limitations, especially when private practice requires patients for economic survival.

Courage, Risks, Advice

Courage is a complex concept and act. Understanding courage requires identifying the motives, act, risks, and consequences. Questioning, criticizing, and challenging convention, and acting without approval of power, are all sources of risk. They require courage! Some acts of courage are momentary and reflexive, automatic responses devoid of any semblance of the consequences, especially the possibility of losing one's life. Other acts of courage are equally intentional in their willingness to risk status, identity, character, and reputation. The acts of courage I have summarized in my life fall within this genre.

I have had to endure insult, calumny, betrayal of trust, baiting, entrapment, defamation, and physical risks of life and limb. I have been called anti-Semitic because I spoke against unbridled Zionism (not Judaism), and because I dared to copublish with an Iranian. I have been called a Mafia member and Mafia Don because of my Italian appearance and style. Speaking fluent Sicilian as a result of childhood learning encouraged stereotypic labels. I have been called a CIA member and assassin because I travelled alone to "strange and exotic" places. It is so easy for bigoted minds to reach conclusions in the absence of information. I am, of course, none of these labels; but when one is considered a threat for challenging convention, labels can be used as punishment.

Today I live alone. I write daily: poetry, poetic elegies, blues lyrics, short stories, brief commentaries, political and government critiques, academic articles for journals and books, and authored books. I endure. I am 76½ years old. I survived prostate cancer of questionable origins (two different types), endless medical disorders, and the growing problems of ageing.

I was diagnosed with cancer at 62. I was at the height of my career productivity. I was told my chances for survival were 50–50. My physician suggested I get close to my children. I resigned after 35 years at the University of Hawai'i. It was painful, but I had suffered much in Hawai'i, as vindictive colleagues and community political forces continued to pursue revenge. As an advocate of cultural determinants of behavior and a critic of Western psychology assumptions, methods, and conclusions, it was easy for others to ostracize me. Thankfully, one of my old behaviorist colleagues had the dignity and grace to tell me, "Tony, you were right, and we were wrong." Amen! It felt good to hear these words, but the scars remained.

My mortality encounter with prostate cancer brought important insights to my life. Among them was an awareness of how fortunate my life has been amid the dark times. How dare I ask for anything more than I have been given? I rose from poverty, underprivilege, abuse, and prejudice to the high ranks of personal and professional achievement. I have received numerous awards, published essential papers and books, helped transform a profession, and achieved stability and stature. And more than anything else, I have been given the privilege and opportunity to question and challenge injustice. I am now, more than ever before, aware that making courageous choices is a requirement for a meaningful life.

References

Judge, A. (2016). *Coming Out as a Radical—or Coming In?* Retrieved May 24, 2017, from https://www.transcend.org/tms/2016/01/coming-out-as-a-radical-or-coming-in/

Marsella, A. J. (1998). Toward a "global-community psychology": Meeting the needs of a changing world. *American Psychologist, 53,* 1282–1291.

Marsella, A. J. (2011). The United States of America: A culture of war. *International Journal of Intercultural Relations, 35,* 714–728.

Marsella, A. J. (in press). *In pursuit of schizophrenia: Reflections on imprecision in professional and scientific assumptions and practices.* Alpharetta, GA: Mountain Arbor Press.

6

Journey to the West

By Jean Lau Chin

Past Influences of My Journey

Journey to the West[1] is a Chinese epic published in the 16th century of the legendary pilgrimage of the Tang dynasty Buddhist monk Xuanzang who traveled to the "West" (India) to obtain Buddhist sacred texts (sutras). Traveling with him were three protectors; one was Sun Wukong, commonly known as Monkey King. Monkey King is a rebellious and extraordinary being, born out of a rock, fertilized by the grace of Heaven. Being extremely smart and cunning, he learned magic tricks and kung fu from a master Taoist. He is able to transform himself into 72 different images, such as a tree, bird, beast of prey, or bug as small as a mosquito, to sneak into an enemy's belly and fight him from the inside. Using clouds as a vehicle, he can travel 180,000 li (miles) in a single somersault. In *Journey to the West,* the Tang priest and his three disciples are put through 81 tests before they can obtain the scriptures and reach enlightenment.

This is my story. I was born in the Year of the Monkey. Immigration is not unlike Monkey's journey, and Monkey's character is not unlike the unbreakable spirit of the Chinese American immigrants who came to this country. Growing up, my parents were Chinese laundry owners, as were

---

1. *Journey to the West* is a Chinese novel published in the 16th century during the Ming dynasty and attributed to Wu Cheng'en.

80% of the immigrant Chinese American families of my generation. It was not an occupation of choice due to the anti-Chinese legislation of the times, which precluded entry into most occupations. I was the youngest of four children, growing up in Brooklyn, New York. My parents emphasized Chinese cultural values and practices during my early upbringing. They insisted on speaking Chinese at home and always reminded us to properly address and be respectful of our elders even if they were wrong. Responsibility to the family to the point of personal sacrifice, hard work, harmony, and modesty were common values of the Chinese culture that were consistently emphasized in my parents' social conversations; it was their way of teaching us and making us proud. It anchored me in my cultural heritage and guided me in professional journey. We lived modestly in the "golden mountain" of the West; it was only in later years that I realized how meager this was compared to our White American neighbors. Coming from a working-class, immigrant family, I know well how chance opportunities can often be so life transforming. It was my high school Honors Program chair who encouraged me to pursue a college education. My ambition was to graduate from high school and become a typist; my mother had finished sixth grade while my father was "more educated," having finished ninth grade in the village back in China. Educationally, I did not have the mentors so common in today's environment. From elementary through graduate school, I was generally the only, or one of several, Asian students in the entire school. I came to expect, as normal, being subject to stereotypic expectations of the "quiet, modest, smart Chinese," being paraded in front of class when Chinese New Year came around and always being asked, "What are you? Chinese or Japanese?"

From high school, my career took a path that neither I nor my family would have dreamed. I received a full-tuition Regents' Scholarship for my undergraduate education and was accepted to Columbia University, a private, Ivy League and world-renowned university. In my naïveté, I chose to go to Brooklyn College, a local, public, no-tuition college, so I could receive a $300 per-semester stipend for my books and expenses. A mentor would perhaps have provided better guidance. I later obtained my doctoral degree in psychology at Columbia University, advanced to management and leadership positions, and became an academic dean at two universities. I became a notable scholar, academic, educator, and clinician in the areas of multiculturalism, diversity, psychotherapy, women's issues, and now leadership.

My journey is amplified by the historical events that helped to shape me and my view of the world. My parents lived against the context of World War II. My mother escaped the Japanese invasion of Nanjing, China, by three days; her ship to the United States missed being bombed by the

Japanese by one day in 1939. The subsequent conversion of China to Communism created an environment of mistrust of all things Chinese in the United States. McCarthyism and the Yellow Peril during the 1950s were rampant. Chinese were subjected to racist remarks and assaults on a daily basis. Messages of "You must be Communist," "You don't belong," and "You are inferior" were commonplace.

In my book, *Learning from my Mother's Voice* (Chin, 2005), I describe my mother as a moral compass who helped me face challenges of leadership despite our differences. She supported my education and my independence despite her attaining only a sixth-grade education and remaining subordinate to my father in the male dominant culture of her times. Her ethics, her nurturing, and her courage influenced my working style and values throughout my career; I recognized the limitations of culture, economics, and historical context that bound her to the life she had.

I did not know I was an American until the age of 22 when I went to Europe. The customs officer in Germany was initially so impressed with meeting "an exotic Chinese"; when checking my passport, he became outraged that I was an "American" trying to pass myself off as Chinese—the answer I had given my entire life in the United States in response to the perpetual question of "What are you?"

Girded by the Chinese Confucian values for education of my parents, I did excel in school. The stereotypic expectations by my teachers of the "smart Chinese" expected me to get good grades; yet these same teachers questioned my ability to speak in public when I was designated as the salutatorian in junior high school. I was often ignored, passed over, or put in my place—made invisible—by others who stereotyped my persona as that of a "quiet, modest, nice, little Chinese girl" who could not possibly be a leader. This taught me how to negotiate the contrasts of East versus West. Being challenged on many levels led me to gain courage, become a risk taker, and innovate in my professional career. I was always the exception!

Experiencing My Professional Journey: A Life of Contrasts

I experienced my professional journey as having lived a life of contrasts. I faced the challenges of living in a bicultural world as a Chinese American woman, facing frequent discrimination, having limited financial resources, and always being perceived as not belonging. I entered the field of psychology at a time when there were only about 20 Asian American psychologists in the country. I often held contrasting roles that took me on an atypical journey in psychology. My identity reflected the contrasts of Eastern and Western values and practices.

In my journey through the ranks to positions of leadership, I was frequently stereotyped because of my ethnicity and gender. Often being different from those who preceded me in my leadership positions, I needed to work to retain my identity and authenticity, which has led to my transformation in the journey. Managing conflicting expectations about me, what I could or should do as an Asian American woman were challenges on my path.

While education and achievement are highly valued in the Chinese culture, my parents perceived a high school diploma as an accomplishment and endpoint given their grade school educations and expectations for women in a privileged male dominant culture. As I advanced, the differences in social class and educational attainment between my parents/community and me had them in awe of what I was doing; more importantly, they could not fathom the meaning of doctoral education much less psychology. My peers who went to college were often the first in their families to do so and stopped at getting a bachelor's degree.

Attempting to integrate the contrasting cultures of East and West is inherently a challenge. The different structure of English and Chinese language is one such contrast, as well as the different emphases on social and cultural values. The mark of a scholar in Chinese is the emphasis on brevity, while in English, the emphasis is on loquaciousness. Sometimes confusing, sometimes misunderstood, these polarities led to my mental agility in shifting contexts. Urges to "speak up" from the West go against the mandate of "don't be so brazen" from the East; urges "to confront" from Western ideals go against those of "promoting harmony" from Eastern ideals. These contrasts required a consciousness and vigilance to contextual cues if I were to communicate successfully.

The differences between the Confucian and Socratic methods of learning and education were subtle but striking in my own education. While Asian methods of learning emphasized drill, active listening, and unquestioning obedience to take in the wisdom of the master teacher in my Chinese school classes, American methods of learning in my American school classes emphasized raising your hand, participating vocally in class, and challenging ideas and the status quo; they are, in fact, different means to the same outcomes of critical thinking and intellectual wisdom. My parents urged an observant and absorbent approach to learning typical of Chinese culture—that is, to be the recipient of knowledge. Early on, I was confused by these differences since I had no mentors to make the translation; I often found my motives and thoughts misunderstood and misjudged.

It was clear that "difference makes a difference," especially in social and professional gatherings. Bringing non-Asians to an all-Asian gathering must be contemplated, as well as being the only Asian in a dominant all-White gathering. Will they feel comfortable with the differences in social customs, food, and values? Do they belong? Often this means creating two different realities or dimensions of authenticity.

A Diverse Career

Not only have my scholarly interests been about diversity, but my professional career also has been diverse. I have held clinical, management, and academic roles; I have engaged in practice, scholarship, research, and administration. I have worked in mental health, health care, academic, and consulting sectors. I maintained a clinical practice for more than 35 years and am a professor of psychology; I held management positions as a mental health clinic director, a community health center executive director, a regional director of a managed care company, and an academic dean at two universities.

In my professional career, there were other contrasts that were characterized by grappling with juxtaposing roles or of being on the outside. When in clinical practice within the community, I was always more scholarly than my colleagues in my publication activity; now in academia, I am more community oriented in my clinical approach to psychotherapy and counseling. I was simultaneously clinical supervisor and executive director of the community health center I ran. I simultaneously maintained a small private practice while also being an administrator. Trained as a school psychologist, my work in primarily clinical settings enabled me to bring cognitive and developmental perspectives to an area dominated by affective and psychopathological perspectives.

These contrasts of culture and profession led to many interesting challenges and dynamics. When conducting clinical supervision of junior staff and trainees while I was executive director, I found them sometimes steering the dialogue to administrative issues. I needed to compartmentalize my dual roles as administrator and clinician to ensure that junior staff and trainees were not avoiding important clinical issues. When seeing patients who were aware of my leadership role in the community, I needed to consider important transference issues because I was not a neutral object.

The diversity in my career and the contrasts in my life, while perplexing at first, transformed me; they enabled me to question, to advocate, and to change. The irony of my first professional presentation reflects this evolution and transformation. Right out of internship, I was asked to give a talk about

Asian Americans at the renowned Boston Psychoanalytic Society & Institute—because there was no one else; my qualifications then were simply because I was an Asian American. I later went on to challenge these biases and preconceived notions in my book, *Diversity in Psychotherapy* (Chin, De La Cancela, & Jenkins, 1993). I began to use narratives as learning tools in counseling and psychotherapy, and qualitative studies as research tools, to study human phenomena that simply could not be captured via surveys and objective quantitative data. I identified the creation of family legends and narratives, and I identified immigration as a traumatic process in the lives of immigrant families.

I challenged these assumptions about standard practices, universal norms, and cultural variation as deviations in my career journey. While stereotypic perceptions about the "smart Chinese" led to expectations of high achievement and good grades, I was often made invisible by opinions, expectations, and actions that stereotyped my persona as that of a "quiet, modest, nice, little Chinese girl," ignored my contributions, and deemed me *not aggressive enough* to take on leadership roles. I was described as a woman leader in the American Psychological Association's (APA) *Monitor on Psychology* (Cynkar, 2007, p. 67): "At 4 feet 10 inches tall, Jean Lau Chin, EdD, doesn't let her height get in the way of taking charge. . . . Many did not expect a petite, Asian woman to be their boss. . . ."

I also held many leadership roles in providing services to the profession of psychology. I have been president of three APA divisions: Society for the Psychology of Women (35), Society for the Study of Ethnicity, Race, and Culture (45), and International Division (52). I currently serve on APA's Council of Representatives and am currently the chair-elect of the Council Leadership Team. I have served on numerous national, state, and local boards and boards and committees of the APA for policy development and advocacy. In achieving these roles, I found that I did not have to be the loudest voice in the room. Rather, I was the one who got things done, who provided a vision for where to go and gained credibility because of my rational, ethical, and collaborative approach to problems and issues. It impacted me because I felt I was making a difference in things I cared about.

Transcendence and Transformation

Transformation and transcendence, both professionally and personally, characterize my professional journey. Often the "misfit," I brought my ability to look at things from the outside to the table. In doing so, I contributed to innovation and change. I was a nonphysician running a health center with a primary identity as a psychologist. I was often the only Asian American in the room, the only psychologist in my family, the only school psychologist in the mental health clinic, and the only woman to hold some of the many roles I held. The diversity and contrast in my experiences enabled me to be transformational. In doing so, I felt I became more innovative and transformational. I could see how stereotypic views of me or the situation could or should be changed. My small size, distinct Asian culture and presence, gender, and different professional training (trained as a school psychologist in largely clinical settings) evoked stereotypic perceptions and expectations about passivity, incompetence, and powerlessness—these perceptions and expectations sometimes silenced my voice; they sometimes made me question my own abilities. However, I strove to remain anchored in my pride about who I was and committed to what I believed. Not only had I learned that my ways of thinking were often different, but I also had learned to advocate for that which I valued, that is, serving the underserved populations, promoting social justice for ethnic minority communities, valuing differences, and advancing cultural competence and inclusivity. I was propelled toward advocacy and empowerment, deeply influenced by the 1960s movements and growing up during the anti-Chinese McCarthyism of the 1950s.

The irony of growing up in *cosmopolitan* New York City was that my racial/ethnic identity was questioned at least weekly: "Are you Chinese or Japanese?" Living through the 1960s, which was keen on empowerment and racial pride, did much to shape my views of the need to value and validate the diverse experiences of all in our training, education, research, and practice.

It has been a journey analogous to the *Journey to the West* of Monkey King and the 81 trials he endured as part of his transformation process (Chin, 2005, pp. 22–26). As Monkey so aptly puts it, though he can leap a thousand miles to get to where he wants in a second, he must accompany the Tang priest on foot for 16 years to reach his destiny and enlightenment; that is, the developmental process of transformation cannot be rushed. It has made me a better person and propelled me on to leadership roles well beyond expectations.

Just as Monkey King needed to fight his demons to learn truth from fiction, my journey also led to self-examination to retain and strengthen my identity. Just as Monkey King's spirit brought him to defy the authority and Supreme Being of the Great Jade Emperor, so did my being different challenge the traditional institutions that marked my professional career. Monkey King reached enlightenment after 81 trials because of his unbreakable spirit, not unlike the challenges and trials I have had to face of racism and sexism, which challenged my competence and suitability for leadership.

I have found my sources of support from the many colleagues with whom I have felt "of one mind" about the things for which we cared. I have found my sources of strength from my drive and passion to fix that which is broken and to heed the frequent reminders of my mother's teachings. I have learned that to resolve conflict sometimes means not to seek integration but to seek divergence in the things we do and the thoughts we have.

Barrett (Barrett et al., 2005) proclaimed, "Psychological theory needs to be representative of the full range of human experience by being based in the experience of all groups of people" (p. 27), when she honored my work and tied my professional contributions and personal stories together in a special monograph on multicultural feminist therapy. In it, she suggested how professional contributions and personal narrative intersect to provide a "powerful understanding about the nature of the intersection of race, culture, class, and gender . . . and the importance of diversity through the lens of contextual identity" (p. 27). She described how I have been "anchored in my multiple group identities and minority status . . . and have woven these into my analysis of the 'assumptive frameworks' for a vision, need for empowerment, and move toward cultural competence to conceptualize the problems inherent in Western psychology" (p. 27), as reflected in my book, *Diversity in Psychotherapy: The Politics of Race, Ethnicity, and Gender* (Chin et al., 1993). These perspectives and lived experiences have enabled me to look at problems from the outside, to ground myself, to entertain innovative solutions, and to advocate for the underrepresented and unheard voices.

Barrett said it well in that *the personal is professional.* I was able to allow her to celebrate my work in ways that my culture considered taboo, that is, not to brag but to let others do it for me. This experience was transforming for me as I learned it was OK to use the subjective "I" pronoun in my professional work. Feminist and multicultural issues are often viewed as too personal and subjective, and hence, as a lesser form of scholarly research.

Courage, Risk-Taking, and Innovation

As the first in my family and community to become a psychologist, and among the first Asian American psychologists in the United States, I found the courage to stand out and follow my passion despite family and community taboos about women's roles and professional taboos about what were acceptable areas of scholarship. As a "misfit," I took risks after measured assessment in areas that others dared not to do or were constrained by the values of the "golden ideal." The diversity of my identity and of my professional roles brought me different perspectives where I was able to look from the outside in and contribute to innovative ways of looking at the status quo and the current situation.

Development as a Multicultural Psychologist/Counselor

My development as a multicultural psychologist is embedded in the multiple cultures of my ethnicity, community, and profession. I learned I needed to be cognitively flexible to ensure accurate and relevant communication. This meant drawing from multiple psychological theories and attempting to both integrate and select those that were most appropriate for the situation, client, and population with whom I was dealing. It meant considering the cultural meaning of practices used in the culture of psychotherapy but perceived and valued differently from the client's culture—for example, the taboo against receiving gifts from patients versus the perceived insult of not accepting tokens of gratitude.

Dubious Firsts

I went on to be first in many of the roles that I took on—sometimes simply because those in my generation as women or Chinese Americans had not yet done so. Here are some of them. I was the first Asian American psychologist to be licensed in Massachusetts. Chinese Americans did not go into psychology because it was not a field that readily led to jobs in a climate where they were already disenfranchised. Besides, this was a "talking" profession. I was the first psychologist to become director of the mental health clinic that had always been run by psychiatrists prior to me. I was the first psychologist to become executive director of the community health center because psychologists simply did not enter primary health care, nor did they typically see themselves as leaders. I was the first female Asian dean at two universities. In these roles, I was told the following upon arrival by several longstanding female administrative assistants: "Do you know I have never worked for a woman before?" They retired soon after.

Women of color have often had to break many barriers to accomplish the things we do. We have had to counter stereotypes about our abilities and expectations that constrain our roles and behaviors. While we are often the first to be there, it is often a dubious accomplishment because it reflects how societal barriers and social expectations of gender and ethnicity continue to shape who has access and exclude those who are different.

For me, my development as a multicultural psychologist has been an experiment of contrasts. We were always outsiders looking in. While scholarship is hailed in the Asian culture, my Toisanese Chinese background comes from a line of peasant farmers with grade school educations. While Asian Americans are known to be "overachievers," they are not expected to be leaders in education. Asian Americans accounted for 13% of bachelor's degrees awarded between 1995 and 2005, when they made up less than 5% of the general population, that is, the model minority. Yet, Asian Americans make up less than 1.6% of senior campus administrators in higher education (Ryu, 2008).

Viewing My Working Style and My Accomplishments

Over the years, comments about my leadership style and my image have ranged from surprise to amazement, since I did not fit stereotypic images of the quiet and passive Asian female. Some comments were compliments. Others were meant to be compliments but belied the ambivalence or micro-aggressions about my gender and ethnicity. I have been described as follows:

1. "You've accomplished so much as a woman. Can you imagine what you could have done if you were a man?"

2. "You're not the typical woman leader. [Why?] You don't micromanage. You don't over focus on feelings or emotions the way most women do."

3. "Don't you know that you are not like us [meaning my being Asian]? You're just too autocratic [this greatly contrasts with how I do lead]."

4. "You don't act like most women. You think like a man [meaning my being logical and decisive]."

My leadership has often been challenged, for example:

1. "I always thought of your role as a glorified program director [instead of a dean]"—an attempt to diminish my role of authority in the system.

2. On collaboration: My reaching out for consensus and collaboration was either deemed indecisive or criticized as being too autocratic. Yet, my male predecessors were often praised for their autocratic leadership.

3. On authority: I have been told about my academic oversight, "You should just sign the dissertations. You mean you actually read them? Why?"

4. On competence: I have been challenged by men who expected me to give them undue respect for their seniority and wisdom or who were angry with me because I did not rely on them for help.

All of these challenges were "over the top," reflecting an expectation that I would behave according to stereotypic behaviors in my leadership, that I would be obsequious or cower in awe of their grandiose and privileged views of themselves vis-à-vis my being this petite Asian female. It was not uncommon to expect me to nurture and feed (as all women should), and not to decide and lead (as this is what men do). Sometimes, it was the women who challenged me more—feeling disempowered in systems where they wanted to "be like the men."

This is not to say that there have not been many positives, or I would not have advanced to the many roles that I did—it took courage, risk-taking, and innovation to get there. My view of my working style is that I am collaborative but firm in my decision making. I take on challenges while trying to actively listen to all perspectives. I infused my leadership within the non-profit community health and mental health sectors with my work in academia. I brought my experiences as a community advocate, promoting community empowerment to negotiating with academia from the inside—moving from the oppressed to the oppressor, promoting relevant training and systemic change. My navigation of different institutional cultures gave me the cognitive flexibility to reframe problems from simply expanding academic knowledge (valued in institutions of higher education) to finding solutions to address contemporary problems (valued in the community). As an Asian American, my experience of racism is personal; my years of advocacy for the underserved enabled me to look at institutional policies and procedures that were unintentionally discriminatory. Hence, cultural sensitivity or awareness is not enough; cultural competence is necessary to contribute to the strength of the system. Marginalizing cultural differences, rationalized as "we're all human," is insufficient; we need to value culture, diversity, and difference as important and central. In contrast, we should not use majority culture as the norm for all other cultural groups who are different. We need to add diversity to globalization as we educate to live and work in a global and diverse society.

This reflects a paradigm shift to revision how we think about race dynamics in the United States and the value of multiple perspectives. When we polarize it in black and white terms, the authentic stories and voices of Asian Americans are largely silenced by either positioning Asian Americans conveniently to align with Whites or ignoring consideration of their unique perspectives. Utilizing the glass ceiling theory (i.e., the concentrations of Asian Americans at lower or middle levels of the managerial ladder) in a study of Asian Americans in higher education and industry, Woo (1994) found that, beginning with the training and recruitment of Asian Americans as graduate students, up through the administrative ranks, fewer and fewer Asian

Americans were noticeable at each subsequent juncture in the pipeline. In this commissioned report, Woo concluded that subtle racism and prejudice are often engrained into systemic aspects of an organization that are difficult to trace back to the actions of individuals or specific policies; the flaw is the inability of organizations to recognize managerial styles that are different from the traditional White male leadership model.

Glass ceiling effects involve looking at the nature of the "fit" between individual characteristics in relationship to specific institutional contexts and expectations that define the contours of barriers or opportunities at different levels. For example, Asian Pacific Americans are more highly rewarded for their educational achievements. When entering the workforce, their occupational performance and talents are often confined to technical areas, and they are commended for their hard work; access to higher levels of decision making, responsibility, and leadership is limited. Their cultural conformity to Confucian values of respect for authority and unquestioning obedience and modesty may, in fact, be negatively valued as conducive to leadership within current institutional cultures, organizational practices, and social dynamics. In other words, Asian Americans may be viewed as less qualified for leadership roles because they are "hardworking, quiet, and modest." These perceptions are often viewed as reflecting personal deficits and are biased by Western definitions of assertiveness as indicative of effective leadership. This is reflected in my personal experience where my "quiet, petite, Asian American" image as an initial perception should not be and has been viewed as being unassertive. I have learned to voice my opinion and to take charge without having to be the loudest voice heard or the first to be front and center.

What Does My Future Journey Look Like?

To look at my future journey, a quote from my oral history book, *Learning From My Mother's Voice* (Chin, 2005), demonstrates the contrasts and similarities of my lived experience with that of my mother:

> Throughout the years, my mother always kept contact with her relatives and maintained her bonds with family, often distant relatives and friends from her past in China. With only a sixth grade education, she was a prolific letter writer although she was self-conscious that her writing was not scholarly enough. . . . As I started graduate school in psychology, I began to appreciate her limitations from a psychological perspective—she did not speak English, she bore the trauma of loss of her mother at the age of 5, her country upon immigration, and carried with her abandonment guilt from leaving her son

when he was 5. Or perhaps it was my journey through life with my mother at my side that helped me to rethink my culture and my identity. (p. 125)

She remained resilient, energetic, and curious (i.e., courageous); she often introduced "teaching moments" in our conversations to remind me of past struggles and future goals. I begin to think of the stories my mother told and retold. I met our ancestors of the past in our travels together:

> As I reconciled the paradoxes and contradictions of these stories, retold to heal the wounds of immigration and an unjust society, my mother and I expanded our emotional and cultural bonds. Now I hear these stories differently and look at my mother in a new light. Where I saw dependency before, I now see her bold and fierce spirit. Where I felt annoyance and impatience, I now appreciate her plight of leaving her home, family and culture. Where I saw contradiction of her obedience to my father versus her challenging of society, I now see them reconciled. In writing her story, I created her immigration legend, and preserved her voice for our children and grandchildren to form our bonds together. (Chin, 2005, p. 125)

This speaks to my journey with my mother (though she is no longer with me) despite our different experiences. I came to realize that we faced the same challenges and transformations as I negotiated a new world of professionalism, of psychology, of mainstream America that were often subject to the microaggressions of making me feel the "lack of cultural fit," of "not belonging," and of challenging my competence and identity. Today, in the 21st century, we look at women's roles in a new light, with options for career and family and freedoms in psychosocial arenas that did not exist before for women like my mother. These new roles require new competencies for women that emphasize choice, flexibility, change, and a willingness to take leadership.

My Advice for Younger Professionals

In *Women and Leadership: Transforming Visions and Diverse Voices* (Chin, Lott, Rice, & Sanchez-Hucles, 2007), the authors identify challenges faced by women in positions of leadership and how feminist principles—collaboration, inclusion, empowerment, and diversity—contribute to leadership. Women are less likely to label themselves as leaders even as they take charge in organizations and contribute to social change. Women of color have different experiences based on their unique cultures, backgrounds, and lifestyles, which often result in their experience of exclusion from key workplace relationships. A Catalyst report (Bagati, 2008) noted that they were more likely to be dissatisfied with overall managerial interaction and support, distribution of key client engagements, access to influential mentors, and access to business development opportunities.

I encourage all women and women of color to distinguish between biases and perceptions about race, ethnicity, and gender that are conflated with the exercise of effective leadership. White male leaders have the privilege of not needing to face these challenges of gender and race. Women and women of color often do not have the opportunities to meet with those who could facilitate access to positions of leadership. Opportunities for modeling behaviors are often absent. Personal, gender, and cultural identities may serve to disadvantage women from learning the behaviors associated with effective leaders while faced with doubts about their potential for being leaders. Males may use their larger physical size to be aggressive or challenge the authority of women leaders when they themselves feel threatened. For example, they may talk over women because their voices will carry; they may physically block more petite women from view. When challenged, they may justify these behaviors as speaking one's mind or suggesting that women just need to jump in.

Typically, we talk of career ladders and climbing the ladder of success when we teach about advancement. However, if aspirations for leadership are to be hidden, if quest for power is viewed as negative, if perceptions and appraisals of diverse women are biased and stereotypic, if the privilege held by White men makes them blind to the denial of access and opportunity, and if women are less likely to be in leadership roles, then what is the path to leadership roles for women and how do we mentor them?

As a result, diverse women often are challenged to be twice as good to counter the biases, perceptions, and expectations. They tend to go overboard. Instead, they need to learn to strike the balance, how and when to be tough and aggressive versus warm and compassionate. They need to create access and opportunities where there are none. As trailblazers, they are likely to meet resistance as the first female to be in such a leadership position. Women may also be unable to accept another woman's authority because they expect or want a man to be in charge and themselves are inculcated to such environments.

The double standard is another dimension of the maze that women need to navigate. Women will be condemned for crying and viewed as not tough enough; yet when they are aggressive just like men, they are condemned for behaving in an overbearing way. Women are expected to be nice.

Access and opportunity are often central to people obtaining positions of leadership. It is being in the right place at the right time. It is the politics of knowing the right people. It is in the opportunity to perform those tasks that bring recognition and provide access to leadership roles. Often women and racial and ethnic minorities are excluded from these opportunities. Women face the challenge of work balance more so than men. Racial and ethnic minority women often find they must choose between their participation in multiple social contexts—those that meet their affiliation needs for race and ethnicity—and those that are useful for ascending to positions of leadership.

Where Does This Leave Us?

In sharing my professional journey, my hope is to convey that the *personal is professional*. My journey of contrasts, transformation, diversity, and firsts can provide insight for counselors and therapists on women's lives. In counseling women, we need to unlearn stereotypes that result in superficial assumptions about women and a one-size-fits-all mentality. Women in the 21st century face new and different challenges (e.g., work-family balance, career and family choices that were not part of earlier dialogues). We need to revitalize the emphasis on cultural competencies and cognitive flexibility that enables counselors and therapists to reframe problems and solutions relevant to contemporary society. Women need to bring all of themselves to the table, including their cultures, lived experiences, worldviews, and social identities that shape their richness and complexity.

We need to challenge and address the perceptions about social gender roles and cultural characteristics that influence the expectations for women to behave in stereotypic ways. We need to make conscious choices about how to respond to microaggressions and not allow them to shape our behavior or constrain our identities. For example, how might ethnic garb distract from your being viewed as a credible leader? How is the display of emotion interpreted?

We need to recognize that there are double standards in expectations of women. While current leadership theories celebrate transformational change, collaboration, and connectedness as ideal leadership characteristics, women leaders who behave collaboratively may find themselves deemed indecisive as leaders while men leaders are complimented.

Does this constrain authenticity or, worse yet, become interpreted as disingenuous? The leadership literature is now replete with emphasis on authenticity as an important leadership characteristic (Avolio & Wernsing, 2008). Yet it does not factor in the influence of ethnicity and gender on that authenticity. In conforming or challenging the perceptions and expectations about our leadership, one must not fall prey to losing authenticity. For example, women tend to undersell themselves in a negotiation. I coach them to learn to put aside their cultural prescriptions and ethnicity when they are negotiating. Don't be modest about your accomplishments or salary expectations when negotiating a position; it does not mean you are being untrue to who you are.

Why did I enter the ranks of leadership? Not unlike many women, I fell into it and was seeking social change. When I look at certain points in my career, it was going to be me or it was not going to happen. I wanted to make a difference. My wish for social justice, to see organizational change, to help people, to promote access to care, to educate future generations to live and work in a global and diverse society, have all driven me toward leadership roles. But it was the perception of my needing "to do it like everyone else" and the expectation that I be the "spokesperson for all Chinese or Asians" that drove me to embrace diversity and cultural competence. My conceptualizations did not always fit what was considered right by "the mainstream." In many ways, I provided the refreshing breath of innovation and difference; at the same time, I posed the threat of change. This has been the biggest challenge of all.

Mentoring Women to Be Leaders

Mentoring women to be leaders is important to help them realistically identify their strengths and weaknesses and understand how these will be related to effective leadership. Mentors are those more experienced individuals helping those less experienced to advance their careers, enhance their education, and build their networks. My advice is to seek out your mentors to help you navigate the maze before you. For mentors, the task is one of identifying promising protégés and urging them in their career paths and role choices. A mentor, then, is someone who believes in you. For mentors, the responsibility is to reach down and pay back when you've ascended to higher levels of authority and leadership. For mentees, it is to seek those to whom you aspire and admire based on core values and career choices.

Women as mentors often have the advantage of sharing in the experiences of bias and barriers that are different from men. Work-family balance, pregnancy, caretaking of family members, and child care are some of the challenges faced by women as they ascend the career ladder. Although men are increasing playing greater roles of coparenting and sharing in the housework, women still bear the burden. Modeling how to juggle living with difference, in two cultures, is something mentors can do for women of color. How does one return to one's culture of origin and community, retain one's identity, and still participate actively in multiple contexts where the tolerance for difference may be lacking? Men can be good mentors, especially when they are able to create access in ways that women may not. Mentors can help women into leadership roles by encouraging them to be there, speak up, work hard, have a vision for where they want to be, and come together for a common cause.

References

Avolio, B., & Wernsing, T. S. (2008). Practicing authentic leadership. In S. J. Lopez (Ed.), *Positive psychology: Exploring the best in people. Vol 4: Pursuing human flourishing* (pp. xvii, 147–165). Westport, CT: Praeger/Greenwood.

Bagati, D. (2008, October). *Women of color in U.S. securities firms.* Women of Color in Professional Services Series. New York, NY: Catalyst Research Reports.

Barrett, S., with Chin, J. L., Comas-Diaz, L., Espin, O., Greene, B., & McGoldrick, M. (2005). Multicultural feminist therapy: Theory in context. *Women & Therapy, 28*(3/4), 27–62.

Chin, J. L. (2005). *Learning from my mother's voice: Family legend and the Chinese American experience.* New York, NY: Teachers College Press.

Chin, J. L., De La Cancela, V., & Jenkins, Y. (1993). *Diversity in psychotherapy: The politics of race, ethnicity, and gender.* Westport, CT: Praeger.

Chin, J. L., Lott, B., Rice, J., & Sanchez-Hucles, J. (Eds.). (2007). *Women and leadership: Transforming visions and diverse voices.* Malden, MA: Blackwell.

Cynkar, A. (2007). Profiles of women leaders. *Monitor on Psychology, 38*(7), 67.

Ryu, M. (2008). *Minorities in higher education 2008: Twenty-third status report* (Report No. 311884). Washington, DC: American Council on Education.

Woo, D. (1994). *The glass ceiling and Asian Americans.* Washington, DC: U.S. Department of Labor Glass Ceiling Commission, Office of the Secretary. Retrieved from http://digitalcommons.ilr.cornell.edu/cgi/viewcontent .cgi?article=1130&context=key_workplace

7

Journey to Advance Equity

A Never-Ending Road

By Cheryl Holcomb-McCoy

Gifted Education Program Teacher:	"He doesn't 'fit' the gifted class. Why would you nominate him?"
Me:	"Because he's my smartest student."
Gifted Education Program Teacher:	"I don't know about that. He doesn't fit the gifted program. Maybe he should just be in a more advanced reading group."
Me:	"No. He meets the program criteria. And most important, he is brilliant, smarter than any of the other students. What do you mean by 'fit'? He's as smart as the other students."
Gifted Education Program Teacher:	"You know. Not a good fit."

This exchange between me and the gifted education program teacher at the school where I started my education career marked a significant event in my career development. Twenty-two years old and straight out of an undergraduate education program, I was a young, energetic kindergarten teacher reacting to what I perceived as an unfair gifted identification process. At the time, kindergarten teachers were asked to identify extraordinary, supersmart students who should be considered for a "gifted program." One student in my class stood out among the others. He was a brilliant African American student with an uncanny memory, third-grade reading and math abilities, and a keen sense of humor. Although a behavior challenge at times, I believed he would do well in a gifted program. Quite frankly, most of his behavioral difficulties resulted from boredom and lack of challenge. Most often he would joke around in "special classes" (e.g., music, art, PE) and other students would follow his lead. I knew the kindergarten curriculum was too slow for him and he needed the stimulation and challenge of an accelerated curriculum.

My colleagues, especially the gifted education program teacher, were aware of his behavioral difficulties in special classes and overtly opposed the idea of him in a gifted program, no matter how smart he was. Instead, they wanted him to be placed in a first-grade reading group and receive behavioral support. All year, they created a "narrative" of him being a troublemaker, unlikeable, too loud, too talkative, a know-it-all, unnerving, and threatening. A five-year old is threatening? No one acknowledged his giftedness and talent. It's important to note that there were several White students nominated for the gifted program with similar behavioral traits. But their behaviors were labeled as "assertiveness" and "leadership skills."

When tested, his scores were in the highest range—clearly making him eligible for the program. Nevertheless, my colleagues continued to see only a low-income, misbehaving, threatening, African American boy who didn't fit their profile of a gifted child in an overwhelmingly White program where children were tracked to the most advanced, segregated, college prep courses and curriculum.

Using my advocacy skills, I went to the principal to plead my case on behalf of my student. The principal, a fair leader who took into consideration the student's placement test scores and my recommendation, determined that he should be considered for the program. Finally, he was offered placement. Interestingly enough, I found out years later that he excelled in the program and matriculated into one of the most prestigious engineering schools in the country! I wonder how many students miss the opportunity to go to selective universities because of bias and faulty identification processes.

This incident marked the beginning of my professional journey and personal mission for ensuring equitable opportunities and well-being for those most vulnerable in our society. For me, two themes have emerged in my life that illustrate and embody what it means to be a professional counselor and educator: (a) a strong desire to improve the lives of others, particularly the most vulnerable; and (b) an appreciation for the resilience of the human spirit. After many years in the profession, I still believe professional counselors can provide the gateway to opportunities through their advocacy for students and families.

As a kindergarten teacher and later as a school counselor in a high-minority, high-poverty elementary school, I observed not only extreme levels of poverty but also extreme bias toward families and children from economically disadvantaged backgrounds. My most profound memories from those early days are the students' faces when they realized I cared and the hope in the eyes of parents when told their child could "be whatever he or she wanted to be." I also remember, just as vividly, when my heart would sink after hearing colleagues' (such as the gifted education program teacher) "negative talk" about families, communities, and even the children in their classes. I carry these early observations with me every day, and they have shaped my career as a professional counselor, counselor educator, and university administrator.

The remainder of this chapter covers aspects of my professional journey that I consider to be significant markers or transitions. The chapter ends with guidelines or tips for young counseling professionals.

Doctoral Studies: The Only One

After serving as an elementary school counselor for five years, I knew I wanted to do more but had no idea counselor education was going to be my academic home. I traveled to Greensboro, North Carolina, from Silver Spring, Maryland, to visit The University of North Carolina at Greensboro (UNCG). I had every intention of only "checking it out" but decided immediately after the visit to make Greensboro home for a while. My initial goal was to attain a PhD and then return to Maryland to open a private practice serving children and families who couldn't be served by school-based counselors. I had recommended community-based counseling for many families only to find that there were limited numbers of counseling professionals with the skills and knowledge to effectively counsel students from diverse backgrounds. So I thought this was a lucrative area for me to pursue.

After a year or so of studying under the guidance of UNCG counseling "greats," such as Drs. Jane Myers, Nicholas Vacc, DiAnne Borders, James Benshoff, and Bill Purkey, I became more committed to a professorial career. Preparing school counselors to be more effective and competent in their work with students and families from historically oppressed backgrounds became more attractive and aligned with my overall personal mission.

Very few of my colleagues and doctoral cohort members shared my passion, commitment, and fervor for a multicultural and equity-based research agenda. So my journey of being the "lone voice" or "solo advocate" to consider cultural difference began. I wrote every paper, including my dissertation, about the impact of culture and/or cultural background on the topic at hand. While my cohort embraced my identity and career focus, being the "only underrepresented minority" was a heavy responsibility and taxing role. Am I further narrowing the perspective of how my cohort and professors see me by advocating for cultural issues to be considered in counseling? Will my questions about culture, race, gender, and "others" alienate me from my colleagues? While risky, the courage to be consistent, persistent, and true to my beliefs paid off. I developed a "reputation" for my early work and focus, which led to several meetings, presentations, and opportunities with accomplished faculty in the field.

Around the same time I launched my dissertation research, the Association for Multicultural Counseling and Development (AMCD) published a new set of multicultural counseling competencies. My dissertation research, including an examination of the AMCD competencies and their relationship with training experiences, became relevant to the field and pivoted my career path quickly. Relevant and timely scholarship makes for an easier career launch!

First Academic Appointment: Balancing Life Roles

I met my husband while in North Carolina. He was a graduate business school student at Duke University, and two years before I graduated, he started his career in New York City. While his move to New York City was a motivator for a rapid completion (three years!) of my dissertation, I was also anxious to start my career. Little did I know in my doctoral program that balancing a new marriage and a new career was the big hurdle—not the dissertation! Late-night writing and preparing for classes became the norm. I was lucky my husband was also starting a new career that required him to work late. The first years of our marriage were consumed with work and trying to "fit in" to our new roles as partner and career person.

It's well known in the literature that women faculty craft and leverage various "alternative narratives" and perspectives as navigational tools amid inequitable, gendered dynamics in the higher education setting. And women of color faculty have even more challenges given that we remain underrepresented at all levels of the professoriate in U.S. colleges and universities.

My first academic position as assistant professor at Brooklyn College of The City University of New York (CUNY), primarily a teaching institution, was a perfect first step in my professional career because of the culturally diverse faculty available to me on campus. Not only were my colleagues diverse in cultural background, but they also possessed a similar passion for pursuing educational equity and cultural responsiveness in K–12 classrooms. When I reflect on this period of my professional development, I immediately think of feeling as if I had found my "intellectual kindred spirits." My colleagues exposed me to theories and concepts of urban education, school reform and restructuring, and systemic change in schools. I busily applied these concepts to my understanding of school counseling practice and roles. And more important, I began applying these concepts to counselor training. These applications were the beginning of my scholarship related to urban school counseling and measuring school counselor multicultural competence.

Second Academic Appointment: On a Roll

I arrived at the University of Maryland, College Park (UMCP), a large research-intensive university, after two years at Brooklyn College. My husband and I agreed that we wanted a family and thus wanted to be closer to our relatives in Virginia and Maryland. Brooklyn College had grounded me in my scholarship but UMCP had the potential to give me the opportunity to write and research in a way that would serve me well later in my career.

At UMCP my publication record progressed, I received excellent mentoring from women (e.g., Jane Myers), and scholars in the counseling field (e.g., Courtland Lee), established my teaching of master's and doctoral level courses, supervised doctoral research, and codeveloped an urban school counseling program. Personally, I became a mother, giving birth to both my son and daughter during my pretenure years. Some would characterize this moment as courageous because many women opt to delay childbearing until after tenure. I consciously decided that I didn't want to wait and didn't see having children as courageous but as a natural next step in my life. My departmental colleagues were supportive and I found a good balance in structuring my time between mothering and academic/career responsibilities.

Around this same time, I joined a wonderful group of African American women who were part of a counselor education faculty in the Washington, D.C., area. They were all untenured at the time. We met on Saturdays not only to craft manuscripts but also to listen to each other's trials and concerns. This peer-mentoring model served us well. We wrote three manuscripts that were published, and more important, we were all successfully tenured.

What's Next?

Receiving tenure gave me some comfort and stability but it didn't satisfy my thirst for making even more of a difference in the field. After securing tenure, I made several conscious decisions—to explore long-term research projects, to mentor junior faculty, and to increase my knowledge of grants and contracts. Like many of the posttenure female faculty members that I observed, I didn't want to spend most of my time on service obligations and miss promotions and institutional rewards connected to scholarship. I began saying "no" to those activities that were not directly related to my professional and personal goals. As difficult as it was to say "no," it was worth it. I no longer spent my time preparing for conference presentations or writing short articles or book chapters. These activities took time away from larger, more significant projects that required more time and effort. As a result of my career shift, I wrote my first successful grant proposal and was able to conduct a three-year research project. Managing a grant project required another set of skills (e.g., project management, budgeting) and knowledge that I had to learn. Growth requires more learning and a willingness to admit one's shortcomings.

Midcareer Changes

There is some debate as to whether one should change jobs frequently. On the one hand, many people think one should keep doing the same job throughout his or her life, whereas others advise multiple jobs are a benefit. For many reasons, I opted to be open to a job change after acquiring tenure. First, after 11 years at UMCP, I wanted to conduct more interdisciplinary research for new proposals and believed that other institutions might be more open and nimble for this type of work. Second, I wanted to build and develop a school counseling program with a focus on school reform, college access, and urban settings. And last, I thought that a change in institution could bring renewed excitement to my career. When colleagues from Johns Hopkins University approached me about joining them, I accepted their offer and gained access to a totally new landscape of higher education. A private selective institution, Johns Hopkins offered collaborative opportunities with top-notch faculty, an entrepreneurial culture, and a reputation for world-class research. Nonetheless, the School of Education at Johns Hopkins lacked tenure (but had long-term contracts) for faculty and was much smaller in its infrastructure (e.g., graduate school only) than UMCP. Tenure, which provides a high degree of job security and a tremendous amount of respectability in the academy, was my ultimate goal at one point in my career. However, during my last years at UMCP, tenure didn't seem to matter as much. Most of my colleagues thought I was making a mistake by leaving my tenured position to go to a faculty position without tenure, even at a prestigious institution like Johns Hopkins.

The transition to Johns Hopkins, with all the pros and cons, turned out to be a good professional decision. I was promoted to full professor and several career opportunities were offered to me. I was department chair for almost two years, vice dean of academic affairs for three years, and vice provost for two years. Although nervous about becoming an administrator at first, it has suited me well. With my children older and more independent, the shift to a 12-month contract and longer hours was not as difficult. A huge difference for me has been embodying the role of "administrator." No matter how understanding I am of faculty responsibilities, as an administrator, comments regarding what "the administration" doesn't know, understands, realizes, or focuses on—any of the host of complaints that can come from the "us vs. them" of faculty and administration—are different when you are an administrator. Whether you like it or not, you are part of that often nameless and faceless body of otherness embodied in that phrase: "the administration." All in all, my intuition about going to Johns Hopkins turned out well. The lesson learned was to trust your gut and resist second guessing yourself.

My Future: Still Advocating for Students

I am very optimistic about my career development and future beyond Johns Hopkins. In fall 2016, I became dean of the School of Education at American University in Washington, D.C., again experiencing a new transition and change in my career development. My family is supportive of the move and as usual, I am juggling family and work. Some of my colleagues were shocked that I was not continuing the central administration track to a provost position. Nevertheless, I see this as not only a chance for me to lead but an opportunity to collaborate more fully with K–12 school districts and community organizations. This move is totally aligned with my initial desire or goal to ensure equitable outcomes and opportunities for our most vulnerable populations through the training of teachers and educators to work in metropolitan and/or city schools.

At some point, I would like to return to a faculty position in counseling, where I can again supervise doctoral students' research. I remain open to the wide array of possibilities that could still happen in my career. Working at and/or leading a nonprofit organization, being a college provost or president, or owning an education/counseling product or service are all possibilities.

Beliefs Guide Behaviors

All of my experiences—research, teaching, service, advisement, counselor supervision, and leadership—are grounded in my belief in the common human experience, which includes a need for self-worth, validation, and belongingness. In essence, since my early days as a kindergarten teacher, I have continued to see the need for human connectedness and resilience. Even faculty members need to feel connected to their departments, and students want to belong and feel welcomed among peers in their counseling programs.

During my tenure as a school counselor, I was awed by children's resilience in spite of their many obstacles. One student in particular made a lasting impression on me. An 11-year-old, high-achieving, Black male with a positive and cheerful personality showed up at my office one day to talk. After a few minutes of chatting, I realized he was struggling with difficult family issues. Given his high academic achievement and happy demeanor, he was not "on my radar" for needing assistance. His story reflected resilience and the ability to push forward through incredible circumstances. This early encounter in my career further enhanced my appreciation for the human experience. In the face of adversity, many (even those as young as 11) have the resilience and capacity to keep moving forward.

I pursued degrees in counseling not only because of my desire to help others but also because of my fascination with human thought and behavior. Recently, I've engaged in exciting conversations with cognitive scientists at Johns Hopkins to explore the connections between their research, based in neuroscience, and counseling process research. Being a professional counselor has enabled me to study and engage in important research that propels the field in new directions. In addition, I continue to "fine-tune" my counseling relational skills (e.g., listening, empathy, reframing, self-reflection), which promote "change" in human thought and behavior. To me, counselor characteristics and/or dispositions are equally important as counseling skills. Honesty, confidence, optimism, open-mindedness, flexibility, stability, and genuineness are ideal characteristics for professional counselors, particularly in light of clients' multilayered problems and dilemmas.

I'm drawn to the profession's more recent focus on advocacy and social justice. A social justice perspective in professional counseling represents a shift from traditional individually focused models to more "client within context" models. I agree with Ratts's (2009) notion that "the social justice counseling paradigm uses social advocacy and activism as a means to address inequitable social, political, and economic conditions that impede the academic, career, and personal/social development of individuals, families, and communities" (p. 160). For professional counseling, an emphasis on social justice expands our capacity to understand the human spirit and enhances our understanding of the impact of oppression on clients' everyday lives.

Advice for Younger Counseling Professionals

It's difficult to give overarching advice about becoming a courageous and innovative faculty member or counselor educator because there are so many factors and personal characteristics (and luck!) that must be considered when making career and/or life choices. My best advice for graduate students is to know your passion and desire for the work you do. Stay committed to your passion and be yourself.

Another seemingly obvious piece of advice would be to do your work well. Fine-tune your skills and/or craft so that no one will be able to criticize your work ethic or desire to succeed. When I was first appointed to an assistant professor position, I read at least five articles a day. I read because I wanted to understand the structure of scholarly writing. Likewise, when I received feedback from editors about rejected manuscripts, I would read the comments multiple times for clarity about the direction of the revised version. Clearly, this is a difficult process. Being able to digest brutal criticism from peers requires thick skin. I definitely have thick skin!

Courage, risk-taking, and innovation require personal confidence and a sense of integrity. For some, these attributes come naturally, and for others, they can be developed. These three traits also require the person to be in a position of receiving few possible consequences. It's much easier to be a risk-taker and to be innovative when tenured and a senior member of the faculty. I recommend that young faculty members accept positions in highly supportive departments where risk-taking and innovation are valued.

Following are a few lessons I learned along my journey:

- *Find your passion.* Be true to you. Find your passion and structure your career around it.
- *Find a support network.* Identify colleagues who understand where you are trying to go ("your goals") and are supportive (avoid naysayers). Good colleagues and friends will keep you grounded and ready for the bumps in the road.

- *Balance work and family.* Finding a "sweet spot" for balancing work and family is a number one priority for young professionals. Find departments and universities that value and support families of faculty. When your family is happy, you can be creative and innovative.
- *Don't fear change.* Change is often what's needed for growth. Action deflates fear.
- *It's okay to struggle.* No one is perfect; we all make mistakes and endure failure. As long as you keep reaching out for support and maintaining the courage to try, it's okay to struggle.
- *Trust your intuition.* Your "gut" will often tell you what you need to do.
- *Hone your skills* (e.g., writing, research). Be good at what you do.
- *Negative things happen to everyone. Attempting to avoid negative events (e.g., manuscript rejection) proves an exercise in futility.* Adversity can often provide an opportunity to strengthen your character, deepen your emotional fortitude, and increase your overall sense of self.

I consider "my professional journey" as in perpetuity. My new administrative position will hopefully lead to more discoveries and innovative structures for ensuring excellent and diverse educators in today's schools. My two life themes—(a) a strong desire to improve the lives of others, particularly the most vulnerable; and (b) an appreciation for the resilience of the human spirit—will continue to guide my work as long as I live.

Reference

Ratts, M. J. (2009). Social justice counseling: Toward the development of a "fifth force" among counseling paradigms. *Journal of Humanistic Counseling, Education, and Development, 48,* 160–172.

8

Prepared Serendipity Mixed With Naïve but Eager Curiosity

By Arthur M. Horne

When one achieves senior status (aka being old), there is the opportunity for reflection. The invitation to prepare this chapter provides that stimulus to examine a number of occasions that have shaped my life, and the opportunity is appreciated. My life has been rich and full and very enjoyable, even during the times and activities many would classify as challenging or even unpleasant, such as low-level jobs to pay for school. I believe the innate personal temperament that helps me find joy in my activities is one of the serendipitous characteristics of my career. Being born of a positive nature has been good for me, and I highly recommend it for all. The core conditions described on the following pages embody my experiencing of the theoretical model developed by John Krumboltz, which he named "planned happenstance" in his excellent career development scholarship (Krumboltz, 2008). His theoretical advances in this area have been a major influence in my life and in the experiences of many in our area of specialization.

A core serendipitous event was being born and growing up in the university town of Gainesville, Florida. My family of origin was predominantly poor, uneducated or undereducated, and rural. However, we lived in a university community where many—even most—of my peers and friends were children of professors or others associated with higher education. Our teachers were often spouses of faculty or were working on or possessed their own graduate degrees. Expectation was that all—or at least most—of us students would do well academically and go on to college, regardless of family circumstances.

School and community were two of a number of early influences that shaped the direction my life has taken. They include the following:

Dealing with birth order. Being first born and an only child for 14 years resulted in a lot of attention and engagement from parents and provided a sense of "special but with high expectations for the family future." Being read to and learning to read early; being included in family conversations and planning; playing lots of games and being supported in activities such as Boy Scouts, church, and school activities; and being coached in sports, all influenced early development that fostered leadership and active engagement.

Being prepared. I was taught early on that wishful thinking seldom solved problems, and that one had to be prepared for the events that came in life. The old Boy Scout motto "Be Prepared" fit well, as it emphasized that serendipitous events would occur, and the prepared person could be advantaged when they do. This was strongly underscored by parents, grandparents, teachers, Boy Scout leaders, and ministers ("The Lord helps those who help themselves"; "Build your house upon the rock"). This became part of the anthem of "Prepared Serendipity," which has been a core lifelong belief for me.

Delaying gratification. My parents and teachers had a common theme: It is better to work hard and keep the eye on the goal to achieve greater rewards in the future than it is to have a lesser achievement immediately. This became evident as I saw others who were not able to delay gratification, either positively (do the homework and then have some refreshments) or negatively (fighting rather than calming down and working out problems).

Reasonable risk-taking. Early exhortations that I remember include "go ahead and try it; nothing risked, nothing gained; leaders don't stand behind the crowd; you are certainly as good as they are—go for it." My father had a way of supporting risk-taking. He never commanded but would say things like, "I'm guessing you know what you need to do to do this. Just try it and see what happens. What would the first step be?"

Teachers opening awareness. Being a student in public schools in a university community with talented teachers provided untold opportunities, such as having music teachers make available opportunities to attend university concerts, literature teachers who knew famous authors who would come visit our classrooms, and art teachers who could access the museums and galleries. Further, having high school faculty teaching psychology, sociology, anthropology, and world issues opened doors of knowledge and imagination undreamed of in many schools at the time. Having a school counselor who actually knew what it meant to be a school counselor—and could run groups for a variety of concerns for students—was amazing. Dating classmates whose parents were psychology professors, or etymologists, or literature faculty members, exposed me to a world far beyond the expectations of most of my relatives living in other communities.

Working as a motivator. I began working in a livestock yard at the age of 14. It was truly dirty, often disgusting work. My father said to me once when I was cleaning manure out of the cow stalls, "That is hard work you are doing, no doubt about it. If you don't want to spend your life shoveling cow crap, you better study your tail off, because only education is going to get you out of this kind of work." It was good advice. The stockyard work put me in contact with many interesting people and helped shape my beliefs that being successful requires hard work but also rests on many more factors than that, including serendipitous events beyond one's control. Everyone in the stockyards worked hard, but that did not always result in success. I worked with persons of color who attended segregated schools, came from families who experienced poverty far worse than mine, and did not really have much of a chance for success as they moved toward adulthood. I remember the sadness I experienced knowing that with all the difficulties I had in my life, at least the opportunity for getting out of poverty existed for me, although not for most of them. At that point in my life, the condition I experienced was not called White male privilege; it was called shame and embarrassment.

Realizing that marriage can help. I was one of the first in the family to graduate from high school, but I married into a family where graduate degrees were the expectation. Becoming a member of a family with a strong educational engagement can certainly shape one's goals and aspirations. Realizing that the family of Gayle, my wife, valued education and supported it in many ways prompted me to join the team—to go for education and the opportunities that would become available as a result of a commitment to lifelong learning and advancing knowledge through teaching, research, and practice. My marital family always supported this commitment.

(Continued)

(Continued)

Colleagues influencing careers. Throughout my academic career, I have worked with great colleagues, people who were able to inspire and encourage me. Truly believing "the whole is greater than the sum of the parts" resulted in teaming up and developing innovative and inspirational programs and interventions. Also, working with leaders who could provide entré into the academic and professional circles resulted in leadership roles becoming available early in my career. For example, my colleague, Merle Ohlsen, had just completed his term as president of the American Counseling Association when I joined the faculty with him, and he provided a number of opportunities, including reviewing books, manuscripts, and program proposals; being invited to conduct workshops and training; and serving on editorial boards and association committees.

Educational Influences

In a family and community setting where educators and parents expected success and accomplishment, regardless of family backgrounds, it was easy to see myself as "one of the group" for whom achievement and accomplishment were a given. That, and being in leadership roles throughout my public school education, created a sense of agency, of self-efficacy for success, regardless of the endeavor. There is a lifelong benefit to mingling with highly competent and achieving classmates, peers, and colleagues—they expect the same of you.

At the university level, I encountered challenges that were substantial, particularly for one without sufficient funds to cover expenses, which resulted in working throughout college, usually 30-plus hours a week. But in the romanticized vision of the poor beating the odds and succeeding, the various work experiences were seen as opportunities rather than challenges, and a lot was learned in the process. For example, working in a large jewelry store and becoming a specialist in selling diamonds to newly engaged college students provided opportunities in sales (persuasion), service, entrepreneurship, and connecting with people, while earning enough funds to continue in school.

My early intention was to be a psychology major. However, I found early psychology courses to be of a general nature and with a strong experimental bias. They were, in short, boring, and for a person focused on finding relevance in my studies, I had little enthusiasm for the Psychology Department. Thus, I chose a much more career-relevant area: English literature and journalism.

Upon completing my bachelor's degree, I became an English teacher, again in the same community of Gainesville, which meant it was very easy to continue with graduate education without having to travel, another serendipitous event. As a teacher, it quickly became evident that English literature, as a topic of study, was a most enjoyable focus, particularly learning about the lives of the authors and how their personal experiences influenced their writing. But teaching English, including all that went with it—spelling, grammar, mundane literature that secondary schoolers were exposed to, endless grading of papers for 180 students at a time—was not. My great enjoyment was engaging and interacting with students, but not as a teacher, and so I looked for a different way to connect with learners. Becoming a school counselor was an easy choice. It took me back to my earlier interest in psychology and applied mental health, including understanding people and their motivations, which was much of the appeal in English literature from the beginning. Moreover, it provided the opportunity to work with young people while providing a service to schools and communities and to be involved in a truly engrossing and thoroughly enjoyable subject matter: counseling and mental health service. I learned early in my counseling program that part of the success of the work we do is in meeting the needs of the clients but also—of great importance—in meeting our own personal and emotional needs in a healthy manner. Working with students helped them and resulted in my feeling accomplished, satisfied, and excited; both sides benefitted.

Beginning coursework in counseling at the University of Florida was one of the greatest experiences of my academic career. The faculty was stimulating, engaged, often charismatic, and very committed to social justice, though we didn't call it by that name then. They influenced me dramatically, to the point that I still refer to their teachings today. The counseling content was thought-provoking, and it was applicable; it connected with me so much more than the undergraduate psychology courses ever did. (The program then, as today, reflected teaching the basics of counseling, assuring that counselors are empathic, warm, genuine, congruent, and concrete in developing relationships with clients. The emphases advocated by many in the field at that time, including Robert Carkhuff (Carkhuff & Berenson, 1977), Arthur Combs (1976), C. H. Patterson (1966), and Carl Rogers (1961), were very consistent with current models of today, including Clara Hill (2009), Allen Ivey (Ivey, A. E., Ivey, M. B., & Zalaquett, 2009), Fred Leger, (1997), Randall Pipes (Pipes & Davenport, 1998), and Thomas Skovholt (2012), but the topics were amazing to me then.

Counseling with students was all I had hoped for. To be able to engage, to understand their life situations, and to help them adapt to the circumstances they experienced was exciting and meaningful. But wait—"help them adapt to the circumstances they experienced"? That belief changed quickly. I can still cite examples of faculty members (50 years later!) challenging my beliefs and expectations as I entered the field. On the topic of helping students "adapt," one faculty member—Sidney Jourard—stated to me clearly and emphatically, "I cannot condone counselors whose goal is to place round students into square holes, and yet that is what passes for school counseling in most of our schools. Help the students find where and how they will fit; don't force them into the predetermined roles that schools assign them." This statement, to me, became the essence of ethical counseling, of a commitment to facilitating growth and development in a socially just and respectful manner.

When I began counseling at my school, again in Gainesville, the director of guidance, who was a retired career military officer, asked, "Horne, all counselors in our school have assigned responsibilities. Do you want sick bay, attendance/record keeping, scheduling, or discipline?" I was flabbergasted. This was inconsistent with all the preparation of my graduate program, but I quickly responded, "Give me discipline." That decision shaped the rest of my career. For the next 40 years I engaged, one way or another, in addressing behavior problems young people were experiencing.

I determined quickly that even with a master's degree in counseling I didn't know enough to be the counselor I thought the students needed. I determined to go on to a doctoral program with the expectation that I would learn what was needed to address the problems of discipline, delinquency, aggression and violence, and all the factors contributing to creating kids who were oppositional defiant disordered, conduct disordered, or otherwise behaviorally challenging. Fortunately, I had a family who agreed to the years of restricted income and limited discretionary time that goes with doctoral studies—at least my wife did; the kids were too young to vote. They supported the move and the shift from teacher/counselor to student, a major contribution to my career taking the direction it did.

Doctoral studies were great! At that time, being a graduate assistant provided almost as much income as being an educator in Florida, and the work was delightful. Being paid to have thought-provoking discussions with faculty and students, developing and conducting research programs because they were interesting and challenging, and justifying studying as "that's my job," all resulted in a most positive occasion. Moreover, the faculty and my peers validated the experiences. They encouraged me to continue, explore, reach out, and to be innovative in my work and to dream large in my plans. It is always good to have your hopes validated by peers and mentors.

Upon finishing the doctorate, I began the job search. I tentatively accepted a position at a student counseling center at a university, but then that university hired one of my classmates for an academic slot. When I learned he would earn as much in 9 months as I did in 12, because he was academic and I was counseling center staff, though we had the same degree from the same university at the same time and I had considerably more experience, I withdrew my acceptance and went back on the open market. That was one of the most fortuitous experiences for me, as I then found an academic position at Indiana State University and had a marvelous 18-year academic experience there.

At Indiana State University I continued my membership in the American Counseling Association (American Association for Counseling and Development at that time), joined the American Psychological Association, including Division 17, Counseling Psychology, and became a licensed psychologist in Indiana. The position provided entry into an academic world of teaching, research, and practice, but it also opened the door to phenomenal opportunities. When I begin studying in counseling, we examined the original works of the developers and innovators of mental health counseling, but there weren't that many models being studied at the time. We had the original leaders in psychiatry, such as Freud and Adler, and the early behavioral writers, such as Skinner and Baer, or in my experience, Krumboltz and Thoreson. Then there were the early leaders in humanistic or person-centered approaches, such as Rogers, May, Maslow, and Jourard. As more models were introduced into our field and we moved toward developing our own literature, it became more difficult for programs preparing counselors to require original text reading. Some collections began to emerge, such as Corsini's *Current Psychotherapies* (1973), in which model developers presented their theories in a structured format in summary form. Corsini's original text had 12 chapters on analytic, client-centered, rational-emotive, behavioral, gestalt, reality, experiential, transactional, encounter, and eclectic therapies. Four decades later we have several hundred models advocated for counseling and psychotherapy, resulting in both a responsibility and the advantages of being an applied psychologist in an academic setting—having the opportunity to grow professionally! Woe to those who assume learning stops with the granting of a degree; learning is a continuous and ever expanding opportunity.

My graduate training had emphasized one-on-one counseling. This progressed to group work, including a variety of group models (encounter, T-, therapy, psychoeducational, etc.). Marriage and family therapy was added to my area of expertise, and a systemic orientation was adopted; family was expanded to include traditional, single parent, GLBT, feminist, and others). The transition from individual to group to family to a systemic orientation led to the adoption of a transcultural/multicultural understanding. With the enhanced focus on the importance of diversity and systemic approaches, our approach to providing counseling and therapeutic experiences for others embraced a commitment to social justice as a core element of our training, research, and practice, and to understanding culture in a systemic manner.

With the broader systemic and inclusive approach to counseling and therapy, there came an awareness that much of our previous work had focused on alleviating the concerns and issues of individuals and groups related to the life circumstances they experienced. But we will never have enough therapists to meet all the emotional and mental health needs of the people of our communities, let alone of our nation or the world. As George Albee (1982) said, "We must recognize the fact that no mass disorder affecting large numbers of human beings has ever been controlled or eliminated by attempts at treating each affected individual or by training enough professionals as interventionists" (p. 1045).

Early in my career, several colleagues and I had the opportunity to consult on a weekly basis with a state training school for boys ages 13 to 17. We established a therapeutic community in which we trained teachers, correctional officers, and other staff on how to implement change programs with the incarcerated youth, and we had great success, by our standards. But I was once asked, "How does your follow-up data look?" We had none but immediately began collecting it. We soon learned that regardless of the level of impact our program was having on incarcerated youth, within six months of release, a majority of them were back in some form of custodial care. Understanding the familial, community, school, and peer influences on behavior led me to dedicate my energies to identifying ways to *prevent* the circumstances that led to incarceration rather than try to "fix" the problems through treatment. I felt a different approach was needed, one focused on preventing problems rather than—or in addition to—treating the persons with the problems. But this required a rethinking of how to invest time and energy, and it also was not as popular a direction as one might think, since it was a redirection from a therapy emphasis to one of prevention. And it was suggesting a rethinking of counselor training and practice. Fortunately, there were others in the field going in the same direction, such as Bob Conyne, and so the journey wasn't as lonely as it could have been.

In our counselor training programs, we had emphasized that our obligation was to the client. But in an approach emphasizing prevention, who is the client? Is it the student you are hoping to influence toward a more productive problem-solving approach? Is it the teacher who may impact an entire classroom when teaching effective conflict resolution and decision-making skills? Is it the school, which hopefully will be developing a safe and welcoming environment for all members of the school and community? Or is it the superintendent, the school board, or state legislators who develop the rules and guidelines for our schools and communities? Did we have a responsibility to students experiencing bullying due to sexual orientation issues to learn to manage the bullying and find ways of protecting themselves from the abuse, or was our responsibility to the classroom, school, and community to implement programs fostering healthy respect for all members of the community? Or both? If both, given limited resources (time, money), what is the top priority? I made the decision to focus more on policy and program development to attempt to affect larger areas of influence. Don't get me wrong—I am proud of our field and thrive on our rich history and enormous contributions to the lives of millions over the almost century-long period of counseling and therapy, but I also want my time and energy to have as large an impact as possible in today's period of reduced resources. I believe energy spent on policy and program development may be as—or more—impactful than the same resources devoted to therapy. I don't like thinking of "either-or," since both approaches are critically important, but I've moved more and more to prevention efforts.

Experiencing the Professional Journey

My professional journey has been very fulfilling but with a few caveats. First, many people say that if they had their life to live over again, they would want to do it exactly the same. I get the point, but I add that while I think my career has been outstanding for me and I've felt privileged and honored the entire time I've traveled the academic path, I've been there, done that. I loved it but would opt for something new and equally as exciting—or even more so—than the life I've had. Many of my closest friends now are in other fields, such as ecology, environmental design, marine sciences, public health, law, and medicine. I would love the opportunity to study those—and other— fields. Part of this awareness came when I was a visiting professor at the University of Otago in New Zealand. I was staying in a college of "senior residents." The other five members of the residence had degrees in other fields and had traveled the world plying their knowledge and skills. Over the months we met daily for discussions, I learned there were other whole worlds to be explored and lived. I would like the opportunity to do that.

This brings the second caveat: I get bored. In my career, I seem to run in approximately five-year engagements, and there is always an overlap of interests, but I get tired of a topic. Working with oppositional defiant and conduct disordered kids was engaging for a number of years, but that led me to working with families of the kids. I received training and certification in marriage and family therapy; that was also intriguing but just for a few years, and then it wasn't. Group counseling and group therapy were focuses of teaching, training, and research—especially related to conduct disordered youth—for about a decade before I lost interest and wanted to do something else. I enjoyed directing our counseling psychology program, but after a decade I thought living through another accreditation experience would drive me out of the field. Being a department head for several years was impactful; it allowed the opportunity to dramatically reorder academic programs and shape the hiring of faculty lines. The opportunity of being at a first-level research institution was what took me to the University of Georgia. Previously, and at Georgia, I was successful in obtaining research funding. I had grant or contract funding for my research for a period of more than 25 years. I treasured the research enterprise and appreciated that the funding freed me up to explore avenues not otherwise accessible. The universities certainly were appreciative, as the indirect costs from grants brought in enormous resources. The University of Georgia even made me a distinguished research professor; indirect funds to a university will do that for a career. For more than a decade, our team had researched reducing violence in schools and families, well-funded by the Centers for Disease Control and Prevention. The three bully prevention books our team had completed related to the project and influenced schools and community agencies. Grants from the National Institute of Mental Health and the Department of Education facilitated developing safe and welcoming schools. But I reached a point of not wanting to write another grant proposal, not wanting to serve on more review panels, not wanting to sweat the budgets and administrative hassles, and—I hate to admit it in writing—not wanting to write another peer-reviewed research paper. I knew what I did not want to do, but I was not sure what I did want to do.

So, after 35 years as an academic, I retired. I quit. I knew I was too young to stop, but I was truly bored with what I was doing, and the expectation for me if I continued was that I would apply for the next grant, keep the enterprise afloat. But I retired. And this was one of the biggest risks I had taken in my career. I believed in prepared serendipity but wasn't sure where it would take me at that point.

Retirement lasted only a brief period. First, I became a fellow with the George Soros-funded Open Society Foundations, which provided educational consultation to universities in the former Soviet Union and Eastern European Bloc countries. I made a number of trips to work with the Psychology Department at Yerevan State University in Armenia, teaching family therapy, group therapy, therapy training, and ethics. The department was examining ways of incorporating Western psychology into its more traditional experimentally focused training program. This was an adventure and a delight, and it certainly was not boring.

In the meantime, people at the University of Georgia knew of my interest in reaching out to larger change issues and asked if I would establish and direct a policy center, including working with young faculty to help them find research support as they moved to influence the policies governing educational practice in Georgia and the nation. With my growing desire to impact and change educational environments, it was a challenge worth tackling but quickly seemed to become bogged down in efforts to find funding and to gain access to the legislative process that influenced so much of education in the state.

Within a year of taking on the policy center, the office of dean of education became available. I was asked to become an interim dean, a position to which I had never aspired. But I agreed to be interim dean with the stipulation that it would be possible to make changes, some being somewhat major, so that the next dean would not have to address some of the problems. That process of initiating change seemed to work well as we tackled a number of ongoing personnel and academic challenges. I was asked to apply to be dean and received the position, so I had the opportunity of completing my career with a five-year term as dean of one of the largest colleges of education (230 faculty members; 5,000 students at that time) in the nation. While I had never aspired to senior administration, I loved it. It was the favorite position I held in my academic career.

The dean position provided me with great leverage for impact, a goal I've had throughout my career. I had senior administrative support; that was a condition for me coming out of retirement and taking the position. I had credibility, for I had retired as a distinguished research professor, had demonstrated skill in obtaining grants, had received teaching awards several times, and had worked with budgets, which is a necessity of any effective administrator these days. I had been a member of the faculty and was pro-academic. Thus, with this wealth of experience, it was possible to be both an innovative and challenging administrator while still being well-accepted by (most of) the faculty.

I was empowered by the position to have influence. Working with a great team of educators in the college, a professional development partnership was established with our community school system. The superintendent was truly dynamic and connected well with our team, and the result was a partnership that has received recognition and awards nationwide. The superintendent, Philip Lanoue, was selected as the outstanding school superintendent in the nation in 2015. The partnership was selected as one of the top professional development programs in the nation, and it is still flourishing.

This was also one of the riskiest moves I made in terms of reputation. I say this because I had an established career and a solid reputation within the field. When one becomes dean, there are many factors over which there is no control. It would have been possible for the experience to go very badly and then for me to be remembered not as a successful academic but as a failed administrator. A substantial number of my colleagues discussed the possibility of career-damaging effects that could come from either poor administrative decisions or factors far beyond my control. But it all turned out very well. There were some very challenging situations (e.g., four straight years of state budget cuts resulting in no pay increases for faculty or staff; the attempt of a very conservative state political movement to challenge public education; college and departmental reorganization to effect more efficient and effective programs), but this experience is one for which I have great pride and satisfaction.

Professional Experiences

A number of professional experiences occurred during my career, which resulted in several learnings:

Know your field. It has been interesting (amazing, really) to realize how many people in our field lack confidence and then to see how that uncertainty can negatively impact their behavior. As a department head, I would have young faculty ask how many papers they had to publish to get tenure or promotion. I always considered that the wrong question. A better approach would be to ask how to garner resources to do the research we are trained to do, how to properly prepare a paper for peer review, or how to get the creative ideas and innovative thoughts circulating in the field. I've not been taken with "safe research or required research," but I am very taken with passion, originality, and enthusiasm for our field. When preparing for doctoral exams, I was confident that the members of my examining committee would collectively know more than I did but that I would have more expertise on my topic than any of them would, and it was fun to joust with them at the orals. The defense became an experience of "taking on the teachers" and establishing a sense of authority and knowledge. The same was true for many events over the years—licensing, accreditation of programs, tenure, and promotion. The challenge was energizing and invigorating, and it helped make the work worthwhile.

Seek advanced training. I started at Indiana State University in 1971. In 1978, I took a leave to work at the Oregon Social Learning Center, one of the leading research centers in the nation studying conduct disordered youth. The program director, Gerald Patterson, and his team were doing some of the most creative and innovative work anywhere. A colleague asked how I ever managed to get such a plum opportunity with one of the premier research centers of the time. I told him, "I applied." But there was more than applying. It was a prepared serendipity experience. I had been conducting small-scale research similar to what the center was carrying out. I had followed the National Institute of Mental Health funding programs and had prepared a grant proposal. I visited the center and presented my work, and that coincided with the National Institute of Mental Health grant being funded to cover my expenses while doing the work. It was an enthralling experience, to be engaged full-time in cutting-edge research with leaders influencing the field of applied psychology. To this day, I feel honored to have been selected as part of the group. The experience changed my research, teaching, and service for the rest of my career. Let's hear it for the occasional sabbatical or research leave experience, which occurred serendipitously at the same time for me.

It pays to write. A number of my colleagues established private practices to earn additional money. I never had the time, as the academic efforts were truly full-time for me, including scholarly writing starting in graduate school and continuing throughout my career. In 1980, I began writing on family therapy and was asked if I would conduct a workshop on the topic. The workshop was for the American Counseling Association European Branch in Germany. I went and conducted the workshop, which was well-received. I was then asked to teach overseas. The next year we—my whole family—moved to Germany, and the experience changed the lives of all of us—forever—in a most positive way. As a result of that experience, I went back to work with various programs and offices in Europe for the next 18 years. Again, a colleague asked how I was so fortunate to get to teach and consult in many places around the world, and the answer was, "I wrote a paper." Again, it was much more. It was writing a paper at the right time that described the work we were doing and demonstrated that we knew our subject matter and were prepared—serendipitously.

While writing papers never provided the income that faculty with private practices may have generated, the process did offer the opportunity of influencing our field. Several papers over the years received recognition

(Continued)

(Continued)

for swaying our research and practice, and that is a most fulfilling (exhilarating?) experience. Writing books, too, has been scary but gratifying. Why is it scary? Putting thoughts out for peers and the field to examine can be somewhat frightening, particularly when it is known that some of the ideas being presented will challenge the status quo. And yet, being willing to risk the criticism, critiques, and even confrontations can be invigorating and revitalizing. But to put oneself out there does require a level of confidence in what is being presented.

Lead a balanced life. My career has been a privilege and one that has required enormous work and time commitments. But throughout the process, a major emphasis of my career has been to have a balanced life, especially with time and commitment to my family. Some colleagues sacrificed family and personal time for their careers, but it has been with great pride and enthusiasm that my family has been central to my life and not only on a personal level; my family has influenced my teaching, research, and service. I have always believed in our field of scholarship and wanted it to influence my family—I truly do believe in creating safe and welcoming families and schools—and I know my family has influenced the counseling field, for the values we hold as family members translate to healthy models for children and schools. For me, family and scholarship were always complementary. Engaging a caring and supportive life partnership helps free one up for risk-taking. When one is secure in the family domain, and there is mutual respect and shared decision making, there is greater freedom to take on risks and challenges in the world. I've been most fortunate that Gayle has been in this partnership for a half-century, and counting on more, and that both children are people I have enjoyed throughout their life span, one of whom is also a counseling psychologist.

Closing Thoughts

The work I've been able to do in counseling has never felt like risk-taking. Risk-taking would be to do "business as usual" or to maintain engagements because they are familiar and don't involve change. Again, don't get me wrong: I value and enjoy ritual and predictability, but I have needed challenge, novelty, and new opportunities. It has never felt risky to take on "sacred cows" or established patterns when other directions appear to be more promising and more consistent with the values and goals of the field of counseling. Taking leadership roles also never felt chancy. They were taken because of an anticipation of being able to make changes and have an impact, and that is, after all, a goal of all counseling. I have been a president of four national organizations, a program director, department head, dean, and editor of two journals. Each time the role was taken because of a belief in the potential for impacting positive change—and that isn't risky; it is betting on the ability to influence organizations and programs. My most fulfilling moments occurred when it was possible to see improvements, changes in a socially engaging and rewarding manner in the workplace, where students and faculty and staff felt safe and welcome, and where a climate of safety resulted in more innovation, creativity, and enthusiasm for being present. My saddest moments occurred when policies, policy makers, and others of influence were able to create environments of worry, fear, and loss of respect for our work and our relationships. Sometimes those conditions were created by members of our own field.

Recently, graduate students asked me about regrets. There have been few, but two stand out. In both cases, I was offered the opportunity to leave the academy and go into free-standing research centers, and in both cases I did not go. The reasons were clear to me at the time. Being a tenured professor is very secure, and at the times the other offers came, I had young children and other family responsibilities and the risks seemed too daunting. I most likely would have done well, and the opportunity to devote myself full-time to research would have been fulfilling and may have resulted in even more impact over the decades. However, I felt it was not just my life and security I was deciding about but my family's as well. Moving to a career that demanded obtaining external funding (grants) year after year seemed too risky at the time, but I've often reflected on the "what ifs . . ." of the decisions.

Over the years I've most valued the people I've encountered—the clients, students, coworkers, colleagues, and the public who supported our efforts. And they supported me, oftentimes encouraging the willingness to challenge the status quo, to be innovative and creative in examining problems and changing the circumstances. They offered support and encouragement for tackling issues and provided care and understanding when success was less than hoped for.

I follow the humanistic/developmental belief that people can grow and be wonderful contributing individuals; but I also believe the opposite—that given fear, threats, and punishment, a life of deprivation and lack of access to fulfill physical and emotional needs result in the problems we encounter throughout the world. We know how to create safe and welcoming environments, but we as a people do not yet have the resolve to make this happen for everyone. We do not lack knowledge and information about creating climates of respect and dignity for all people; what we lack is the knowledge of how to bring about what we know. Thus, there is a need—a demand—for future leaders to challenge the current circumstances and bring the changes we so urgently require. I call upon you, the reader, to be one who commits to making these changes happen. They won't occur in this lifetime, but through more and more people committing to effecting change, we can be moving in the direction that will be fruitful for everyone.

References

Albee, G. (1982). Preventing psychopathology and promoting human potential. *American Psychologist, 37*, 1043–1050.

Carkhuff, R., & Berenson, B. (1977). *Beyond counseling and therapy.* New York, NY: Holt, Rinehart and Winston.

Combs, A. W. (1976). *Perceptual psychology: A humanistic approach to the study of persons.* New York, NY: Harper & Row.

Corsini, R. (1973). *Current psychotherapies.* Itasca, IL. Peacock.

Hill, C. (2009). *Helping skills: Facilitating exploration, insight, and action* (3rd ed.). Washington, DC: American Psychological Association.

Ivey, A. E., Ivey, M. B., & Zalaquett, C. P. (2009). *Intentional interviewing and counseling: Facilitating client development in a multicultural society.* Pacific Grove, CA: Brooks/Cole.

Krumboltz, J. (2008). The happenstance learning theory. *Journal of Career Assessment, 17*, 135–154.

Leger, F. J. (1997). *Beyond the therapeutic relationship: Behavioral, biological, and cognitive foundations of psychotherapy.* New York, NY: Routledge.

Patterson, C. H. (1966). *Theories of counseling and psychotherapy.* New York, NY: Harper & Row.

Pipes, R. B., & Davenport, D. S. (1998). *Introduction to psychotherapy: Common clinical wisdom* (2nd ed.). Boston, MA: Allyn & Bacon.

Rogers, C. R. (1961). *On becoming a person.* Boston, MA: Houghton Mifflin.

Skovholt, T. M. (2012). *Becoming a therapist: On the path to mastery.* Hoboken, NJ: Wiley.

9

My Journey as a Chinese Immigrant Counseling Psychologist

By Y. Barry Chung

I appreciate having this opportunity to write a story about myself. I am a big fan of learning from stories and narratives. I actually learned something about myself from writing this chapter. I hope that my story will be a source of support and inspiration for others, and I look forward to learning from other stories in this book.

Past Influence

I grew up in a poor family of seven in Hong Kong in the 1960s, as the youngest of five children. My earliest memory of our home was a small studio with a bunk bed—my parents slept in the bed on the lower level and all five children, all about two years of age apart, slept on the top level. I remember falling to the floor in the middle of the night and going back to sleep, until my parents heard the noise and woke me up. My mother still recounts the story when we had to borrow rice and milk from our neighbors to feed the children. My parents both worked, and my older sister joined the workforce when she was only 11. With her additional income to the family, we began to do a little better financially.

As children we all learned to do housework and cook for the whole family. The budget was very tight, and I learned how to buy groceries and make dinner within means for a family of seven every day. It was this early childhood experience that taught me to be independent, budget-minded, and creative given the limit of resources (both in money and time). Going to school full-time, managing housework and dinner, and finishing my demanding homework meant that every day involved long hours of hard work. My parents were so busy working that they did not have time to monitor my schoolwork. I was a good student and did not need anyone to make sure that I did all of my homework and studied for exams. I enjoyed getting good grades of which my parents could be proud. In a sense, I really took it for granted that everyone in the family was self-sufficient. I did not know if there was another way.

Looking back I think my early childhood experience groomed me to be a person who is independent, self-motivated, proactive, hardworking, achievement oriented, and embedded with a sense of responsibility to care for others. I also learned to become resourceful and do my best to create opportunities.

I became a Christian when I was 17, and that contributed a lot to my desire to be in a helping profession. Most of my cohort at church wanted to be teachers, but I wanted to be a social worker. At that time Hong Kong had very few opportunities for higher education. By chance I learned that attending college in Taiwan was an option, and I took the Taiwanese college entrance exam that resulted in being admitted to the National Taiwan Normal University, a very reputable university in Taiwan. Because of my science track in high school, I had access only to science majors in college (my major as a freshman was industrial arts education). I was determined to change my major in my second year and ended up choosing educational psychology and counseling rather than social work. That was the beginning of my career in counseling psychology. Upon graduation, I applied for graduate studies in the United States because that was a very common aspiration among Taiwanese college students. I was accepted to the University of Illinois at Urbana-Champaign where I received my master's and doctoral degrees in counseling psychology.

An amazing thing was that I never had to pay tuition after high school. My undergraduate institute was a teacher education university—students had their tuition waived, in addition to free housing and a living allowance every month. I also received financial aid in all of my years in graduate school. Without these forms of financial aid, I would not have been able to pursue postsecondary education as a young man from a poor family.

Some may think that I was courageous and a risk taker to go to Taiwan and America alone to pursue my education, especially when I did not have any certainty of financial means. I guess my upbringing had prepared me well to be independent and self-driven. I also learned to be innovative in exploring and creating opportunities to access resources beyond my financial means, resulting in my admittance to a free and quality education in Taiwan and successive financial aid opportunities in graduate school.

Professional Journey

I was lucky enough to have Dr. Lenore W. Harmon as my doctoral advisor. When I was in graduate school, I pretty much wanted to grow up to be like her. She was editor of the *Journal of Counseling Psychology* at that time, and my research and writing skills benefited greatly from her mentoring. Dr. Harmon's expertise in vocational psychology had great influence on my focus on career development research. I developed my own research interests in multicultural counseling and sexual orientation issues because of my cultural background. As an international student (and later immigrant) from Asia, I was keenly aware of racial and cultural issues in ways I had never experienced in Hong Kong. I also came out as a gay man in graduate school, which was another significant life event and experience. Collectively, these experiences and identities contributed to my research programs in career development, multicultural counseling, and sexual orientation issues.

Since graduation in 1996, I also became increasingly invested in professional leadership. I was often a leader in school, usually by teacher appointments or peer nominations. Interesting enough, I do not remember ever volunteering or running for these leadership positions. I think I was elected or appointed leader because of my height and/or good grades. I either gladly or reluctantly accepted these appointments or nominations.

I had no interest in pursuing leadership in the profession. However, the persistent encouragement and persuasion by some, particularly Drs. Mark Pope and Linda Forrest, changed my career. In 1998, Dr. Pope convinced me to run for the position of Trustee-at-Large of the National Career Development Association (NCDA). As a tenure-track assistant professor, this was really not my priority, but I could not say no to my mentor. I ended up winning that election, which was my first significant leadership in the field. I enjoyed serving on the board of directors of the NCDA and agreed to run for a second term, which I also won. During my second term, there were senior leaders of the NCDA who asked me to run for president, and I kept saying no. By the time I finished my second term as trustee, I finally agreed to run for president.

I have to say that I enjoyed my NCDA presidency and I learned a great deal—not only about professional issues but also about how things work in the business world. It was gratifying to be able to work on presidential initiatives such as international collaborations and multicultural career practice guidelines.

My leadership experience in the NCDA caught Dr. Forrest's attention. She has devoted much of her life to professional leadership and mentoring new leaders. She encouraged me to think about leadership in the Society of Counseling Psychology (SCP) and the American Psychological Association (APA). In 2007, I was elected to the position of SCP vice president for education and training and APA's Board of Educational Affairs. It was shocking to everyone that someone like me, with no prior APA leadership experience, was elected to a major governing board of the APA. I can only attribute this to a village of people who worked behind the scenes to advocate for me. Subsequently, I was elected SCP president and to the APA's Board for the Advancement of Psychology in the Public Interest, Membership Board, Council of Representatives, and Finance Committee.

I never really understand what contributed to the success of my elections to the aforementioned leadership positions. Maybe others see something in me that I fail to recognize myself. However, I did come to the following conclusions about what helped my journey in leadership. First, I am willing to say yes. There were times when I was not confident that I could be elected or that I could do the job, but I said yes when people I trusted saw the potential in me. I have blind spots about myself and realized that I would never find out if how well I could do if I never put myself in those positions. Second, I learned to campaign. Campaigning was really not in my nature. I remember the first time I was nominated for an APA committee. Dr. Forrest told me everything I needed to know about campaigning, but I didn't follow her advice and lost that election. Since then I have learned to step out of my comfort zone and to adopt the tactics of campaigning. I have been winning elections ever since I started to campaign. I still feel a bit awkward promoting myself; but if I didn't know how to succeed in this system, I would not have had an opportunity for professional influence through my leadership positions. Third, I learned to help others to become leaders. Dr. Forrest is my number one role model in this regard. I actually become a better leader when I try to teach others about leadership (much like I learn a lot more when I teach a subject matter). Also, leadership is more effective when you have a critical mass of supporters who share similar values. By mentoring more leaders, there will be more of a critical mass. My desire to train more leaders led to my presidential project to create a Leadership Academy for SCP. This initiative has now become a standing committee of SCP.

To me, the most satisfying thing about leadership is that I can make an impact on promoting social justice, cultural sensitivity, and public well-being. This means that I have to learn to address sensitive topics in ways that people will listen and be open to change. Of course this is often not easy. Challenging the status quo often makes some people uncomfortable or upset. There will be resistance and sometimes unkind or even brutal counteractions. One time I was working with a committee composed of very seasoned and well-accomplished White men. I was the only one in the group who was nonheterosexual and a person of color, and I was also the most junior in experience. While discussing a sensitive topic, some of the email and conference call exchanges were very culturally insensitive and even insulting. I was very upset and hurt and did not know how to deal with these well-respected scholars who would never say these things outside of the committee. I was already feeling burnout from other leadership experiences involving racism and heterosexism, so I was having an existential crisis. I went home that night and told my partner, "I need a vacation, by myself. I don't know where I am heading, and I don't know when I will come back. Will that be ok with you?" My partner responded, "Sure, take your time. Come back when you are ready. I will be here taking care of our dogs." So the next morning I jumped into my Mustang convertible (I guess I was having a midlife crisis) and headed south from Atlanta, Georgia, driving all the way to the end (Key West, Florida) without a hotel reservation. That likely was one of the craziest things I have ever done. But I needed to be alone and sort out my thoughts and feelings. I did have a good time staying at bed and breakfasts and resorts and hanging out at swimming pools and beaches. I did a lot of thinking and reflecting, particularly when I was driving. I drove home a renewed man after one week on the road. I was ready to face my challenge again. Within a few months, I took a new job as department chair in Boston. I was actually ready for more leadership. What happened on that trip? I am not sure. I guess I just needed to lick my wounds and think about all the great people who came before me and paved the road and everyone in my support network who is always there for me fighting similar challenges as mine. I was alone, but I didn't feel alone. Taking this time for self-care was what I needed to prepare for more challenges. Indeed, I have taken on more challenging leadership positions in my place of employment and in the profession, and I continue to find leadership the most satisfying aspect of my professional work.

Another existential issue I had was the balance between investing in research versus leadership. In the early stage of my career, I spent a lot of time on research and writing, and I enjoyed making professional contributions that way. As I began spending more time on leadership, I had to struggle between balancing the two and wondered if I was still a scholar. Over time I resolved this existential crisis, because I realized that I was making contributions via leadership in ways that are different from research. The impact of leadership could be very immediate and direct (versus waiting for someone to read your research article and make use of your findings and recommendations). For example, I had advocated in a research article that journal editors and editorial board members should receive training in multicultural research methodology and implicit bias, to avoid multicultural papers being unfairly reviewed and rejected. When I served on APA governance, I was able to make that suggestion as a policy for APA journals. This kind of experience is very gratifying, and it continues to strengthen my commitment to leadership involvement. I am glad that I found a niche for my professional development, one that is worth my time and effort, despite difficulties associated with advocacy through leadership.

One other issue I want to discuss is the balance between work and personal life. I am a work-oriented person, and I have to work hard to maintain a balance with my personal life. As a full professor with tenure, I still work more than 40 hours a week. Typically my work days are 10 a.m. to 7 p.m. Monday through Friday, plus Sunday afternoon. I do not work at home except checking email (more like reading and deleting rather than responding, unless there is an emergency). This has worked out pretty well for my partner and my dog. I guess not having children allows me to devote more time to work. I believe that work and personal life balance is subjective, depending on personal situations. One cannot use a set number of work hours to judge whether there is a balance. It is about prioritizing based on one's values and passion, as well as resources available. I learned to be more efficient and to accomplish more when I work, and I devote myself totally to my family and social life when I am not working. When people spill over their work and personal life on each other, they end up not having a good balance.

Connection Among Professional Life, Courage, Risk-Taking, and Innovation

I believe that people change because of many factors, chief among them happenstance, learning, and self-agency. Happenstance contributes to people being in certain environments and having certain experiences. For example, by happenstance I was born in a poor family of seven in Hong Kong, with few resources. I was born with certain cognitive and physical abilities and was lucky enough to not have an accident or injury that had a major influence on my body or ability. I was exposed to certain learning experiences afforded by happenstance. With limited financial means, I learned skills to be independent and to care for others. My academic aptitude led to my success in school, and my emotional intelligence contributed to my positive learning about social behavior and my learning to be a leader. Finally, self-agency affects happenstance and learning experience. A person can exercise some control over happenstance (e.g., maximizing opportunities). When I was in high school, by chance I learned about applying for college in Taiwan, over a lunch with my peers. Although everyone was excited about this opportunity, I was the only one who followed through and took the entrance exam. My self-agency took advantage of the happenstance and altered the rest of my life. I said yes to colleagues who nominated me for leadership positions. I followed my mentor's advice to campaign for elections. Without actively taking charge of happenstance and engaging in positive learning, my professional life would have been quite different.

To me, courage, risk-taking, and innovation are functions of self-agency. When facing challenge, a person with strong self-agency will exercise courage—to take on new and/or bigger responsibilities, to tackle something even without sufficient self-efficacy, and to take risks that could result in failure or a losing status. To maximize success, this person will engage in innovation—to consult others, try new strategies, use new methods, and step out of one's comfort zone. I remember the days when I had self-doubts about my ability to pursue certain leadership positions. It took courage to accept the nominations (which is also risk-taking because I might lose face for not winning or get elected and have to take on new roles that will pose challenges to my ability). I also innovated by following my mentor's advice to campaign but to do it in a way that fits my personality. I stepped out of my comfort zone and learned to be more competitive in the mainstream leadership culture, yet I didn't betray who I was. In doing so, I realized that human beings actually have a lot more flexibility and potential than one may realize—there are many facets of each individual to be uncovered if one has the courage to take risks.

For early career professionals, my advice is to be open-minded and allow oneself to expand. Take charge of your happenstance (e.g., commit to attending convention social hours so that you increase opportunities to meet new colleagues who may lead to new work opportunities; pay attention to LISTSERV announcements and actually apply for things that you want, rather than saying to yourself that you won't make the cut). Have the courage to say yes to new opportunities, even if you don't think you can do it. Take risks and tap into new resources to overcome challenge. Be creative and innovative—be willing to step out of your comfort zone and learn new strategies and methods. Embrace your self-agency. My colleague,

Dr. Nancy Schlossberg, once told me the story of showing her student one drawer of accepted journal article submissions and several drawers of rejected ones. She concluded that, "A successful person has more failures than the failures do."

For my midcareer colleagues, my aforementioned advice is not too late for you. Remember my midlife crisis of driving all the way to Key West by myself? We all can be courageous, risk-taking, and innovative. If not now, when?

My Work Style

I am not sure how I would categorize my work style. I guess the first thing that comes to mind is that I am an organized worker. I always have a clear picture what I need to accomplish and in what time frame, so I am able to get things done on time (most of the time). If I ever need to negotiate for a deadline extension, usually it is for writing projects (like this book chapter). This is because I can multitask quite well, but when it comes to writing, I need blocks of time to focus. I cannot write an hour or two one day and pick up a few days later. I am most efficient if I can have undivided attention to my writing. However, I usually have a high demand on my workload, so finding blocks of time for writing often becomes a challenge. For that matter, I have to learn to say no to invitations for writing projects. When I do accept invitations, it is mainly because I want to involve students as coauthors. It is rewarding to mentor them and see their excitement in getting things published.

I also have a reputation for being very timely in responding to email. I organize and achieve most of my work via email (e.g., communicating, submitting work, organizing events). I delete emails when the work is done; I love to delete emails! My goal is to leave work every day with only one screen page of email in my inbox (that is about 10 emails on a smart phone screen). This is an ambitious goal, and I accomplish it infrequently. However, I always keep that goal in mind, which means I often review all of the emails in my inbox, prioritize them, and find ways to get work done and delete as many emails as I can. This strategy has kept me organized and productive. Of course, being an administrator in my day job and leader in professional organizations, I know that my students and colleagues appreciate my timeliness in responding to email and getting work done (well, most of the time anyway).

As a leader and administrator, I sometimes face challenges when people treat me in certain ways because of their stereotypes about various aspects of me (e.g., being Asian, a man, an immigrant, gay, younger looking than my age). For example, without knowing much about me, a colleague might stereotype my leadership as authoritative because I am an Asian man, or that I am compliant, submissive, and nonassertive because I am Asian. Others might undermine my authority and disrespect me because I look younger or because I am an ethnic minority. Yet others might assume that I have inferior English ability because I am an immigrant and speak with an accent. I am not afraid to show how I might not be what they assumed of me. I am assertive and I do challenge authority figures when the situation calls for it. I have exerted my authority and demanded proper job performance when dealing with someone who wants to walk all over me and get away with his or her selfish desires. I am also more democratic, collaborative, and kind than some might assume because I am an Asian leader. Yes, some of these actions require courage and risk-taking. I have learned a lot throughout the years from my mentors and colleagues about how to be very tactful in confronting someone, asserting myself, and engaging someone in a difficult dialogue. When I didn't do well, I tried to learn from my mistakes. The other helpful mindset is that I always have options. Some people are afraid to take risks because they fear they may have too much to lose (e.g., losing their job, lowering their chance of being reelected). I believe that I have options and I don't deserve to be treated unfairly or disrespectfully. I try to deal with problems that I face, and if things don't work out, I can always find an environment that fits me better.

My Future Journey

I understand that people's priorities and aspirations may change, depending on life circumstances, critical incidents, and their personal and professional growth. I have a good momentum for leadership development, and I enjoy it, so most likely I will keep growing with leadership involvements. What I would like to achieve is to pursue leadership beyond counseling psychology and maybe beyond psychology. In a sense, I am already pursuing leadership positions beyond counseling psychology, such as my elected positions on APA governance. I enjoy learning more about other specialties and issues in psychology (e.g., serving on the Council of Specialties in Professional Psychology, APA Board of Educational Affairs, APA Membership Board). My recent participation on the APA Council of Representatives and the Finance Committee opens up a whole new world of experience. In previous roles I could focus on a special domain in psychology (e.g., educational affairs, public interest). But these newer roles require knowledge of a much broader scope of what is happening in APA and psychology. For example, just as I began to serve on the APA Finance Committee, I realized that I needed to have more knowledge of budget proposals of various units and initiatives before I could work with the committee on prioritizing funding allocations. This required a very steep learning curve, but it was a challenge that I welcomed.

I also aspire to pursuing leadership or administrative positions beyond psychology. I am intrigued by the idea of using my psychological skills to lead people of different disciplines to achieve common goals and advance their own disciplines (e.g., serving as a college dean or chief diversity officer). I have role models who are doing excellent work in those roles (e.g., Drs. Rosie Bingham, Andy Horne). Counseling psychologists could be great leaders beyond psychology because of our training in interpersonal skills, group dynamics, consultation, career development, multiculturalism, and social justice advocacy. In light of racial incidents on university campuses, counseling psychologists could help to make a positive change in racial climate. Furthermore, when people from other disciplines understand more about the positive impact of psychologists and psychology, they will be more supportive of psychology training programs. We have lost quite a few counseling psychology doctoral programs at research-intensive universities. Maybe we should support more counseling psychologists to move into university administrative positions so that they can make an impact at the college and university levels and showcase the value of psychology training. I want to be part of that process of wider scope change.

Advice for Students and Early Career Professionals

As discussed previously, I encourage students and early career professionals to develop and strengthen their self-agency so that they have more influence over happenstance and positive learning, which will lead to being more courageous and willing to take risks. This is particularly relevant to members of underrepresented groups who have fewer resources, are disenfranchised, and are targets of discrimination—and I consider myself one of them. We can turn things around by creating opportunities, being innovative in tapping new resources, and taking risks to advance our life and career. It won't be an easy process, but there are people before us who have paved our path, and there is a village of people who support us, even though sometimes we forget about them. We are stronger together, so we need to create a critical mass. That's why being open to being mentored and supported, and committing oneself to mentoring and supporting the next generation, are keys to success. I was lucky to be surrounded by many wonderful mentors and peers, and I learned to accept their support and mentoring. I found out that I should give myself a chance, especially when others believe in me before I believe in myself.

For educational programs, I offer the following advice. Students can benefit from more mentoring and encouragement outside of the classroom. Faculty can inform students about all kinds of opportunities (e.g., assistantships and financial aid, job openings, grants, awards, volunteer and committee work, nominations for elections, research and publication opportunities, calls for presentation proposals) and encourage them to apply. By doing so, faculty could have a positive influence on happenstance for students and increase their self-agency. Students often shy away from seeking and taking advantage of these opportunities because they lack self-efficacy. I advise my students to actively seek out whatever they want to achieve, and I share my own stories to encourage them. I actively nominate my students and junior (and senior) colleagues for honors and awards. That was how I was mentored and supported, and I want to pay it forward. Once they have some successful experience, their self-agency will be strengthened and they are more likely to take risks. They will have more courage to try new things and face challenges. I believe that this kind of mentoring and support can have a very significant impact on the personal and professional development of students.

Final Thoughts

When I was first approached to write this chapter, I was very excited and happily accepted the invitation. I never thought I could write some sort of autobiography that could be published professionally. I think this narrative approach for empowerment and positive change is a great idea. Stories could be very powerful and influential, particularly when they are accompanied by good music!

As I write this chapter, I am grateful for this opportunity to reflect on my life and career and to identify themes that are evident in my professional journey. I realized that I have come a long way—from growing up in a poor family in Hong Kong to being a tenured full professor at a major research university in the United States. I tried to articulate the themes of my journey—happenstance, learning, self-agency, courage, risk-taking, and innovation. I hope they make sense to you. I am certainly more aware of these themes after this writing exercise. For that matter, I would encourage you to try it—write your own story and try to make sense of your journey. Or, if you are a faculty member, ask students to do it in your class. I consider myself to be still in midcareer, and I count on utilizing my self-reflections and learning from this chapter to further develop myself. If my story has helped you in any way, I will be most honored and gratified.

10

Public Policy's Highly Personalized Nature

By Patrick H. DeLeon and Omni Cassidy

The views expressed are those of the authors and do not reflect the official policy or position of the Uniformed Services University of the Health Sciences, the Department of Defense, or the United States Government.

A Lifelong Journey

Over the years, I have come to appreciate that being involved in the public policy/political process reflects one's chosen lifestyle and fundamental value system, considerably more than representing a "job" or professional identification. There is no such thing as a nine to five, five days a week, policy position. To be successful, one must be passionate about one's personal mission and at the same time, appreciate that others often have different perspectives and different priorities. Above all else, one must be flexible. When colleagues ask if I am enjoying "retirement" today, I usually respond that I have never really worked; I have just been fortunate to have kept doing that which I enjoy. Politics and involvement in the public policy process are intimately intertwined. This is a lifestyle, with its own language, culture, and history, far more than most outside of the system will ever appreciate.

As an individual who has always found psychology, and by extension interpersonal relationships, to be fascinating, I want to note up front that the more one becomes intimately involved in the political process, the more important it is to cultivate a sense of personal priorities. Throughout my professional career—which includes serving on the U.S. Senate staff and as the American Psychological Association (APA) president and now teaching graduate students—I would frequently take the time to have informal coffees with colleagues and discuss how we saw the nation evolving. Not surprisingly, these breaks from the office turmoil would often turn into talking about personal and family issues. These Senate staff colleagues were highly educated and clearly accomplished. Yet their public and private personas were often quite different. I soon came to appreciate how lonely high-level positions can be and the serious toll they can take on one's loved ones—fostering divorce, children struggling academically and dropping out of college, substance use, and even suicide attempts. I quickly appreciated that I was neither better nor brighter than they were and thus, I would have to make a conscious effort to learn from their experiences. The public policy journey can become all-consuming, and it can also be truly satisfying.

Approximately half of those elected to the U.S. Senate possess a legal background; with business being quite popular, particularly in the U.S. House of Representatives. Those trained in the health professions are a distinct minority in both legislative bodies, although there are a surprising number of elected officials who have previously been engaged in a wide range of educational endeavors; this is similarly true for their staff. Nevertheless, those with a mental health background soon find that both the subject matter that interests them, as well as the way that they think (i.e., process information), are often quite fundamentally different than for those who are engaged in politics. When I finally retired in the fall of 2011 as U.S. Senator Daniel K. Inouye's chief of staff, I had served with him for over 38 years, thereby having been there quite a bit longer than most of my colleagues. In fact, when I retired, I had been serving longer than any of the other sitting senators at the time.

A Personal Journey

Prior to coming to the U.S. Senate as a University of Hawaii School of Public Health intern (beginning on the first day of the infamous Watergate hearings), I had worked for the State of Hawaii Division of Mental Health for almost five years, where I was very active with the Hawaii Government Employees Association, the state employees' union. Prior to that, I served as a field assessment officer for two Peace Corps training projects that were based on the Big Island of Hawaii. Currently, I am teaching part time at the

Department of Defense (DoD) Uniformed Services University of the Health Sciences (USUHS) in the Daniel K. Inouye Graduate School of Nursing and the Department of Medical and Clinical Psychology, exposing their graduate students and faculty to the nuances of health policy. When working on the Hill, USUHS and nursing were two of the areas that I spent a considerable amount of time focusing on. At USUHS, we host highly informal weekly seminars with invited speakers who have themselves helped shape national policy. Students also complete field experience and three brief written reports that further expand their knowledge of national policy and policy making (DeLeon, Sells, Cassidy, Waters, & Kasper, 2015).

The following from my coauthor and a USUHS graduate student helps to describe the immense values of the seminar: (Cassidy) There are no words to express how invaluable an experience it has been to be exposed to the public policy process through the seminar at USUHS. Every speaker comes to the class with a plethora of knowledge and experiences that allows students to learn about the elements that go into—not just *knowing* but *doing*—policy. In many ways, each week, trainees in the course have the opportunity to "sit at the feet" of those who have gone before us, who have stood on figurative cliffs and seen the storms raging ahead. For most of the students who have spent so much of their time (including that of many of their mentors) in their own little worlds on the beaches, the perspectives from the people on those cliffs are nothing short of incredible, eye-opening, and one might even say earth-shattering. Indeed, once you have a chance to talk to someone with that worldview, or better yet, visit the top of the cliff, it is hard and maybe even impossible to be satisfied with your little world on the beach. That is precisely what the course affords—a complete paradigm shift. Fortunately, this paradigm shift is coupled with an obligation to give what you have to make things better for those on the beach—the local communities, the states, the nation, and the people we are called to serve.

For instance, one of the recurring themes that the class speakers keep raising is that to make a real difference in the public policy process, one must be persistent and personally involved (i.e., present), as well as appreciate the importance of taking advantage of whatever opportunities are presented, especially those that are truly "unexpected." To succeed, one must be willing to fail and to learn from those "mistakes." Almost none of the speakers (including several retired surgeon generals, two secretaries of the Department of Veterans Affairs, White House colleagues, and several former APA presidents) ever seriously expected to be where they were. And yet, in retrospect, their personal journeys now seemed quite reasonable to them. Each opportunity had led to another unexpected challenge. It is as if one is floating down a meandering river, rather than marching along a straight and predictable path. Further, as one of the speakers specifically noted, as you progress along your career, your close colleagues often become your competitors for a seemingly limited number of positions. Being at the top can be quite lonely. And those who disagree with you can be rather forceful (if not highly personal) in their opposition. Accordingly, one must possess a heartfelt vision for what one wants to accomplish in one's life and value accomplishing seemingly "little steps." Those who succeeded also frequently noted that although praise is perhaps comforting, in the long run, the underlying mission is far more important than personal recognition.

Early Formative Years

Reflecting back, there were a number of significant social/environmental factors that undoubtedly influenced my own future career. During World War II, my father served overseas in the U.S. Army, and my earliest memories are of my mother and living in the church home where my grandfather was a Russian Orthodox priest. His congregation, and thus our neighborhood, comprised many Russian families who had lost everything when they had to flee for their lives as the Communists took over. I will never forget the time my grandmother (who I believe was 13 when she gave birth to my mother) pointed to pictures of Russian citizens being hung and emotionally exclaimed, "Those are your relatives!" I was the church altar boy and loved baking the bread, which was to be served during the Sunday service, on weekends with my grandfather. My biggest fear at that time was losing control of the incense chain as I swung it back and forth during the service.

I vividly recall during my first confession when, before I could say anything, my grandfather proclaimed that I had nothing to confess, and subsequently, the time down at the beach, when he informed me that he was slowly dying. By all accounts, my grandfather was a very successful priest. When he died, his colleagues came from all over the world, parading around the church to honor him. Soon after his death, however, my grandmother refused to ever again attend that church, as their lay leadership was unwilling to pay for his tombstone. As an undergraduate at Amherst College, I would at times spend the evening sniffing Drambuie and reading foreign literature. One night, it suddenly came to me—my grandfather was an atheist priest. No wonder he had been so successful at comforting those who had lost everything.

Much later I came to appreciate that even when you know that you have done the right thing, there are many who feel empowered to undercut your accomplishments for their own personal reasons. One must learn to always keep one's ultimate objectives in mind, notwithstanding whether or not they may be popular at the time. A vision for the future can be very useful during those personally challenging times.

In graduate school, I had a horrific auto accident on an icy highway en route to visit friends at the University of Michigan. In the operating room, I recall the surgeon urging me not to fall asleep, as I could feel no pain. One of the nurses suddenly gasped that my blood pressure was drastically falling. I had just passed a rather difficult statistics exam that morning, and I was determined to graduate. I began to focus my thoughts and suddenly heard voices exclaiming that my blood pressure was rising. They removed as much glass as they could from under my scalp and 100 stitches later, they sutured me up. The local newspaper proclaimed, "Man Scalped by Car Windshield." A physician friend of my mother's was informed that I should have died and that I should not have recovered. That summer he asked her if I would be willing to undergo an extensive neurological examination, as he simply could not understand how I survived, let alone returned to graduate school. My mother's comment to me was that the state had actually billed her for the cost of replacing the guardrail that didn't hold my Austin-Healey. I guess my time had not yet come. Interestingly, the couple I was going to visit knew that I would not make it for dinner that evening, and the wife stopped cooking the special meal she had planned.

Perhaps a Personal Barrier—Perhaps Not

Another significant factor (again, that one appreciates only in retrospect) is the realization that I have always had a serious hearing loss, due to being one of the "sulfa babies" of the World War II era. During grammar school, I recall spending hours with a special teacher, whom I now assume was a speech therapist, and reading out loud from the local newspaper every night at the dinner table. One time my father got visibly upset when an article I was reading criticized the Mafia, but that is a different story. My parents made sure that I attended small, private schools where there would be considerable student-teacher interactions. I did very well in school and interestingly, I particularly enjoyed learning Latin and several foreign languages, as well as playing various team sports. The summer after my senior year in high school, I attended a special Russian-language camp. We were in a rural part of the USSR when the American U-2 pilot was shot down. The quick and decisive actions taken that evening during a "spontaneous mob response," by whom we assumed were KGMB agents, was very much appreciated by our visiting class.

At Amherst College, I soon learned that oral languages (including Spanish) were very difficult, if not impossible, to understand. This, combined with my earlier decision to stop studying "all the time," resulted in a very difficult first year. I had simply never understood that I really could not hear what people were saying; I guess lip reading came naturally to me. Again, in retrospect, this approach to interpersonal interactions definitely shaped what I learned during my graduate psychology studies and especially how I approached providing therapy to patients. Humorously, near the end of graduate school, I learned, by chance, that Purdue University at that time required a language proficiency. I successfully petitioned for Spanish—my rationale being that I was interested in working in rural America and emphasized the increasing number of Spanish-speaking immigrants. I spent the summer being tutored by the wife of a fellow graduate student and took the exam, which fortunately was in a written format. Soon thereafter, I received a call from a professor who indicated that he was responsible for grading the graduate school Spanish examinations and wanted to meet with me. I had enjoyed the exam—lots of history, poetry, colloquialisms, and so on—and went to see him. He wanted to know if I was Spanish. I am not; my parents were Russian and Italian. Apparently, my score on the language exam was the highest he had ever seen. Several weeks later, I stopped in a small book and newspaper store that specialized in foreign publications. I picked up a Spanish newspaper and could no longer read it. I had essentially memorized the language for the test and then deleted it from my memory, although today, every once in a while, I will listen to a Spanish-speaking television show without realizing it.

Family Influence—Role Models

I grew up in a family in which both parents were lawyers and actively engaged in local Democratic politics. My mother was the second female attorney in the State of Connecticut. Near her deathbed, she informed me that she had failed the bar examination the first time she had taken it, and 40 years later she had received the letter from the bar examiners formally informing her of the time of her oral examination. "If I were a man, I am sure that they would have asked me the next day why I did not show up for the examination. Instead they failed me," she said. The following year she passed. I vividly recall a number of political events she hosted in our new home, including one Christmas party when sadly no one came. This was at a time when the Irish Catholics controlled the country clubs and most of the political positions, including those on the judiciary. One evening at dinner my father indicated that he had been invited to join the local Catholic country club where most of my friends went on weekends. If I wanted him to, he would join; however, he really did not want to, as they had never previously invited any Italians or members of the Jewish faith to become members. I deferred to his wishes, and the following year the first Jewish country club opened up in our area and invited him to become a member.

I also recall that in grammar school, some of the faculty thought I would never be able to go to college; in college, I remember fellow students laughing when I mentioned one day during our public speaking class that I would eventually be going to law school. Nevertheless, during my senior year at Amherst College, I had been accepted by both the psychology graduate program and law school.

A Decision to Be Made

I really enjoyed psychology classes, although I did horribly on the Miller Analogies Test (again, the scores being heavily influenced by that hearing loss). I had always known that eventually I would become a lawyer. Law was a career path that seemed predetermined—probably because I grew up in a family of lawyers. That summer I had to decide which to attend first, having enrolled in both the psychology program and the law school. Although my father had been able to attend two different graduate programs simultaneously, without either faculty being aware of the other, this would not be possible in my case, since Purdue University and the University of Connecticut were quite a distance apart.

I realized that if I went to law school first, the future was highly predictable. I would undoubtedly become involved in local politics and eventually run for governor. With both my parents being active in numerous community organizations, especially those representing the non-Irish Catholic elements of the state, I felt my prospect for success was quite good. However, that journey was too predictable. Thus, "I took the one less traveled by. And that has made all the difference." (While at Amherst College, I had taken up photography and became the campus newspaper photographer. As a result, I was able to interact with Robert Frost.) My father was highly disappointed and became disengaged in politics, focusing more on his thriving law practice. During my internship at Fort Logan Community Mental Health Center (currently known as the Colorado Mental Health Institute at Fort Logan) in Denver, Colorado, I again enrolled in law school. Finally, it was not until after starting my internship with the U.S. Senate that I eventually graduated from the Columbus School of Law at The Catholic University of America in February 1980.

At the funeral service for my father during a very cold New England winter day, a black limousine arrived and a familiar face appeared that we had not seen in ages. She called me by the name that we had not heard for decades, kissed the coffin, and said, "We just wanted to express our best wishes." Her driver was wearing only a black T-shirt and was impressively muscular; the assembled crowd was silent. Later on, I finally understood my father's frustration that dinner eve when he had exclaimed, "Never criticize those you do not know." Yes, I have no doubt that I would have been elected governor of the State of Connecticut and then perhaps U.S. Senator, with their support.

Our Nation's Capital

From the fall of 1973, for nearly the next 40 years, I worked on Capitol Hill for U.S. Senator Daniel K. Inouye and eventually retired as his chief of staff at a time when the Hill was becoming more and more partisan and, equally important, as my grandchildren began walking. When I arrived, it was the first day of the infamous Watergate hearings; when I retired, Barack Obama was president. During that time we had a number of fascinating experiences, especially learning how Congressional staff often have the unique opportunity to move between the various branches of government and/or into the highly lucrative private sector. At one point, for example, I attended a small chief of staff dinner with several members of the U.S. Supreme Court, listening to their stories as to how two of their members had themselves served on the Senate staff. Over time, I came to appreciate the extent to which my current colleagues would eventually move into different high-level policy positions. Undoubtedly, I could have done the same. However, my wife was increasingly involved in the daily lives of our two grandchildren and thus moving from the Washington, D.C., area to accept the positions that most intrigued me was not a viable option.

A Case Example—Postdoctoral Training

One individual, Tony Principi, whom I consider a true friend and colleague, served on the Republican staff of the Senate Armed Services Committee. We traveled together to visit the Denver headquarters of the Department of Defense Civilian Health and Medical Program of the Uniformed Services (CHAMPUS; now known as TRICARE). A Vietnam veteran, he eventually was selected to serve as Secretary of Veterans Affairs under two Bush Administrations, and then, for a very brief period of time, he returned as staff director of the Senate Committee on Veterans Affairs (VA) before entering the private sector. He was one of my class speakers at our USUHS health policy class and was thoroughly engaging with the students.

I was serving on the APA board of directors when fellow Purdue University graduate Jack Wiggins became president. I asked Tony, who was then VA Secretary, if he would be willing to meet with us. During that meeting in his office, we asked him if he would initiate a postdoctoral training program for his psychology corps. We noted that the chief VA psychologist was supportive of such an initiative. Tony asked for a rationale. I stated, "You are a Vietnam veteran." He spontaneously responded, "Those experiencing posttraumatic stress [disorder] (PTSD) need specialized care." Although historically the largest employer of psychologists, at that time the VA only offered predoctoral training. Postdoctoral training was quite rare, even within the private sector. Once the VA began its initiative, the APA soon thereafter instituted the process of accrediting postdoctoral programs. Today, retired senior VA psychologist Bob Zeiss reports that over 400 postdoctoral positions are funded annually, providing a wide range of health psychology experiences (personal communication, April 1, 2016). In essence, as a direct result of that meeting, the federal sector became the catalyst for what is today considered psychology's integrated health care initiatives. Personal relationships in many ways are the key to substantive policy changes, far more than most will ever realize. In this particular case, these relationships opened the door for an entirely new expansion of health psychology—one that simply could not have been foreseen in 1992.

From a Far-Off Vantage Point

Over time, one begins to appreciate that working on the Hill offers a rather unique vantage point for observing impending change in the status quo. APA visionary and legislative activist Gene Shapiro once chided me: "You are not smarter than most of your colleagues." And I would fully agree. Serving on the Congressional staff provides constant exposure to a wide range of sources of excellent information, as well as to the efforts by those who perceive themselves (or their clients) as directly impacted by institutional change. On the Hill, one is surrounded by staff colleagues who are extraordinarily bright, dedicated to the success of their bosses, and highly knowledgeable. Lobbyists, in particular, can possess fascinating backgrounds. Congressional hearings are a trove of history, data, and aspirations. Certain themes continue to surface, and one gradually comes to appreciate the personalities (and value systems) of those involved. Some are honest brokers of accurate information; there are those who primarily utilize emotional arguments and those who are driven by narrow self-interests, almost to the exclusion of caring about the impact of their actions on the lives of others. Some of these individuals act as if they do not understand that tomorrow will always come and that those whom they mislead (or intentionally harm) will have long memories.

In many ways, serving on Capitol Hill is analogous to standing on a cliff high above the beaches of an enclosed cove. One can see the storms approaching long before those swimming or sunbathing can. To shout out a warning of an impending huge breaker or tsunami does no good, as you are too far away to be heard. Nevertheless, the pounding waves do arrive and have an immediate and forceful, if not destructive, impact. What was going to happen seemed so obvious from afar but apparently not to those most directly affected.

A Case Example—Prescriptive Authority ("RxP")

When engaging in the public policy process, it is important to be attuned to the potential "unintended or unanticipated consequences" of what one is contemplating, as well as the overall context within which one is operating. Although perhaps sounding somewhat negative in orientation, this approach can actually be quite positive. We have learned that unexpected or unanticipated consequences can be especially beneficial/creative in nature. Several decades ago, I began focusing on the serious lack of access to quality mental health care (today frequently referred to as "behavioral health care") that those living in rural America and from economically disadvantaged backgrounds were experiencing (i.e., "health disparities"). The more we researched this area, the more compelling the data became. From essentially every vantage point, society's historical excessive reliance on psychotropic medications (often inappropriately prescribed) for addressing behavioral, economic, and cultural/racial issues was overwhelming. Considerable data existed indicating that children, the elderly, women, people of color, and so on, were consistently inappropriately medicated by licensed health care practitioners, who were supposedly subject to professional ethics committees and state governmental oversight. It also became clear that within the physician prescribing population, those practitioners with specialized mental health expertise (i.e., psychiatrists) were not the primary prescribers of psychotropic medications. Instead, almost 85% of some psychotropic medications ordered were by nonpsychiatrists (Mark, Levit, & Buck, 2009). From a public health/social policy perspective, this was unacceptable.

Over the years, I have admittedly been somewhat disappointed by the extent to which the profession of psychology has expressed very little interest in serving those who are truly underserved (DeLeon & Kazdin, 2010). This is the population that President Lyndon Johnson envisioned being served by his Great Society initiatives. It was expected, for example, that the network of Federally Qualified Community Health Centers (FCHCs) that he established would provide comprehensive primary care (including integrated mental health care) for those who could not afford health insurance or were unable to receive services from the private sector. FCHCs were to accept all patients, regardless of their income or socioeconomic status. This is also that segment of our society for which Medicaid (and today, President Obama's Patient Protection and Affordable Care Act [ACA]) was developed. Yet very few psychologists or their state associations have ever expressed interest in being recognized under Medicaid or being employed by FCHCs. Their expressed rationale has been that, "These programs do not pay enough for my services." As highly educated health care professionals, many of our psychology colleagues genuinely seem to be unaware of their special societal obligation to address society's most pressing needs, which comes with their unique/special status. These FCHCs are now known as Federally Qualified Health Centers (FQHCs).

The DoD has a long history of training and effectively utilizing those personnel that it requires to fulfill its underlying mission, for example, the utilization of medical corpsmen (or medics), which eventually became the model for physician assistants (PAs) in the civilian sector. The DoD possesses its own PA training program at Fort Sam Houston, Texas, which today is considered to be the world's largest and most prestigious military medical training center, representing 14 medical specialties. Senator Inouye envisioned that the military could develop a special training program for its psychology corps, providing them with psychopharmacological expertise. He appreciated the policy significance of the reality that DoD medical personal have never been restricted by state professional practice acts. In fact, it was Senator Inouye who modified the underlying authorization statute to require all health care professionals who treat patients to be licensed by at least one state jurisdiction.

During a Christmas break, I had lunch with the relevant House Appropriations Committee health staff member and shared the senator's vision with her, noting that once operational, there would undoubtedly be considerable "pushback" by organized medicine. She was supportive, and during the subsequent Senate Appropriations Committee deliberations on the fiscal year 1989 DoD appropriations bill, relevant language was included: "Casualties related to combat stress reactions are predicted to be in the range of 20 to 30 percent during a sustained combat scenario. Properly trained military mental health professionals can recover up to 75 percent of these casualties for return to full duty within 72 hours. . . . Appropriate and timely intervention is highly effective in the prevention of future stress-related problems (e.g., lost man hours and productivity, increased substance abuse, family violence, suicidal behavior, and voluntary separations from the service)" (DeLeon, Fox, & Graham, 1991, p. 389).

During that year's House–Senate appropriations DoD conference deliberations, follow-up language was included directing the DoD to establish a "demonstration pilot training project under which military psychologists may be trained and authorized to issue appropriate psychotropic medications under certain circumstances" (DeLeon et al., 1991, p. 389). The Assistant Secretary for Health Affairs issued a memorandum directing the Army to begin a pilot project by September 15, 1988.

As expected, organized psychiatry raised considerable objections, and the following year, the Senate (and later, the House–Senate appropriations conferees) included rather strong language addressing the DoD's apparent unwillingness to follow the previous year's conference directive. "The conferees agree that the Department cannot ignore direction from Congress and therefore should develop such a training program in fiscal year 1990 . . . the pilot program (should) be designed so that military psychologists could be trained and authorized to issue appropriate psychotropic medications to military personnel only. Issuance of medications to DoD beneficiaries should be addressed after review of the success of this pilot program" (DeLeon et al., 1991, p. 389).

At one point during the subsequent staff deliberations, the DoD proposed the establishment of a fast-track fellowship in clinical psychopharmacology, which would be implemented prior to the end of fiscal year 1990. Under this particular proposal, two psychologists would be assigned to the PA course at the Army's Academy of Health Sciences at Fort Sam Houston for approximately four months. Upon completion of that training, they would begin a clinical practicum on the inpatient psychiatric service at Walter Reed Army Medical Center or Bethesda Naval Hospital. Many articles have been written detailing the ensuing negotiations and impeccable quality of care provided by prescribing military psychologists (Fox et al., 2009).

On June 17, 1994, APA President-Elect Bob Resnick and I attended the graduation ceremonies at Walter Reed Army Medical Center for Navy Commander John Sexton and Lt. Commander Morgan Sammons as they became the first graduates of the DoD psychopharmacology training program. In all, 10 psychologists, representing all three services, eventually graduated from this initiative, which ultimately became the catalyst for several civilian Masters in Clinical Psychopharmacology training programs, as well as prescriptive authority for psychology throughout the DoD and the U.S. Public Health Service. A significant RxP state legislative quest has evolved, with increasing success being obtained over the years. Perhaps the importance of focusing on the clinical needs of real people was finally becoming paramount to psychology's leadership, especially at the state grassroots level.

Prophetically, a 1992 APA Task Force Report to the Council of Representatives, chaired by Michael Smyer, concluded the following: "Practitioners with combined training in psychopharmacology and psychosocial treatments can reasonably be viewed as a new form of health care professional, expected to bring to health care delivery the best of both psychological and pharmacological knowledge. The contributions of this new form of psychopharmacological intervention have the potential to improve dramatically patient care and make important new advances in treatment" (Smyer et al., 1993, p. 403). Bob McGrath, who is one of the original futuristic thinking architects of psychology's civilian RxP training initiatives, estimates that currently there are at least 1,750 graduates of these programs (personal communication, April 1, 2016). And for those with an appreciation for history, in August 1995, the APA Council of Representatives formally endorsed prescriptive authority for appropriately trained psychologists as APA policy. Substantive change does take time, and once begun, there is no turning back the clock.

A Frequently Asked Question

It is quite reasonable to wonder if I miss serving on the Hill. Those were extremely exciting times, and I am confident that we were able to make a real difference in the lives of many Americans. At times, I do think that, "If only we could return to our former position for a week or so, we would be able to ensure that this or that policy or administration priority would be changed." Or, "If we had only known this then . . . ." However, a National Football League (NFL) analogy is undoubtedly more apt. To play in the NFL, one has to be good. To be able to continue to play for a significant period of time, one has to truly understand the game. But with the passage of time, one's body simply cannot take the daily pounding, no matter how good one might have been.

A dear friend and colleague who served in the Hawaii legislature once commented: "Politics is for the young." She is fundamentally correct. The longer one stays, the more one finds that other staff members seem to be younger and younger. For example, whereas once we could have informal discussions about some of the unique issues facing rural Hawaii and Alaska, it eventually became necessary to be rather directive in what we were requesting. In the past, we could facilitate committee staff members being creative on our behalf in developing acceptable solutions from the vantage point of their committee's jurisdiction and culture. We gradually were dealing with staff directors and elected officials directly, rather than with those on the front line of crafting legislation. The fun of legislating was slowly disappearing. And, with the entire Congress becoming increasingly partisan, successes were seemingly more and more difficult to obtain.

We were successful in having "earmarks" (Congressional directed spending) long before they were so named and vilified by the popular media. Strategically placed funding did make a real difference in developing creative solutions, for example, in effectively encouraging women to pursue careers in science, technology, engineering, and math (STEM); opening up the legal and health care professions for Native Americans; establishing FQHCs throughout rural Hawaii; fostering timely Native Hawaiian and Alaskan Native cultural activities; and developing a concentrated focus on the unique needs of children, which is unquestioningly the accomplishment of which I am most proud. Children have always been far more than "little adults"—with their own unique strengths and needs—although many clinicians and policy experts have never seemed to appreciate this. Each of these activities has its own interesting story.

This has been an exciting journey, and now the time has come to focus on other venues. Today, that has become exposing the next generation of educated leaders to the opportunities and challenges they will be facing if and when they decide to become personally engaged in the public policy process. Our challenge now is to *get them excited* about their potential, rather than focusing on specific solutions. I still do keep in contact with a number of my former colleagues. Nevertheless, the skills necessary for today's challenge are quite different; and, as one might imagine, this has become a profound personal learning experience. Aloha.

References

DeLeon, P. H., Fox, R. E., & Graham, S. R. (1991). Prescription privileges: Psychology's next frontier? *American Psychologist, 46*, 384–393.

DeLeon, P. H., & Kazdin, A. E. (2010). Public policy: Extending psychology's contributions to national priorities. *Rehabilitation Psychology, 55*, 311–319.

DeLeon, P. H., Sells, J. R., Cassidy, O., Waters, A. J., & Kasper, C. E. (2015). Health policy: Timely and interdisciplinary. *Training and Education in Professional Psychology, 9*, 121–127.

Fox, R. E., DeLeon, P. H., Newman, R., Sammons, M. T., Dunivin, D. L., & Baker, D. C. (2009). Prescriptive authority and psychology: A status report. *American Psychologist, 64*, 257–268.

Mark, T. L., Levit, K. R., & Buck, J. A. (2009). Datapoints: Psychotropic drug prescriptions by medical specialty. *Psychiatric Services, 60*, 1167.

Smyer, M. A., Balster, R. L., Egli, D., Johnson, D. L., Kilbey, M. M., Leith, N. J., & Puente, A. E. (1993). Summary of the report of the ad hoc task force on psychopharmacology of the American Psychological Association. *Professional Psychology: Research and Practice, 24*, 394–403.

11

Buscando Mi Propio Camino

A Journey of Professional Identity and Honesty

By Edil Torres-Rivera

¿Quienes somos? Somos un Pueblo compasivo, porque hemos sufrido mucho; somos un Pueblo pacífico, en cuyo escudo de armas el Pueblo de San Juan Bautista tiene un Cordero que a mí se me antoja que no es otro que Aquel que quita los pecados del mundo. . . . Somos un Pueblo humilde; somos un Pueblo pobre, donde la vergüenza todavía vale más que la plata, donde la honradez todavía vale más que la plata, donde la honradez todavía vale más que cualquier otra medalla de honor. Somos un Pueblo que tiene tres patrias, y sin embargo no tenemos dominio sobre ninguna de ellas hasta la fecha.

—Pablo Rivera Álvarez, as quoted in Cordasco
and Bucchioni (1973, p. iii)

M y story and professional journey can be summarized by this quote, which explores the existential questions of a colonized country—that has suffered under two colonizers—that prides itself as existing with very spiritual and humble characteristics, such as compassion and honesty.

My story was further elucidated in the dedication of my dissertation, which read as follows:

> This dissertation is the culmination of a long journey that began with a dream of becoming a more acceptable helper, a liaison for social change, and an equalizer for the people of the public housing projects on my beloved island of Puerto Rico. However, to get to this point in this long journey I cannot begin to thank the two very important people in my life and who without their help I could never even dream of completing this monumental task. Thanks Drs. Michael P. Wilbur and Janice Roberts-Wilbur, you are, were and will be always part of my life. (Torres-Rivera, 1996, p. 4159)

This journey began many years ago when, in the public housing project where I was raised, I began to question relationships, happiness, inequality, and social conditions. My mother, without much education herself, knew that in Puerto Rico an education was the only way out of the housing projects, so she encouraged me to pursue my education (Gracias Titi, tu eres la mejor madre de mundo). At that time, I realized that an education was a way to freedom and that my teachers were the guides toward that promised freedom. Every one of them has been a real and idealistic role model. Therefore, I would like to thank the mentors and heroes who guided and inspired me: Don Pedro Albizu Campos (Dr. Michael P. Wilbur reminded me of this great Puerto Rican national hero); Don Eugenio María de Hostos (el educador de América), the inspiration of my educational hunger; Doña Julia de Burgos (Dr. Janice Roberts-Wilbur reminded me of this giant among women); and finally, a man who has held his principles and has reminded all of us in Latin America about the meaning of the term "Patria": Don Fidel Castro. To those intellectual giants, thanks for the inspiration.

As I mentioned earlier, the other types of role models were those who were closer to me. They included my elementary school teachers, Mrs. Caraballo, Mrs. Corchado, Mrs. Veléz (gym teacher), Mr. Hernández, Mr. Ortega, and Mr. A. Veléz; my junior high school friend, Nelson Peña; my high school teacher, Mr. Pizzini; and my friend, Germán Soriano. These individuals inspired me to go the extra mile and to remember that silent heroes are those heroes who count the most. Mrs. Corchado taught me to stand up for myself against bullies and abusers. Mrs. Veléz, Mr. Hernández, and Mr. J. Veléz provided me with the necessary encouragement to believe in my abilities. Nelson Peña, Germán Soriano, and Mr. Pizzini taught me how to value my intellectual abilities in the classroom and in real life and helped me figure out how to grow up and survive in the housing projects by using my intellect to outsmart the streets and dangers, especially since it was unpopular to be smart in that environment.

What do the two previous quotes mean regarding my professional development? Like anyone else, my professional journey is an integration of personal experiences and education. My path involved an ongoing struggle for clarity and balance, which at times seemed daunting, while other times seemed easy.

Early in my life, I became aware of oppression and the effects of colonialism and poverty in the lives of my family and my neighbors. The awareness allowed me to experience differences that at times were more about socioeconomic status and access to services and opportunities that I also understood to correlate to skin color and education as I grew older. Thus, the first quote above speaks to my Puerto Rican personality, which is based on my life as a spiritual being who incorporates peacefulness, respect, and humility as more important qualities than status and money. My personality and culture also treasure honesty as more valuable than any badge of honor. Added to these qualities, I find myself as a person who lives in a culture where we, as people of Puerto Rican descent, are without any real control over our country.

However, while that is the basic traditional Puerto Rican personality and my Puerto Rican identity, some of my experiences and upbringing have transformed my personality into something a little different. There have been significant influences that shaped my life, leading me to a professional educator, healer, and helper, and leading me to be the professional educator, healer, and helper that I am today. The fact that I grew up in a rough neighborhood required high levels of resilience, forcing me to become an adult before I understood what being a child meant. I had to quickly learn how to have endurance and persistence to manage the situations I was faced with daily. These skills were instrumental in contributing to my ability to understand the academic world. Clearly academe is not as brutal as the environment of the public projects, but academe did present an element of deceitfulness and dishonesty similar to what I experienced in the projects. A key difference is that in the projects, the deceit, lying, and cheating was frequently well-known by everyone involved, whereas in academic settings, this type of behavior was oftentimes hidden from view and could not be seen directly. Thankfully, the intellectual heroes of my childhood supported my potential and cultivated my intellectual capacity to deal with the adversity of my reality growing up. Concurrently, my real-life mentors, such as my mother, brothers, and my friends, added to my base personality and identity as a strong Puerto Rican man with strong moral and humanistic convictions, allowing me to absorb the ideas that my intellectual heroes provided to me and helping transform me into a "free thinker." Taking this base of life instruction, where I nurtured my cultural identity along with my spirituality, courage, compassion, and knowledge, provided a basis to more fully come into my own both intellectually and spatially. A person who significantly impacted me during this developmental time in my journey to becoming a helper was my grandmother, who was a spiritual healer in Puerto Rico ("espiritista"; Torres-Rivera, 2005).

Although my grandmother was a spiritual healer, as a 12-year-old growing up in the projects, this type of work had no appeal. While very much aware of the social problems of the Puerto Rican people and understanding and experiencing the poor living conditions of people in the public housing projects of Puerto Rico, I was drawn to work as a lawyer to help poor people combat inequalities and oppression. Over time that interest changed, very much influenced while in the United States Army, where I gained an understanding that to help others you cannot just change the environment without changing people's minds and their outlook on life (Memmi, 1957).

It is important to point out that while I became aware of discrimination and oppression early in my life due to the circumstances in which my mother found herself (poor, uneducated, and single, with three growing boys), my awareness of cultural differences and racism did not come to play a role in my life until I joined the U.S. Army in 1979. My first experience was during basic training, when all non-English speakers were placed in a special training program that added another eight weeks of basic training. It was interesting to see that all people of color seemed to be in one platoon, which the drill sergeants called the "gangster platoon." It seems like my time in the Army was very much riddled with experiences of racism. I was regularly passed up for promotion and positions of leadership, watching people from the dominant culture selected for positions for which I was well qualified.

Even so, I took every opportunity to gain access to numerous opportunities provided by the Army, despite the persistent racism and discrimination that was present during every posting. After my basic training and first military occupation training, I was assigned to Fort Stewart, Georgia. While I was stationed at Fort Stewart, I had the opportunity to change my military occupation specialty from combat medic to behavioral science specialist. In that particular military occupation specialty, I was able to train as a substance abuse counselor as well as a discharge planning coordinator and a mental health counselor, which changed my life. Once I finished my training at Fort Sam Houston in San Antonio, Texas, I was deployed to Giessen, Germany, to work as a substance abuse counselor in Kirch-Göns. Each of these experiences provided me with the opportunity to learn and grow as both a professional counselor and as a person of color in a White-dominated world. The words of my mother and grandmother echoed in my head, "lo que mata, engorda," which means what does not kill you will make you stronger. The hardship of each experience gave me the courage to seek the next challenge, as another of my mother's "dichos" motivated me, "nacismos sin ropa, todo lo que optenemos es ganancia," meaning that we are born with nothing, therefore, everything that we have is gained.

During these times, almost everything that I did was a risk. As the older son of a single mother, I learned early in life that apart from my mother, the only role models that I could follow were in books and/or in "cuentos" and "dichos." The "cuentos" provided me with an invisible map of life and how to live and maneuver my life successfully, while the "dichos" provided me with a set of instructions on how to navigate the map of life and find meaning and direction. Oftentimes without role models I felt that I was on a journey by myself, creating my own path, yet even so, I could feel that my mother, grandmother, and ancestors were always there with me, helping me take chances and challenging me to move into the unknown. My solo journey was even more pronounced, since during this time I didn't have any role models with the intellectual capacity to teach me how to be creative.

While my mother and my grandmother were (and continue to be) very influential people in my life, it also is clear that their capacity was limited in teaching me how to be even more resilient and tenacious than they had been to combat oppression and to deal with the adversity I was facing in my expanding world. From their teaching and courage, I inherited the indomitable spirit of seeing the best of people and the strength to continue in my search for equality and commitment to open doors for others. Thus, my preacademia upbringing was strongly influenced by my mother and grandmother and was greatly supplemented by intellectual real-life and fictional heroes that I learned and dreamed about from books, "cuentos," and "dichos."

Academia

While in the Army I was able to finish my bachelor's and master's degrees and then began pursuing a doctoral degree. The most influential people during that journey were Drs. Michael P. Wilbur and Janice Roberts-Wilbur, two of the professors in my master's program. It was on this journey, with my personal experiences in the Army, where I learned that my passion for helping was rooted in and related to colonialism (Memmi, 2000). As I further developed, it became clear to me that social justice must complement the cultural approach (Strega & Brown, 2015) that I was developing in my studies and life.

There were two highly significant moments during my journey in academia. One was when I completed my doctoral degree. This was profound, especially since I was the first person in my family to obtain a college degree. The second moment was when I hooded my first doctoral student in 1999 at the University of Nevada, Reno. For years, my academic advisor (Dr. Michael P. Wilbur) told me that I knew more than I allowed myself to believe and that eventually that would become clear to me. This did not occur until I began to teach and supervise students and experienced reaching students, seeing how I played a significant part in helping others preparing to be "effective" counselors. As time progressed, I was also able to see that my approach to research was helping others create a different paradigm to combat oppression. I grew to realize that my contribution was valuable, with the perspective of native or indigenous knowledge that was rooted in the experience of coming from a colonized country.

The adjustment to the culture of academia has been a constant challenge to me as honesty and directness did not seem to be part of that environment. Additionally, the rules about how to be "part" of academe are not necessarily compatible with my cultural values, such as humility and lack of ambition (Bourgois, 1996). This dichotomy has contributed to my constant search for acceptance and the need to prove myself at every turn. Nonetheless, it is that struggle that has provided me with the necessary tools to understand how to be a helper and a leader. My understanding of counseling and psychotherapy has evolved from believing that people are in a helpless position to believing that people are resilient enough that my job as a counselor is one of collaboration and companionship to help clients move from helplessness to empowerment (Watkins & Shulman, 2008).

The challenge to modify myself from being honest and direct to being more tactful and careful when I relate to others in academia has presented my biggest challenge, as this makes me feel like this adapted behavior strips me of my identity as a person and as a cultural being (Wah, 2002). Thus, trying to keep my dignity and integrity seems to be a never-ending process. In this struggle, as in previous years, it seems that my strength comes from my extended family in Puerto Rico. Adding to the strength are my students as well as my research and writing. It has also been helpful to create separate compartments that create distinct differences where I can be my real self as opposed to the person I am when living in toxic environments, such as the work environment. Interestingly, even within university environments that were dramatically different from my culture or upbringing, I found the classroom to be a sacred place that was safe, where I could work with and train future professionals. This experience is similar to other people of color in academia, and I, like so many others, have paid a price and continue to pay a price, with experiences such as being passed up for promotion, being fired, being called a thug, experiencing numerous microaggressions, and in one particular position, being escorted out of the classroom because two dominant culture students did not feel comfortable with the lecture about privilege and colonization. Nonetheless, despite all of these obstacles and hardships, at night I find solace sitting down in my small place and listening to salsa music, smoking a Puerto Rican cigar, and having a cup of coffee, all of which take me to the place where my ancestors provided a safe space. Oftentimes in these moments, I will receive an email from one of my former students or some other student from around the world who might be struggling with the decision to join academia, writing something like this: "Not only am I inspired by your authenticity and genuineness when identifying systems of oppression within our field but also your wealth of knowledge about the field. I would greatly appreciate the opportunity to meet with you." These types of correspondence help reinforce that everything has been worth it.

The last three years of my career have been probably the most difficult of my twenty-plus years in academia. Fundamentally, I believe that people are good. Contrasting with this belief are the current challenges I am faced with by the presence of individuals in my professional career who seem to be without boundaries or a sense of morality. Nonetheless, the idea that everything takes place for a reason and the truth will be revealed to me at the proper time helps keep me grounded.

Lessons Learned

The lessons that I have learned on my journey are to have patience and hope, to trust my instincts, and to never assume that people can understand you, even if they state that they do. I also learned that in academic life, having the ability to remain truthful to oneself is the best medicine. In fact over the years, it seems to me that principles of liberation psychology and Gestalt therapy have become my most key ingredients for living life to the fullest. That is, I learned to be concerned with the present rather than with the past or the future; to deal with what is present rather than with what is absent; to experience the real; to stop unnecessary thinking; to express rather than manipulate, explain, justify, or judge; to not restrict my awareness; to not accept "should" or "ought" other than my own. It is important when taking risks to accept the consequences of your decisions. Furthermore, in the end, everything will be as it is meant to be, and if you do the right thing, the rewards will always be sufficient to maintain your identity of being humble, courageous, peaceful, and true to the essence of a Puerto Rican man (Martín-Baró, Salvador, & Salvador, 2007).

Recommendations for New Counselors

For new counselors, my recommendations are probably the same ones that I would share with anyone who is willing to learn and take risks. Listen, observe, take a chance, wait your turn, be polite. Learn to talk when you need to; however, don't be afraid. Be honest, and express yourself as long as you remain honest. Honesty can be defined as the following: "(a) perception—the ability of the professional to be aware of her or his sensory perceptions; (b) feedback—giving and receiving feedback that is in harmony with the professional's sensory perceptions; (c) directness—the ability to display candor and to be open, moving beyond the 'everything is all right' pretense; (d) recovery skills—which are sequential to directness, as directness may create conflict or discomfort to the client, and the professional may need to respond with care, acceptance, and empathy; (e) confrontation—the ability to recognize and point out incongruity; (f) self-disclosure—the ability to be real and transparent; and (g) interpretation—a clear understanding of the client situation" (Torres-Rivera, Phan, Maddux, Wilbur, & Arredondo, 2006, p. 38).

Conclusion and Future

As I approach the age when people in the United States retire, I am beginning to dream about my return to my homeland to do the work that I left behind in my communities and public projects. Such a move would allow me to remain in the United States while working with the people who could benefit from my expertise and passion back in the paradise island of Puerto Rico. I am ready for the most compelling challenge in my professional journey—to work with my people.

References

Bourgois, P. (1996). *In search of respect: Selling crack in El Barrio*. Cambridge, England: Cambridge University Press.

Cordasco, F., & Bucchioni, E. (Eds.). (1973). *The Puerto Rican experience: A sociological sourcebook*. Totowa, NJ: Littlefield, Adams.

Martín-Baró, I., Salvador, S., & Salvador, E. (2007). *Hacia una Psicología de la Liberación, 22*, 1–11.

Memmi, A. (1957). *The colonizer and the colonized* (H. Greenfeld, Trans.). Boston, MA: Beacon Press.

Memmi, A. (2000). *Racism*. Minneapolis: University of Minnesota Press.

Strega, S., & Brown, L. (Eds.). (2015). *Research as resistance: Revisiting critical, indigenous, and anti-oppressive approaches* (2nd ed.). Toronto, Ontario: Canadian Scholars' Press.

Torres-Rivera, E. (1996). Puerto Rican men, gender role conflict, and ethnic identity. *Dissertation Abstracts International Section A: Humanities and Social Sciences, 56*(10), 4159.

Torres-Rivera, E. (2005). Espiritismo: The flywheel of the Puerto Rican spiritual traditions. *Interamerican Journal of Psychology, 39*, 295–300.

Torres-Rivera, E., Phan, L. T., Maddux, C. D., Wilbur, M. P., & Arredondo, P. (2006). Honesty in multicultural counseling: A pilot study of the counseling relationship. *Interamerican Journal of Psychology, 40*, 37–45.

Wah, L. M. (2002). *Last chance for Eden.* Berkeley, CA: StriFry Seminars & Consulting.

Watkins, M., & Shulman, H. (Eds.). (2008). *Toward psychologies of liberation.* New York, NY: Palgrave Macmillan.

12

A Journey From a Single-Wide Trailer to the White House

By Dorothy L. Espelage

As a "military brat" growing up in Virginia Beach, I never imagined that I would find myself in my career sitting in White House conferences advocating for youth and their families in the United States. In fact, I largely lived in survival mode day-to-day, so that did not leave time to daydream about the future. My stepfather was career Navy and was gone six months of each year, and my mother a waitress who struggled with depression, which left me and my siblings largely unsupervised and on our own most of the time. However, our street block was filled with military and civilian families with a lot of kids, and the neighborhood would turn out to be a source of protection for us. There were many positive adult role models like my friends' parents who provided us with spaces that were safe, consistent, and nurturing. There begins my journey through a multitude of experiences with protective adults, including our neighbors, babysitters, girl scout leaders, coaches, teachers, and librarians.

The Big Chill

Throughout my childhood, I was intrigued by human existence, the meaning of life, and found myself analyzing the behaviors of everyone around me.

A career in psychology came as a natural option given my obsession with the human psyche. However, career or vocational training in my house was limited to the roles of my parents—an enlisted military father and a mother who was a waitress. What these two roles had in common was they both required a strong work ethic and an ability to get up early and work with a wide range of individuals. That is where my strong work ethic was spawned, but I really had to turn to television to get exposure to other professions. Television in the 1970s did not offer many career options for girls and women, so it was not until the 1980s when I started to explore career ideas. In 1983 (a perfect time to start thinking about college), a movie called *The Big Chill* was released, and it was my first exposure to a wide range of professions. For those of you who have not seen this movie, it is about a group of college friends who graduated from the University of Michigan and come together for a friend's funeral. This friend killed himself. He was a scientist who battled with the meaning of life and depression. These friends spend the weekend following the funeral catching up for lost years, partaking of libations, listening to Motown music, and questioning how they lost sight of their social justice intentions and ended up "selling out." The cast of characters includes a female doctor, a female lawyer who was going to save inner-city families but took a job with a corporate law firm, a writer who instead of finishing his novel writes for a well-known celebrity magazine, an actor who plays a detective, a writer who gave up writing stories to be a stay-at-home mother and wife, and finally an injured Vietnam vet (Nick) who always dreamed of having a family but sustained an injury that makes that an impossibility. This loss has left him empty and closed off from society.

As you can see, this movie was an excellent introduction to several careers that I could consider as a woman from a working-class and military family. But one scene really stuck with me. Nick spends most of the weekend filming himself and interviewing his friends about their experiences after college. In one of the scenes, Nick plays the role of interviewer and interviewee and pretends to interview himself. At one point, the interviewer says something to the effect of, "So you are ABD in clinical psychology from the University of Michigan? How is it that you cannot finish the dissertation," to which he replies, "I *chose* not to finish the dissertation." What was ABD? At that time there was no Internet to look this up quickly and it was not listed in the encyclopedias that we had on the bookshelf at home, so I had to wait until I got to school the next day. The first thing I did when I got to school was go straight to the library to get a book on doctoral programs in psychology and ask my librarian about the term ABD. For the next few years, I would watch this movie over 100 times; I analyzed every conversation and dissected each character. I analyzed the ways in which each character interacted and how they made sense of their life decisions. Sam, the divorced actor, regretted having an affair in his marriage and was fearful that he would not be a good father to his children. I watched how Nick was so troubled by his experiences in Vietnam, and his way of coping was to push everyone away from him. I was fascinated by how the characters blamed themselves for their friend's suicide. They each thought they could have prevented it. I watched how Meg, the female corporate lawyer, regretted that she put her career first and now had to figure out how to have a child. I learned several things that still resonate with me today: (a) Life is not fair; (b) most careers come with sacrifice; (c) career-oriented women are treated differently than men; (d) life is not endless; (e) success requires hard work; and finally, (f) I wanted to be in a career that gave back to society.

These characters motivated me to keep working hard in school because I wanted to be successful and I wanted to go to college. I did not want to wait tables after college. I wanted more. I enrolled in Advanced Placement (AP) math and science classes when given the opportunity. There were only six of us in my high school AP classes, and we became very close. All of us had the same goal in mind—to attend college. But I wanted to set myself apart from them. I convinced my science teacher that I should take an independent research class to conduct a science experiment. Each Sunday night I watched *60 Minutes;* I remember watching a segment on the preservatives in hot dogs (e.g., sodium phosphates) and how they are linked to diseases. I remember going to the library searching for research on these preservatives. I spent mornings and weekends designing an experiment to test the impact of monosodium glutamate (MSG) and phosphate on the offspring of fruit flies called Drosophila. Only now do I recognize that I designed a randomized clinical trial when I randomly assigned the fruit flies to different levels of MSG (e.g., .001, .01, .05 concentrations). My study hypotheses were supported—fruit flies who were exposed to the highest levels of MSG had offspring with impaired wings. I recall going to a lab at a local college to examine the wings of the offspring.

One-Way Trip to the City—Richmond, Virginia

We now fast forward to 1986, my senior year in high school. As a student athlete in AP classes, it was only natural that my teachers assumed I would apply for college. But college was never discussed in my house, despite the fact that I was in AP classes, competed in math competitions, and won science awards for my experiments with fruit flies. But a small miracle happened. I was walking in downtown Roanoke, Virginia, and saw a sign for an open house for Virginia Commonwealth University (VCU) in Richmond. I convinced my cousin Robin to go with me, and we were encouraged to apply. Having no idea what I was doing, I applied, and several months later I received a letter of acceptance. Robin got in, too. We were headed to the city and capital of Virginia. I worked that summer on the lake to save money for college and was excited for the next chapter of my life.

That summer, my stepfather died of Agent Orange exposure at the age of 52 as a result of three tours in Vietnam. Because he spent 30 years in the military, and because the military recognized that his death was due to Agent Orange, they offered us compensation—if you will—for his service. This came in the form of $400 a month toward educational expenses for his stepchildren. I was able to go to college because of this $400, plus a waitress position at Bob's Big Boy the first year of college, and then a transfer to work at the JW Marriott in Richmond for the following four years. Yes, I took five years, for several reasons. First, I could never register for classes in advance because I had to make money during the school breaks to pay my tuition and books. Thus there were times when I could not get into classes. Second, I had to work Friday nights and doubles on Saturday and Sunday (start time 5:30 a.m.; end time 11 p.m.), so I was never able to take a full load, as there was no time on weekends to study. But I was grateful to be in college.

When Robin and I arrived in Richmond to pick a major and register for classes, there were no computers at registration, only a large hall filled with tables with signs for the various majors—math, physics, education, biology, psychology, and so on. My mind went right back to *The Big Chill* and I then reflected on my interests and successes. I loved math and competed in math competitions. But I thought it might be too hard for me to be math major. I won competitions for my experiments with fruit flies, where I randomly assigned them to various levels of MSG. But I wasn't sure I wanted to consider being a female scientist. To this day, I am not sure why I hesitated to pursue a degree in a hard science. Perhaps there wasn't enough encouragement at home. What about Nick and his doctoral work in clinical psychology? Yes, that I could do. I walked briskly over to the psychology table and registered for college classes!

Search for Research Opportunities

I had done enough research on doctoral programs in psychology to know that I needed to conduct research as an undergraduate student to be competitive for graduate programs, especially because I was at a state school, not a private school, which was not seen as particularly strong in undergraduate education. So in my normal assertive and socially skilled fashion, I started knocking on doors to ask about joining labs. I found myself first working in a "rat lab," where I was a research assistant for Professor Robert Hamm who ran a federally funded lab that tested the effects of components of anti-anxiety medications. I enjoyed my time there, but I really fell in love with research when I started to work with Professor Shari Ellis in her developmental psychology studies. Her research focused on peer relations, and more specifically, friendships. She gave elementary school children tasks to create conflict, and these interactions were videotaped for later coding. This was my first introduction to research outside of a research laboratory and my first introduction to human subjects research. I had found my calling. Not only did I want to be a clinical psychologist, but I wanted to also focus on developmental psychology. After spending hours of watching and coding interactions between friends and enemies in these videos, I started to value the potential restorative nature of friendships.

Please note that my love for math continued, so I took calculus classes for fun at VCU. There was something about the finality of solving a math problem that excited me. Despite Professor Farley's (my calculus professor) attempts to persuade me to pursue graduate study in math, I did not have the confidence to make that change. Thus I was off to create a competitive resume for graduate school.

Next Challenge: Graduate School Applications

Professor Ellis was instrumental in my applying for graduate school, and she gave me what turned out to be best advice: "In addition to applying for PhD programs in clinical psychology, apply also to a few master's programs as a backup." I applied to the top U.S. PhD programs in clinical psychology—and did not get into any of them. But I did get into several terminal master's programs, including one in Virginia, Radford University, which was close to my family. In a small program of only 12 students, I found myself in graduate school pursuing a degree in clinical psychology. But I was not there to get a terminal degree; I was there to prepare for my PhD applications that would be going out the following fall.

I had to get to work. I needed to find a professor who was willing to supervise my master's thesis, but this was not easy in a teaching institution. After knocking on many doors, I found Professor Jeffrey Chase, who was willing to help me design, conduct, and write a research study. We designed an experimental study using the Stroop color-naming interference task, which requires individuals to name the color of a word (e.g., red); an interference is created because the word is blue but displayed in red font. So, I adapted this to screen women with and without eating disorders to see how much interference was created when they had to color-name words related to eating and body image. I randomly assigned these women to a neutral condition or eating-disordered Stroop tasks. The outcome was how long it took them to name the color of the words. As hypothesized, women with eating disorders were delayed when color-naming eating-disordered or body-related words (e.g., cake, toilet, vomit, fat) in comparison to the neutral group and in comparison to women without disorders. I fell further in love with hypotheses and analyzing data. Although we submitted this for publication, it was rejected, but I learned a lot in the process.

Round Two: Graduate School Applications

The second time was the charm, but it would not come without a major challenge. During my graduate study at Radford University, I took classes with students in counseling psychology, so I came to understand the differences between clinical and counseling psychology. I was so excited to have been introduced to the field of counseling psychology because it seemed to focus on the strength of humanity, in comparison to clinical psychology, which focused more on psychopathology. So this second time around, I applied to both clinical and counseling psychology PhD programs and was really excited when I got invited for an interview at Indiana University. My sister Sarah had agreed to drive with me to the Midwest in the middle of winter. I would first interview for a clinical psychology program in Chicago and then we would make our way to Bloomington, Indiana. I recall saying to myself, "A snowstorm? How bad could it be?" I was determined to make it to Indiana University for the interview. As a purposeful planner, I ensured that we left Chicago early to allow for plenty of time to get to the interview. This was a smart decision, because only one lane was open on the interstate from Chicago to Bloomington, and we encountered whiteout conditions. It took us over six hours to get to Bloomington, but we made it. It was not a snowstorm but a blizzard. I found my way to the education building and learned that I was the only applicant who made it, although several faculty members were there. As I recall, I interviewed with Professors Bell, Kurpius, Froehle, and Ridley, among others. Indiana University would be my home for the next three years.

Now the Journey Gets Real

Now that I found my way into a PhD program in counseling psychology, the journey continued at breakneck speed. During my master's program at Radford University, I spent a lot of time talking to professors in the various programs to see how they ended up at a teaching university versus a research university. I learned that there were a number of skills I would need to be competitive for an academic position in a research-intensive university. These included developing strong quantitative research skills, mastering writing and managing grants, and learning to write for publication. I was off. I enrolled in every quantitative class available and quickly learned who on campus was grant funded and inquired about working in their lab. I was successful in finding a well-known child clinical psychology faculty member. Professor Alexandra Quittner was doing work in the area of eating disorders but was largely working with families managing cystic fibrosis. Her scholarship was heavily funded by the National Institutes of Health, which gave me an opportunity to learn about this funding agency. To maximize my exposure to her studies, I took a lab coordinator job when it opened up. At the same time, I was hired as a graduate student to evaluate a violence prevention program for Professor Kris Bosworth. This project was funded by the Centers for Disease Control and Prevention (CDC), which would be a federal agency that would support my work in years to come. My three years at Indiana University also allowed for great mentorship from Professors Froehle and Ridley, two counseling psychology faculty members who encouraged me to write for publication and to network within our profession and beyond. Within three years, I had learned about building a federally funded research program and how to manage a laboratory and supervise undergraduate and graduate students, and I had started to appreciate the challenges associated with publishing. Through the mentorship of Professors Quittner and Bosworth, I carved out two lines of research that were keeping me busy with ideas: (a) assessment in eating disorders and (b) school-based bullying.

Next Step: Tenure-Track
Position in a Research I University

In October 1996 I was several months into my predoctoral internship at the Durham VA Medical Center, and it was time for the next step in my journey—time to apply for a tenure-track job at a research-intensive university. Although I enjoyed some aspects of clinical work, I felt that direct clinical work with no research component left me unfulfilled at the end of the day. I wanted to have a greater impact on societal issues like eating disorders and youth aggression. I submitted applications for tenure-track positions all over the country. To my surprise, several weeks after searches closed, the phone rang. It was Professor James Rounds from the University of Illinois at Urbana-Champaign, a faculty member in one of the highest ranked PhD programs in counseling psychology. I could hardly talk to him—I was in shock! "Yes, I can make an interview on December 6th." The interview consisted of two long days of meetings and a job talk. The job talk was well-attended and there were several challengers in the audience who made sure I was on my toes. I guess I passed the test of these senior faculty members who appeared to have their own agenda, which is best summarized as attempting to have me fall on my face. That was not going to happen. Life had thrown me too many challenges to give up now. I recall flying out of Champaign after the interview, feeling exhausted but also myself smiling as I reflected on my journey up until this point. Not two days later, the phone rang and I was offered the job! Little did I know when I flew out of Champaign that it would be my academic home for the next 20 years.

Over Two Decades of Scholarship to Impact Policy

Here I am a counseling psychologist and endowed professor of educational psychology with over 22 years of research experience in the area of peer victimization and bullying. I have conducted over 30 school-based survey studies to identify risk and protective factors of bullying, peer victimization, sexual harassment, homophobic teasing, and dating violence. I have secured over $7 million in external funding, and the portfolio is growing. The most comprehensive investigation was funded by the CDC—a three-year, longitudinal study on the intersection of bullying, sexual violence, and now dating violence (funded by the National Institute of Justice) among a large, diverse sample of middle and high school students. I was also principal investigator on another CDC-funded grant that was a three-year, randomized, clinical trial evaluation of a bullying-prevention curriculum in 36 middle schools and involved 3,600 sixth-grade students. This work was extended into a currently funded CDC grant evaluating a social-emotional learning program in another 28 schools, with a focus on working closely with school staff to recognize and prevent violence.

School-Based Bullying Involvement: Social-Ecological Investigations

Prior to my work, research on school-based bullying was limited, and what was being studied focused on individual characteristics of the youth involved. I introduced the field to the notion that school-based bullying is best understood from a social-ecological perspective, in which bullying is viewed as behavior that emerges and is maintained through complex interactions among multiple socialization agents. As principal investigator, my cross-sectional and longitudinal investigations include targeting individual characteristics (Espelage, 2004), familial influences (Espelage, Bosworth, & Simon, 2001; Espelage, Low, Rao, Hong, & Little, 2014), and environmental factors (Espelage, Polanin, & Low, 2014) as pertinent correlates of bullying during early adolescence. These studies are heavily cited and are the basis of many prevention programs.

School-Based Bullying Involvement: Social Network Analysis Studies Point to Peers

My early work on bullying (Espelage & Asidao, 2001) suggested that bullying during early adolescence is a group phenomenon where cliques of students seek out victims. As principal investigator, I designed several rigorous investigations to examine systemically the influence of aggression within peer groups during early adolescence. In several network studies (Espelage, Green, & Polanin, 2012; Espelage, Green, & Wasserman, 2007; Espelage, Holt, & Henkel, 2003), we found support for the homophile hypothesis that youth who engage in these behaviors socialize one another to adopt the same behaviors. This scholarship has been used to argue for prevention programs that address the peer norms around bullying during early adolescence.

Bullying Is a Precursor to Sexual Harassment During Middle School

Until recently, research on bullying among middle school youth did not consider how it might be related to sexual harassment. In fact, much of this scholarship has focused on high school and college samples. As principal investigator of several longitudinal studies, my colleagues and I found that bullying is causally linked to the use of homophobic language and perpetration of sexual harassment as early as sixth grade (Espelage, Basile, De La Rue, & Hamburger, 2014; Espelage, Basile, & Hamburger, 2012; Espelage, Low, Polanin, & Brown, 2013; Espelage, Van Ryzin, Low, & Polanin, 2015). These studies have been used to argue for the development of bully prevention programs that include discussions of sexual harassment in U.S. middle schools, which is an area that is virtually ignored in current school-based programs. This research is also driving bully policies at state and national levels.

Evaluations of School-Based Social-Emotional Learning Programs

Despite the costs of bullying, the impact of bullying-prevention programs in the United States has been disappointing, especially in middle schools. I have spent the last 10 years arguing for the implementation of evidence-based programs that have been developed for youth in the United States, rather than the common practice of adopting curriculum from other countries (Espelage, 2013). As principal investigator of three randomized clinical trials of school-based, social-emotional learning, we published results showing significant reductions in aggression and victimization in U.S. middle schools (Espelage, Low, Polanin, & Brown, 2013, 2015). In addition, we found reductions of bullying perpetration among students with disabilities who completed the social-emotional learning program (Espelage, Rose, & Polanin, 2015). These studies are driving prevention efforts in schools across the United States by highlighting the need to develop and evaluate programs with American children, rather than adopting programs from other countries.

A Long Journey That Is Just Beginning

Indeed, my journey continues and I believe I might just be getting started! I am proud of the some 35 PhD students who have worked in my lab and have gone on to do great things in academia at research and teaching institutions; those who are engaged in direct service at medical hospitals, veterans' hospitals, university counseling centers, government agencies, private sector organizations, prisons, and in private practice; and those who serve as psychologists in the military or run their own practice. My more than two decades at the University of Illinois at Urbana-Champaign flew by because of these students who formed my academic families. I am happy to say that the families are growing, with these students nurturing the next generation of students (my academic grandchildren). My colleagues and mentors throughout the years at Illinois (you know who you are) and mentors across the world (you know, too) are all responsible for my success, and I will be forever grateful. As I think back to the single-wide trailer that I called home for so many years in Moneta, Virginia, and the old school bus where I would study for my high school exams, I am very appreciative of my journey.

These are the lessons I learned: (a) Take risks and do scary things where success is not guaranteed; (b) do things outside of your comfort zone; (c) hold tight to your values and do not back down when faced with adversity or resistance; (d) grant writing is a skill and an art, and it takes time to learn how to do this—keep writing; (e) ask for help and mentorship; (f) publishing requires persistence; (g) collaborate often; (h) not all people have your best interests at heart, so be careful; (i) there are people with whom you will work who will take advantage of you and take credit for things they do not deserve; and (j) not all individuals are good collaborators.

I also value the Virginia family that continues to support my work despite being so far away. Uncle Paul, thank you so much for your support. I will never forget when I left the White House Conference on Bullying in 2011 (yes, they let me in) and you called me to say that you were so proud of me. Cousin Robin Brown, it has been a long time since we walked the streets of Richmond at VCU. I am proud of your work in social services, and together we are helping families. Here is to my brother, who introduced me to science and math, and to telescopes (he made one in high school), and continues to encourage me in my work. Thanks to my sisters Sarah and Catherine, who brought into my life six nieces and nephews who remind me often that sometimes work is not the top priority (not that much, but enough), and play has to happen from time to time. Of course, I could not have done this without all of my awesome, fun colleagues and friends who inspire me every day. Finally, I am grateful for endless support from Ray and his beautiful children.

After 19 years at the University of Illinois at Urbana-Champaign, this "military brat," who has moved many times, is faced with a scary thing. I accepted a position at the University of Florida and will move my entire family to continue my career there. I am following my own advice and taking a big risk to try something different. Many of my colleagues are intrigued by this decision to move. They asked, "How did this come about?" There are so many reasons: (a) In a state where the governor has no budget and does not value higher education or the sacrifices university research professors make to do this work, quality of life and family time suffer; (b) returning to a psychology department where they fund their graduate students is attractive and might allow me to write fewer than 10 grants a year; (c) as I manage my Raynaud's disease, I decided that my health mattered; and (d) being close to the ocean is also attractive.

References

Espelage, D. L. (2004). An ecological perspective to school-based bullying prevention. *The Prevention Researcher, 11,* 3–6.

Espelage, D. L. (2013). Why are bully prevention programs failing in U.S. schools? *Journal of Curriculum and Pedagogy, 10,* 121–123.

Espelage, D. L., & Asidao, C. S. (2001). Conversations with middle school students about bullying and victimization: Should we be concerned? *Journal of Emotional Abuse, 2*(2–3), 49–62. doi:10.1300/J135v02n02_04

Espelage, D. L., Basile, K. C., De La Rue, L., & Hamburger, M. (2014). Longitudinal associations among bullying, homophobic teasing, and sexual violence perpetration among middle school students. *Journal of Interpersonal Violence, 30,* 2541–2561.

Espelage, D. L., Basile, K. C., & Hamburger, M. E. (2012). Bullying experiences and co-occurring sexual violence perpetration among middle school students: Shared and unique risk factors. *Journal of Adolescent Health, 50,* 60–65.

Espelage, D. L., Bosworth, K., & Simon, T. R. (2001). Short-term stability and prospective correlates of bullying in middle-school students: An examination of potential demographic, psychosocial, and environmental influences. *Violence and Victims, 16,* 411–426.

Espelage, D. L., Green, H. D., & Polanin, J. (2012). Willingness to intervene in bullying episodes among middle school students: Individual and peer-group influences. *Journal of Early Adolescence, 32,* 776–801.

Espelage, D. L., Green, H., Jr., & Wasserman, S. (2007). Statistical analysis of friendship patterns and bullying behaviors among youth. *New Directions for Child and Adolescent Development, 118,* 61–75.

Espelage, D. L., Holt, M. K., & Henkel, R. R. (2003). Examination of peer-group contextual effects on aggression during early adolescence. *Child Development, 74,* 205–220.

Espelage, D. L., Low, S., Polanin, J., & Brown, E. (2013). The impact of a middle school program to reduce aggression, victimization, and sexual violence. *Journal of Adolescent Health, 53,* 180–186.

Espelage, D. L., Low, S., Polanin, J., & Brown, E. (2015). Clinical trial of Second Step© middle-school program: Impact on aggression & victimization. *Journal of Applied Developmental Psychology, 37,* 52–63.

Espelage, D. L., Low, S., Rao, M. A., Hong, J. S., & Little, T. D. (2014). Family violence, bullying, fighting, and substance use among adolescents: A longitudinal mediational model. *Journal of Research on Adolescence, 24,* 337–349.

Espelage, D. L., Polanin, J., & Low, S. (2014). Teacher and staff perceptions of school environment as predictors of student aggression, victimization, and willingness to intervene in bullying situations. *School Psychology Quarterly, 29*, 287–305.

Espelage, D. L., Rose, C. A., & Polanin, J. R. (2015). Social-emotional learning program to reduce bullying, fighting, and victimization among middle school students with disabilities. *Remedial and Special Education, 36*, 299–311.

Espelage, D. L., Low, S., Van Ryzin, M., & Polanin, J. (2015). Clinical trial of Second Step© middle school program: Impact on bullying, cyberbullying, homophobic teasing, and sexual harassment perpetration. *School Psychology Review, 44*, 464–479. doi:10.17105/spr-15-0052.1

13

My Professional Journey

By Melba J. T. Vasquez

Tell me, what is it you plan to do with your one wild and pre-
cious life?

—"The Summer Day" (Oliver, 1992)

Presidency of the American Psychological Association

The most wonderful, exciting, humbling, and intimidating period in my life
was my service as president of the American Psychological Association
(APA). The decision to run, the process of campaigning, the election, and the
period of service were all part of that phase of my career. It was exciting
because it was one of the most stimulating, challenging, joyful, and empowering experiences of my career. It was humbling because I felt that as a
woman and a Latina, I was representing diverse parts of the membership
who had rarely served in the APA presidential role, and I so much wanted to
serve well. It was intimidating for multiple reasons, including the incredible
responsibility that I felt. I was the first Latina, first woman of color, and only
the 13th woman to serve as president out of about 120 presidencies.

The influence of one's various identities on career choice is powerful. Our
ability to envision options for ourselves as viable can depend on how we have
seen others with whom we identify. I found that various aspects of my

identities were significant in both challenging and allowing me to consider certain options. Did my identity as a Latina, from a working-class background, first-generation college student, encompass serving as a president in the American Psychological Association? Was it acceptable that I did not attend Ivy League universities? What did it mean that I was a full-time independent practitioner, and while I publish as a scholar, I do not work in the academy?

Other women of color had run for APA president and had served as inspiration for me to do so. Diane Willis, Alice Chang, and Rosie Phillips Bingham had blazed the trail to campaign and run for president. The efforts they demonstrated put the notion in my (and hopefully many others') consciousness that it was an option for someone like us. I thought, "If they can take the risk and live with dignity for having contributed to the effort despite not 'winning,' then I can too." I was also cognizant of the three men of color who had been elected as APA president: Kenneth B. Clark, PhD (1971); Logan Wright, PhD (1986); and Richard M. Suinn, PhD (1999). A few years after my election, another man of color and the first Latino, Antonio Puente, was elected to serve as president in 2017.

I had been very active in the APA since the early 1980s by serving on various boards, committees, task forces, and councils of representatives (the policy-making body of the APA). I very much enjoyed the experience and opportunity to influence policy in the profession of psychology through leadership service on the APA, the Texas Psychological Association, and other related psychological associations. I am aware of having entered a different level of leadership service when I ran for (at the encouragement of Laura Brown) and was elected president of APA Division 35, Society for the Psychology of Women (1998–1999), and then, inspired by Rosie Phillips Bingham to run for and be selected president of APA Division 17, Society for Counseling Psychology (2001–2002). I had published and provided a significant number of presentations, workshops, and keynote addresses at conferences and other gatherings.

I was encouraged to seek the APA presidency for approximately 10 years before I seriously considered running. Gomez et al. (2001) and Cheung and Halpern (2010) indicated that women, especially women of color, may have a tendency to not consider leadership roles until they are fully prepared. They wait, hold back, and are concerned about speaking up. The studies of women leaders that Gomez et al. and Cheung and Halpern interviewed reported a pattern of unintended leadership development. In the early stages of their careers, none of the women planned on making it to the top of their professions. This was certainly true for me.

During my campaign for the APA presidency, I had significant support from friends, allies, and colleagues. Many of my supporters encouraged their universities; state, local, or regional psychological organizations; APA divisions; or other groups to invite me to speak. I provided approximately 45 keynote presentations, workshops, and symposia in about 25 states for a year and a half. Those of us without the visibility of significant undergraduate textbooks and other symbols of visibility have to work hard to become visible, since electability, particularly that of APA president, is related in large part to name recognition. It is the only position in the APA that is elected by the full membership.

I was elected at the end of 2009. I served a three-year term as president-elect, president, and past president (2010–1012). I am still aware of how fortunate I am to have had that experience. To this day, I believe it is possible that I was elected due to the 2008 election of Barack Obama, who may have inspired our members to consider that diverse leadership might be productive for the APA.

My presidency was very exciting, and I was able to get a bird's-eye view of the incredible wonderful work that the APA does. I was able to give expression to some of my values, such as designating "social justice" one of the themes for the annual APA convention in August 2011 in Washington, DC. I represented the APA during my presidential year at the Society of Psychology Interamerican XXXIII Congress in Medellin, Columbia. The Interamerican Congress represents numerous Latin American countries and is attended by thousands of psychologists from those countries; I was treated like a "rock star" as the first "Latina" president of the APA—what an honor and responsibility. I couldn't help but feel embarrassed that my Spanish is only moderately fluent; I gave my keynote address partly in English and partly in Spanish. Fortunately, excellent translations were provided (English, Spanish, French, Italian), and participants were kind. I also represented the APA at the 12th European Congress of Psychology in Istanbul, Turkey; the Caribbean Conference of Psychology in Nassau, Bahamas; and during my past president's year, the XXX International Congress of Psychology in Cape Town, South Africa.

Along with APA staff member Rhea Farberman, my spouse and I attended the Voice Awards at Paramount Theater in Los Angeles, which the APA sponsors with the Substance Abuse and Mental Health Services Administration and the Center for Mental Health Services. The Voice Awards program honors consumer/peer leaders and television and film professionals who educate the public about behavioral health. It was a very inspiring event.

APA attorney Shirley Higuchi and her family were involved in ensuring that APA helped sponsor the dedication and grand opening of the Heart Mountain Interpretive Center near Colby, Wyoming. It was on the site where U. S. citizens of Japanese ancestry were imprisoned during World War II. This event was also very moving, poignant, and powerful! I was so proud of

APA's involvement with these events. Travel to various meetings, conferences, and events was a large part of the role during the three years of serving as president-elect, president, and past president.

I facilitated two meetings of the council of representatives and numerous meetings of the board of directors. My special presidential initiatives included appointment of task forces to examine psychologists' perspectives on grand challenges in society, including immigration, discrimination, and educational disparities; and three very hardworking task forces produced the reports, all available on the APA website:

- *Crossroads: The Psychology of Immigration in the New Century* (American Psychological Association, Presidential Task Force on Immigration, 2012)
- *Dual Pathways to a Better America: Preventing Discrimination and Promoting Diversity* (American Psychological Association, Presidential Task Force on Preventing Discrimination and Promoting Diversity, 2012)
- *Ethnic and Racial Disparities in Education: Psychology's Contributions to Understanding and Reducing Disparities* (American Psychological Association, Presidential Task Force on Educational Disparities, 2012)

I also appointed a Joint Task Force for the Development of Telepsychology Guidelines for Psychologists. The guidelines were developed by members of three organizations: the APA, the Association of State and Provincial Psychology Boards, and the APA Insurance Trust. This allowed for the development of one document that could represent a diverse range of interests and expertise characteristic of the broad profession of psychology, including technology, ethical considerations, licensure and mobility, and scope of practice.

How Did You Do It?

People have literally asked, "How did you do it? How did you get elected to a majority White organization? How did a Mexican American who grew up in a working-class family in San Marcos, Texas, the oldest child of parents with elementary educations, who picked cotton during some summers, become president of the APA?"

Although I don't know the specific answer to that question, I will describe my development, with a focus on factors that I suspect contributed to my evolution as a leader. My early childhood, birth to about 6 years of age, was close to ideal. I was the first child born to two first-born parents and thus had a special place in their respective extended families. I had eight aunts and uncles on my mother's side of the family and seven on my father's side. I had the benefit of caretaking from them and all four of my grandparents.

In retrospect, I realize that I was warmly "held" not only in the context of my extended family but also in my community of Mexican Americans. I grew up in a segregated community, and one of the ways that our community coped with discrimination and prejudice was to form a very close and strong resilient "village." I was not aware of discrimination nor of the relative poverty in which we lived until I was about 6 years old.

Going into public school for first grade was traumatic. I had gone to Catholic School for kindergarten and loved it. Therefore, it was confusing to my parents that I cried daily for weeks upon entering first grade in public school. I had not reacted in that way in kindergarten, in Catholic School, where my experience was that the atmosphere was warmer; the nuns were from Mexico, and the "lay teachers" were Mexican American. I realize in retrospect that I experienced a cold, chilly environment in the treatment of Mexican American children in the subsequent public school setting, relative to what I was used to. I attended public school for three years, and then my parents moved from the farm where they worked to "town." My siblings and I were able to attend Catholic School again, and I attended fourth to seventh grade. Catholic School contributed to providing an organized work ethic, consistent with my parents' orientation. The transition to eighth-grade in public school was challenging but mostly fine. I remember that teachers seemed surprised that I was a good student. I suspect that their stereotypes contributed to their inability to see the strengths and abilities of those of my peers, and coming from Catholic School in the seventh grade, I did not know to hide my abilities to fit their expectations.

I attended a public high school during the mid- to late-1960s, and civil rights issues were clearly present, even in a small town in central Texas. Texas was one of the states that enacted the poll tax, a payment required to register to vote as a device for restricting voting rights after the right to vote was extended to all races by the 15th Amendment. The poll tax was abolished when I was 15; my parents had been very vocal about the unfairness of such a tax in order to vote and actively worked to rescind it.

Social segregation was in full force, and Black and Latina/o students rallied together to support each other to obtain leadership positions in high school. The societal context, including in our community, was one of angry empowerment to change the oppressive and discriminatory processes that we knew were prevalent. I believe that the combination of my role as a good student, and social skills learned in the context of my large, extended Latina family with values of "personalismo," led me to become a leader fairly quickly. Several Mexican American and Black students were the first representatives of our respective groups to be elected to various offices and key positions (class officers, National Honor Society and Student Council officers, class favorites, cheerleaders). The racial/ethnic minority members of our local community (all of our parents) were very supportive, and they themselves were running for city council and school board at about the same time. This period of time was challenging, exciting, difficult, and painful, and it was the beginning of my period of anger.

Resilience as an Outcome of Challenges

Fortunately, my parents guided us to direct anger into productive, social justice advocacy. Despite having only elementary educations, and despite being of the working class, both my parents were politically involved at the grassroots level, engaged in civil rights activities, and articulated a strong belief in and support for education. In fact, they influenced all of their children to obtain at least associate's degrees, and all my siblings are contributing members of society. I am proud of my siblings and of my hardworking parents. My mother obtained a GED and a bachelor's degree (while I was in graduate school); she served on the local school board and eventually became director of a community action program, part of President Lyndon B. Johnson's War on Poverty. I was able to observe that well-designed social programs could help provide opportunities for families and individuals to increase the quality of their lives. My mother is now in her mid-80s and is still very active in her community

I am a first-generation college student. I obtained my undergraduate degree from my hometown university, Southwest Texas State University, which was then a Teacher's College (now Texas State University). I majored in English and political science and obtained a secondary teaching certification. I taught in a middle school for two years in New Braunfels, Texas, while I worked on a master's degree in school counseling. Toward the end of the master's program, one of my professors, Dr. Colleen Conoley, for whom I had worked as a work-study student throughout my undergraduate program, encouraged me to apply to the counseling psychology program at The University of Texas at Austin, 30 miles north of my hometown. I have to admit that I did not know what a doctorate in counseling psychology consisted of or what it prepared one to do. Dr. Conoley tried to describe what a counseling psychologist was and assured me that it would be a good fit. She was right. The opportunities for employment as a counseling psychologist have been abundant, and I thoroughly enjoy all the work I do, even when there is a bit of drudgery (such as sitting and writing).

I must say that it was also the encouragement of several undergraduate professors who, in effect, "prepared" me to consider that my identity may indeed incorporate the possibility of one who was capable of graduate school. A sociology professor encouraged me to seek a master's degree in sociology, a constitutional law professor encouraged me to seek a law degree, and an English composition professor told me that she rarely gave "A's" in her class, and I achieved one. The lesson I learned is that it is so important to be willing to provide feedback and encouragement to students and others who display talent. They may not know about their strengths without that mirroring of feedback.

I was told upon entry to the doctoral program that it was a four-year program. Because I did not have a psychology background, I had to take three "vestibule" courses, so I took summer classes every year of my program to catch up and finish on time. At the end of my first year in graduate school, I received an APA Minority Fellowship grant that provided partial financial support for the last three years of graduate school, which helped considerably. I was in the first cohort of recipients of that wonderful fellowship (1975). The directors of the APA Minority Fellowship program, Drs. Dalmas Taylor and then James Jones, also served as mentors and facilitated entry into the profession by encouraging fellows to attend national conventions and participate in leadership activities.

I graduated from the APA accredited scientist-practitioner Counseling Psychology Program from The University of Texas at Austin in 1978. Although I did not have minority faculty, most of the ones there were helpful and supportive, and my peers in the graduate program were largely supportive. Participation in national conferences allowed for exposure to mentors "from afar," including Drs. Marta Bernal and Amado Padilla.

Career Activities as a Counseling Psychologist

I consider myself fortunate to have had the opportunity to explore the career paths and opportunities of a counseling psychologist. I have found the doctoral degree in counseling psychology to open doors to a varied, diverse, outstanding, and highly rewarding career. I began my career as a university counseling center psychologist at Colorado State University (CSU), where I also held an assistant professorship in the Psychology Department. I taught graduate courses in the doctoral program in counseling psychology and also supervised doctoral practicum and interns. In addition, I provided individual, group, and relationship psychotherapy to university students. I consulted with faculty and staff, served as advisor for student organizations, and conducted an ethnic minority needs assessment for the vice president of student affairs, Dr. Jim Banning.

I also provided numerous workshops on topics such as stress management, test-taking skills, communication skills, date rape, and death and dying. I had wonderful mentoring from the director of the Counseling

Center, Dr. Donna McKinley, and from the head of the Psychology Department, Dr. Richard Suinn. My graduate school peer, Anna Gonzalez (now Sorensen), took a job on the faculty at CSU a year after I was there. The mutual peer support (personal and professional) we provided each other throughout graduate school and our early career was invaluable. That support continues in our lives to this day.

After four years at CSU, during which time I became training director of the APA-accredited training program, I took a similar position at The University of Texas at Austin, where I did virtually the same kind of work for an additional nine years. Director Dr. David Drum was also a kind and supportive mentor; I met colleagues and peers who have become lifelong friends.

My life partner, Jim H. Miller, moved with me from Austin, Texas, to Fort Collins, Colorado, where we married in 1980. He took a large cut in salary to support the prioritization of my career. After four years, we moved back to Texas, as we considered it was "his turn" to prioritize his career. We have alternated in prioritizing each other's goals, reflective of a very long-term and mutually supportive relationship. Jim was a school principal, and he eventually took early retirement and obtained a second master's degree, this time in social work.

Since 1991, I have been in full-time independent practice, when Jim and I went into practice together. Although I had considered exploring an administrative role as director of a university counseling center, I decided to try independent practice; I had a small part-time practice an evening or two a week during my university counseling center years. I found that I love full-time independent practice. In addition to providing individual, group, and relationship psychotherapy, I have at times provided assessments for individuals entering various careers (e.g., police work, religious service). I have served as an expert witness in civil court on such issues as sexual harassment, workplace discrimination, sexual assault, and therapist violations (e.g., therapist-client sexual violations). I have provided consultation for various businesses, agencies, and nonprofit organizations regarding personnel issues and conflict resolution and have provided leadership and other skills training as well. I have been invited to serve as an instructor at various universities, but I have not had time to prioritize that activity. Instead, I have given talks to various classes each semester and have served as a visiting professor for brief periods. I provide workshop and keynote presentations to various organizations and universities. At the time, independent practice was much more lucrative financially than university counseling center work. Counseling center salaries have increased in the past few years; the gap between independent practice income and income in other settings may no longer exist.

Scholarship Activities

Although both my counseling center work and my independent practice are considered applied positions, and neither has required me to publish, I have served as author and editor, and I have published extensively. I am coauthor of three books, including five editions of *Ethics in Psychotherapy and Counseling* (Pope & Vasquez, 2016), *How to Survive and Thrive as a Therapist* (Pope & Vasquez, 2005), and *APA Ethics Code Commentary and Case Illustrations* (Campbell, Vasquez, Behnke, & Kinscherff, 2010). I have published more than 80 journal articles and book chapters and served on the editorial boards of 10 journals. I have met some of my coauthors during leadership activities. For example, while serving on the APA Ethics Committee in the mid-1980s, I met Ken Pope, who was also serving at that time. We developed a copresenter, coauthor relationship that continues to this day.

I enjoy the role of scholar and consider my writing and conference presentation activities to be part of my passion for lifelong learning. Most doctoral programs in counseling psychology produce *scientist-practitioners* who have an identity as both scientist (or scholar, or researcher) and practitioner. I write in the areas of professional ethics, psychology of women, multicultural psychology, leadership and supervision, and training. I am invited to provide keynote addresses, workshops, seminars, and other presentations at commencement services, in state and national conferences, and for various groups across the country on topics in those related areas.

Other Leadership Activities

I began this piece describing my role as president of the APA. Leadership service is a professional activity that I enjoy very much. In addition to roles I mentioned previously, I have served in various leadership roles in the APA, including as president of Division 17, Society of Counseling Psychology, and of APA Division 35, Society for the Psychology of Women. I was also elected to serve as the 2006 president of the Texas Psychological Association. My experience in initiating new, major projects include cofounding (with Rosie Phillips Bingham, Derald Wing Sue, and Lisa Porsche) the National Multicultural Conference and Summit in 1999 (now held every two years); APA Division 45, Society for the Psychological Study of Culture, Ethnicity and Race, for which I served as the first council representative; and APA Division 56, Trauma Psychology, for which I served as the first treasurer. I also provided leadership on the APA board of directors.

I have served on various task forces that have addressed difficult and challenging issues in psychology, such as the APA Council of Representatives Task Force Report on the World Conference Against Racism (2004–2005); the APA Task Force on the Revision of the Model Licensing Act, chair (2006–2010); the APA Implementation Work Group, chair (2014); and the APA Commission on Ethics Processes, cochair (2016). I have been fortunate to observe the conflict resolution skills of several colleagues, such as Sandy Shullman, Rosie Phillips Bingham, Linda Forrest, and many others. Learning to listen and communicate to increase understanding (as opposed to "winning"), as well as "standing still" in the face of difficult—at times cruel—treatment, allow for the possibility of moving a difficult dialogue or challenging conversation to a different, productive level. Learning to be assertive in a "hearable" way is part of that skill set.

Recommendations From Lessons Learned

Perhaps one of the most important lessons I have learned is that one develops confidence largely as a result of risk-taking. Taking risks to pursue goals, such as developing more skills, obtaining credentials, or applying for leadership positions, are important strategies that can result in the development of confidence, even if those risks are not always effective. To take risks, one must be willing to face and transcend fear and to move through the anxiety involved.

Acquisition of credentials and special skill development can help us set career goals, manage time and resources, find and provide mentorship, and balance family and work life. Ongoing assessment of skills that may be needed is an important goal to continue to develop one's career.

Persistence is an important variable that determines success and achievement. Knowing when to persist and when to adjust goals and expectations is an important, evolving skill. Only those who persist make progress, but at times, unattainable goals or toxic environments may lead to depression, anxiety, and despair (Vasquez & Daniel, 2010). Work hard, and be as prepared as possible for tasks and responsibilities.

It is important to remember that mistakes are a part of life. The fear of confirming negative stereotypes can result in shame and embarrassment when we make mistakes; a goal is to correct what we can, learn from the mistake, and move on, without allowing mistakes to define us. Knowing how to transform hurt, pain, and rejection into positive, constructive energy is another important skill to develop.

Engage in self-care. You are the only person who can ensure that you prioritize exercise, which can help with stress, anxiety, and depression. Eat healthily, and work on maintaining a good balance of work, rest, and leisure activities.

Effective communication, an aspect of "emotional intelligence," involves the skills of clear communication, the ability to be assertive in a "hearable" manner, and the maintenance of civility, even in the face of challenges.

Nurture and maintain relationships. Seek and provide mentorship. It is gratifying to engage in mentoring the next generations. We have achieved what we have because earlier generations of men and women fought hard to make things better so that we all today have more opportunity than those who came before us. Do not necessarily "write off" individuals with whom you disagree or who engage in microaggressions. I have found that most everyone is capable of growth and change, and over time, someone with whom you once disagreed about a topic may be a partner or ally in another context.

Engage in advocacy for the promotion of the profession, as well as for social justice. The profession of psychology is a great foundation to make contributions to society. Application of the knowledge, values, and principles of psychology can help promote quality in the lives of individuals, families, and groups.

The Importance of Family Relationships

I want to acknowledge my family, including my late father, Joe Vasquez Jr., who was very loving and validating, and my incredible role model, Ofelia Vasquez, who has accomplished so much, most recently the founding of the Centro Cultural Hispano de San Marcos; the museum part of the Centro was named after her in 2015, at its four-year anniversary. Both of my parents had only elementary educations, yet they strongly encouraged all of us to achieve as much as possible. I have six younger, amazing siblings and I am proud of them all. As I said earlier, I was lucky to grow up in a community where I felt "held" and supported at a substantial level, emotionally. I am so appreciative that my mother has created a literal structure so that others may experience that as well.

I want to acknowledge my spouse, Jim H. Miller, former school principal who became a clinical social worker—we were in business together for 25 years! Not only has he been very supportive and served as a significant and helpful consultant to me, but he keeps me balanced by helping me have fun and enjoy life! He makes me laugh. I just feel tremendously lucky. His daughter, Cecilia, a very smart and effective school teacher, has taught me much about how to deal with reconstituted families, and I am so grateful for the love and connections among us.

My professional journey as a psychologist has been rich, stimulating, and rewarding at many levels. I am so appreciative to my spouse, family, and friends for the support I have had throughout. I feel very fortunate to have been highly productive in my psychotherapy and consulting work, my scholarship, and my leadership activities. I have received over 40 honors, awards, and recognitions for activities and contributions that I have loved. I have had a wonderful career!

I want to thank all of those who have become virtual family members over the years; sometimes even those whose paths have crossed briefly have provided a wonderful connection that sustains. I hope it is mutual.

> I slept and dreamt that life was joy. I awoke and saw that life was service.
> I acted and behold, service was joy.

> — Rabindranath Tagore (Radice, 2005)

References

American Psychological Association, Presidential Task Force on Educational Disparities. (2012). *Ethnic and racial disparities in education: Psychology's contributions to understanding and reducing disparities.* Washington, DC: Author. Retrieved from http://www.apa.org/ed/resources/racial-disparities.aspx

American Psychological Association, Presidential Task Force on Immigration. (2012). *Crossroads: The psychology of immigration in the new century.* Washington, DC: Author. Retrieved from http://www.apa.org/topics/immigration/report.aspx

American Psychological Association, Presidential Task Force on Preventing Discrimination and Promoting Diversity. (2012). *Dual pathways to a better America: Preventing discrimination and promoting diversity.* Washington, DC: Author. Retrieved from http://www.apa.org/pubs/info/reports/promoting-diversity.aspx

Campbell, L., Vasquez, M. J. T., Behnke, S., & Kinscherff, R. (2010). *APA ethics code commentary and case illustrations.* Washington, DC: American Psychological Association.

Cheung, F. M., & Halpern, D. F. (2010). Women at the top: Powerful leaders define success as work + family in a culture of gender. *American Psychologist, 65,* 182–193. doi:10.1037/a0017309

Gomez, M. J., Fassinger, R. E., Prosser, J., Cooke, K., Mejia, B., & Luna, J. (2001). Voces abriendo caminos [Voices forging paths]: A qualitative study of the career development of notable Latinas. *Journal of Counseling Psychology, 48,* 286–300. doi:10.1037/0022-0167.48.3.286

Oliver, M. (1992). *New and selected poems: Volume one.* Boston, MA: Beacon Press.

Pope, K., & Vasquez, M. J. T. (2005). *How to survive and thrive as a therapist: Information, ideas and resources for psychologists in practice.* Washington, DC: American Psychological Association.

Pope, K., & Vasquez, M. J. T. (2016). *Ethics in psychotherapy and counseling: A practical guide* (5th ed.). New York, NY: Wiley.

Radice, W. (Ed. & Trans.). (2005). *Rabindranath Tagore selected poems.* New York, NY: Penguin Books.

Vasquez, M. J. T., & Daniel, J. H. (2010). Women of color as mentors. In C. A. Rayburn, F. L., Denmark, M. E. Reuder, & A. M. Austria (Eds.), *A handbook for women mentors: Transcending barriers of stereotype, race and ethnicity* (pp. 173–188). New York, NY: Praeger.

14

Common Themes of Courage, Innovation, and Risk-Taking

By Frederic P. Bemak and Robert K. Conyne

Writing this book was both a labor and a passion. Both of us (Fred and Bob) feel deeply committed to creating the highest quality training and clinical practice for psychologists and counselors, to challenge social injustices, construct new methodologies, and advocate for organizational change as a means to improve how and what we do professionally. For each of us, this has been an aim for our entire professional careers.

I (Fred) began my career as an Upward Bound summer counselor working with low-income, high-risk youth. Seven years later, I was the director of that Upward Bound program in a position as one of the youngest (if not youngest) directors of a federally funded Upward Bound Program in the country, having seven years of experience getting a firsthand look at the devastating effects of poverty, discrimination, racism, and social injustice. The Upward Bound experience, combined with national consultation and training throughout the United States and international work throughout the globe, further exposed me to human suffering, injustice, marginalization, bigotry, and hatred, and provided the foundation for my life's work through psychology and counseling. The result has been a lifelong quest to better understand and improve the human condition through work in the public sector, in universities, and in over 55 countries as a consultant, trainer, and invited presenter.

I (Bob) have been swimming upstream in my personal and professional journey these many decades. Growing up in the remote and impoverished North Country of upstate New York, flush against the Quebec-Vermont border, in a family that didn't enjoy many resources, I learned early to appreciate the underdog role and to value the importance of hard work and good fortune in life. Buoyed by undergraduate scholarships and graduate fellowships and internships, upon graduation I was able to enter the counseling and psychology professions. I felt graced and had a passion for helping to develop underemphasized directions that I had concluded (fueled by my study of social and public science at Syracuse University and community psychology at Purdue University and a postdoctoral internship at University of California, Berkeley) were important: group work, consultation, prevention, ecology, and social justice. The "long and winding road" I've been traveling has required finding like-minded souls (such as Fred) and supportive university working environments and professional associations to persistently challenge the professional status quo through teaching, training, consultation, research, and scholarly production to embrace not only personal change but also system change. This book is a part of that overall effort, where authors share their own remarkable personal and professional stories in pursuing courageous change.

Indeed, for this book, we carefully selected well-known leaders in psychology and counseling to describe their lives. Each person we identified has been in leadership roles that involved taking chances, challenging traditional thinking, and improving the practice and service in their professional domains. Contributing authors included deans, vice provosts, department chairs, American Psychological Association presidents, American Psychological Association and American Counseling Association division presidents, winners of significant national awards, a senior-level national politician, and individuals assuming high-profile national positions that challenged mainstream practices they believed were detrimental and/or created barriers to high-quality training and practice. It is an honor to have such an esteemed group of colleagues collectively sharing their experiences and describing their life's journeys and hearing how they utilized their talents and skills in ways that were innovative, courageous, and risky in order to significantly improve their profession and the world around them.

Because each author in this book is well-known in his or her professional circles, we were particularly interested in how each of them handled and incorporated three dimensions into their careers, that is, possessing courage, taking risks, and being innovative. We believe these three dimensions are especially important in creating change, in advocating, in steadfastly fighting for social justice, and in improving how we train and practice as psychologists and counselors. A number of the contributing authors describe their unwavering determination as leaders in the context of great resistance and rejection of their ideas and vision. At other times, they describe the importance of using their skills to garner support for change and innovation. Regardless, each contributing author speaks to how and where courage, risk-taking, and innovation were important components in their journeys and the issues that came into play as they manifested these qualities.

Some Shared Themes in Courage, Innovation, and Risk-Taking

First, Your Turn: Themes You Have Identified in the Chapters

As we read the moving stories of the 12 contributors, a number of common themes begin to emerge. Before reading our discussion of them, take a moment to reflect on these stories and see if you can identify up to five common themes. List and describe them here:

Theme 1:

Theme 2:

Theme 3:

Theme 4:

Theme 5:

Now, Our Turn: See How "Your" Themes and "Ours" May Connect

Clear Sense of Self

One overarching theme was that taking risks, having courage, and being innovative in leadership roles were intensely personal endeavors that required a very clear sense of oneself and an ability to maintain vision and persevere even with strong "pushback" and rejection of one's ideas and values. DeLeon (note: all quotations of DeLeon are contained in the DeLeon and Cassidy Chapter 10) shared that it is important to keep your "ultimate objectives in mind" without regard to popularity. Similarly, Holcomb-McCoy commented on the importance of introspection and an acute self-awareness that many of the authors talked about as essential in risk-taking leadership roles. She said, "Growth requires more learning and a willingness to admit one's shortcomings." Chung added how important it is to not betray who you are as a person, while Espelage noted the significance to "hold tight to your values and do not back down when faced with adversity or resistance." Marsella's recommendation—"You cannot be anything other than your unique self. Know it and treasure it"—nicely summarizes the importance of having a solid sense of self.

Learning From Mistakes

Poignantly, many of the authors addressed the critical need to embrace mistakes, failure, and resistance when one takes risks and promotes change. Arrigo warns others that, "preparation for failure is essential in order to continue," while Vasquez shares how making mistakes is simply a part of life. DeLeon goes even further, indicating that, "To succeed, one must be willing to fail and to learn from those 'mistakes.'" Generally, the authors believed that risk-taking and mistakes go hand in hand, with a key element being to benefit from lessons learned rather than to lose one's hope, vision, and passion for innovation and risk-taking.

Personal Strength

The reality of taking risks and being innovative is further complicated by feelings of being alone in the work. Many of the authors talked about being by themselves with their ideas and vision when they challenged established contemporary thought or practice. Marsella spoke of how at times it was scary to be unaccompanied and unsupported with his ideas and vision as he promoted new ideas and challenged mainstream theory and practice, yet even so he maintained the focus and courage to continue, while Espelage talked about doing "scary things" even when there was no guarantee of success. As a leader in the counseling field, Torres-Rivera shared never to assume that people understand you, while DeLeon talked about his loneliness in a career as a senior-level political figure and how to manage times of isolation.

Social Support

In balancing the alienation of being a leader who takes risks and is innovative, there was consensus among the authors that having social support was essential. Bowman describes how she lacked support during parts of her training and professional career, which led her to understand the importance of being supportive of her own students and faculty. Others, like Vasquez, Chung, and Horne, spoke about the significance of family and extended family, while Prilleltensky, Chin, Holcomb-McCoy, Chung, and others spoke about the critical need for collegial support. Many of the authors beautifully described how essential it was to have others who guided, acknowledged, mentored, and supported their work, providing sustenance as they took professional risks and confronted ways of training and practicing that were deeply embedded in the traditions of the profession.

Passion and Commitment

Many of the authors identified the passion for their work as vital in counteracting the estrangement from others. Several of the authors transformed their passion into a driving force that became an important quality in their leadership and helped them stay on the path to promoting positive change and growth. Passion and commitment were identified as key factors in being courageous and innovative and in taking risks. Chin wrote, "I have found my sources of strength from my drive and passion to fix that which is broken," while Marsella described how he was motivated to be courageous, stating, "I did not hesitate for most of my life to condemn injustice, to denounce war, and to be a voice for the voiceless." Torres-Rivera speaks about his lesson from the maternal side of his family that gave him courage: "The words of my mother and grandmother echoed in my head, 'lo que mata, engorda,' which means what does not kill you will make you stronger." Similarly, Vasquez, Espelage, Arrigo, Holcomb-McCoy, and others noted their commitment to a higher ethical standard and strong motivation to improve the lives of others, which was highlighted throughout their work and careers.

Multicultural Differences

Several of the authors spoke about how their race, ethnicity, and gender were important in defining both who they were personally and professionally. Bowman shared her moving life story of finding her identity as a psychologist through culture and feminist principles, which have remained an important foundation for her work and worldview. Chin eloquently portrayed her balance of integrating Eastern and Western cultures and the importance of both being a woman and a woman of color, with challenges about being Chinese helping her to gain and sustain courage and become a risk taker. Marsella described the influence of being an immigrant and the impact on his development and connection with the world, while Espelage spoke to the impact of seeing and experiencing women being treated differently than men, helping to shape who she is as a person and psychologist. Prilleltensky had a different experience; living in five countries and speaking three languages fluently exposed him to diverse cultures and social policies so that the movement between countries and cultures helped deepen his ideas and perspectives. These authors and others, each with their own unique backgrounds as people of color, women, and immigrants, beautifully described their journeys as psychologists and counselors, who, through their experiences, developed their own identities as leaders who stood out from the crowd with courage and the confidence to introduce new ideas and take risks.

Socioeconomic Forces

Another interesting theme was that 7 of the 12 authors described their childhood backgrounds as those of being raised in poor, working-class, and/or immigrant families, which became a driving force in their own pursuit of being successful and creating positive and meaningful change. In their description of their earlier lives, the seven authors movingly described the impact and influence of these roots on developing their sense of self and their relationship to the world. Torres-Rivera talked about how his upbringing in a public housing project forced him to "become an adult before I understood what being a child meant." Chung explained how he had to learn to be resourceful, independent, and self-driven, all qualities that he cherishes today. Marsella attributes his focus on diversity to "the profound differences I was compelled to negotiate" regarding his immigrant families' adaptation to the new and strange culture when they resettled in the United States in Cleveland, Ohio. It was clear in the majority of the stories that the authors' family roots strongly shaped their personhood and who they became as professionals and individuals. (Please note that although 7 of the 12 authors shared the influence of their poor, working-class, and/or immigrant family's childhood on their carrying courage, being innovative, and taking professional risks, this was not a question that was specifically asked of the authors as they developed their chapters and thus may also have impacted some of the other five authors.)

Additional Themes

A number of other themes were raised by the authors that were significant as they related to their leadership and qualities of courage, risk-taking, and innovation. Espelage, Horne, Prilleltensky, Torres-Rivera, DeLeon, and others shared about the importance of patience, delayed gratification, hard work, and persistence. Holcomb-McCoy emphasized how one should not fear change and should grow to trust one's instincts. Arrigo, Vasquez, Chung, Bowman, and others talked about the importance of embracing failure, mistakes, and challenges as learning opportunities rather than experiences to diminish one's passion, vision, courage, and creativity. Horne wrote about how he transformed risk-taking to become normative, observing, "Risk-taking would be to do 'business as usual'." Marsella described his experience of being liberated when he gave himself permission to move beyond an acceptance of one worldview. Many of the authors shared about maintaining an important equilibrium of work with family and self-care, such as Bowman's discussion of the value of including personally unique and enjoyable activities in one's life, such as baking or making handcrafts. Vasquez reminded us to maintain an ethical stance in our work and be assertive "in a hearable way," while Horne shared with us his belief about "reasonable risk-taking." Arrigo described her constant search for "something more," which was complemented by Espelage's recommendation to get out of our comfort zones. DeLeon encouraged us to work with the next generation to get them excited about their potential, rather than focusing on specific solutions.

In Summation: Your Last Turn

You may recall from Chapter 1 that we suggested five discussion questions and encouraged you to apply them to the contributions of each of the authors. Now that you have read all of the stories, as well as this final chapter, we ask you to return to those questions and reflect on how they may pertain, across-the-board, when considering all 12 of the authors' stories. If you have the opportunity to discuss your reflections with a partner, we strongly encourage you to do so.

Book Discussion Questions

1. Overall, identify three lessons you can take from the professional journeys of all 12 authors.

2. What seem to be "key" factors supporting the authors' progress toward becoming courageous?

3. How did the professional journeys of these authors include courage, risk-taking, or innovation—or all three?

4. Indicate any connections between your journey so far and those of the 12 authors.

5. Suppose you were to meet with these authors. What questions would you ask them, and what would you most like to discuss with them?

This book is filled with the richness of the experience and life journeys of 12 highly accomplished psychologists and counselors. We began the book with an aim to illuminate how major figures in psychology and counseling embraced courage, innovation, and risk-taking in their lives and professional careers. The authors tell us intimate personal stories and share deeply moving insights about how they did what they did and how they achieved what they achieved while incorporating courage, innovation, and risk-taking. The themes and lessons learned are a treasure trove. We hope you enjoy and learn from these magnificent role models for your continued development, for our profession, and for our world.

About the Editors

Frederic P. Bemak is a professor and academic program coordinator of the Counseling and Development Program and director and cofounder of the Diversity Research and Action Center at George Mason University. He is also the founder and director of Counselors Without Borders. Fred began his career working in Upward Bound, where he later became the director, providing a foundation for his lifetime work in cross-cultural psychology. He has held administrative faculty positions at Johns Hopkins University and The Ohio State University. Fred has over 100 publications in professional journals and book chapters, and he has coauthored five books. He has provided extensive consultation and training with governments and organizations throughout the United States and internationally in over 55 countries. Fred has received three Fulbright Scholarships to work in Brazil, Scotland, and Turkey, been a World Rehabilitation Fund International Exchange of Experts fellow in India, and received a Kellogg International fellow award to work and study throughout Latin America and the Caribbean. He held visiting faculty appointments at the Federal University of Rio Grande do Sul in Brazil, University of Queensland in Australia, Universidad Iberoamericana in Mexico City, and the National Taiwan Normal University in Taiwan. Fred is an invited speaker at numerous national and international forums and has received a number of awards, including the American Counseling Association Kitty Cole Human Rights Award and the American Counseling Association Gilbert and Kathleen Wrenn Award for a Humanitarian and Caring Person. He is past president of Counselors for Social Justice and a fellow of both the American Psychological Association and the American Counseling Association as well as the recipient of an Honorary Professorship at Amity University in India.

Robert K. Conyne, PhD, is Professor Emeritus in Counseling at the University of Cincinnati, a licensed psychologist, and a licensed professional clinical counselor. He compiled 42 years of professional experience as a professor, department head, program director, counseling center psychologist, and student affairs administrator. Among Bob's many awards are the following: fellow of the American Psychological Association (APA; Divisions 13, 17, and 49), the American Counseling Association (ACA), and the Association for Specialists in Group Work (ASGW); endowed chair and distinguished professor (Seattle University); Eminent Career Award (ASGW); Lifetime Achievement Award in Prevention from the APA; Distinguished Alumni Award of Distinction from Purdue University; Soros International Scholar to Kyrgyzstan; and Fulbright Senior Scholar Specialist (Chulalongkorn University, Thailand). He served as second editor of *The Journal for Specialists in Group Work* (1979–1985) and as president of the ASGW (1995–1996) and the Society of Group Psychology and Group Psychotherapy of APA (2009–2010). Bob developed the ACA Emerging Leaders program, which he led for the first six years. In recent years, he has worked extensively providing preventive mental health services and administrative consultation to U.S. military personnel and their families. He has produced well over 200 scholarly publications and presentations, including 22 books in his areas of expertise (group work, prevention, and ecological counseling), and he has provided broad international consultation in these areas. Bob and Fred Bemak have pursued joint interests in group work, international relations, social justice, and the study of professional journeys.

About the Contributors

Jean Maria Arrigo is an independent social psychologist and oral historian. Her doctoral dissertation (Claremont Graduate University, 1998) and later studies explored epistemology and ethics of military and political intelligence. To advance moral discourse, she created theater performances and brought together social scientists, ethicists, and military intelligence professionals in numerous conferences, symposia, projects, and publications. A Rockefeller Fellowship on Violence and Culture at the Virginia Foundation for the Humanities and Public Policy (2001) and a visiting scholar position at the University of Texas Institute of Medical Humanities in Galveston (2003) fostered these activities. Among her archival efforts, Jean Maria established the Oral History Series on Ethics of Intelligence and Weapons Development at The Bancroft Library, University of California, Berkeley; the Intelligence Ethics Collection at Hoover Institution Archives, Stanford University; and the American Psychological Association (APA) Psychological Ethics and National Security (PENS) Debate Collection at the Duke University Human Rights Archive. Her organizational service includes APA PENS Task Force member (2005), International Intelligence Ethics Association conference chair (2005–2007), Southwest Oral History Association president (2007), Psychologists for Social Responsibility Steering Committee member (2010–2013), APA Council of Representatives member (2014–2016), and Coalition for an Ethical Psychology military liaison (2007–present). The American Association for the Advancement of Science acknowledged Jean Maria's contribution to psychological ethics in national security with its Scientific Freedom and Responsibility Award in 2015.

Prior to psychology, Jean Maria studied mathematics (BA, University of California, Berkeley, Phi Beta Kappa, 1966; MA, University of California, San Diego, 1969) and also taught mathematics part time in San Diego colleges for 11 years. Her comanagement of a vegetable farm in Upstate New York (1974–1976), development of a storytelling troupe in San Diego

(1978–1992), and escort of indigenous human rights leaders in Guatemala (1986) also inform her ventures as a psychologist.

Sharon L. Bowman, PhD, HSPP, ABPP, LMHC, is professor and chair in the Department of Counseling Psychology, Social Psychology and Counseling at Ball State University. She is also a psychologist in private practice in Muncie, Indiana. She earned her doctoral degree from Southern Illinois University Carbondale. Her internship was completed in the counseling center at the University of Delaware. Sharon's research and clinical interests are in supervision, mentoring and training, disaster psychology, and broadly defined issues of diversity. When not reading emails, she is often found either testing a new recipe in her kitchen or playing with one of her many fountain pens.

Omni Cassidy received her BA in psychology with a minor in women and gender studies from Washington University in St. Louis in 2010. She matriculated into the Clinical Psychology dual-track program at the Uniformed Services University of the Health Sciences in Bethesda, Maryland, in 2012. As an undergraduate, Omni volunteered with the Weight Management and Eating Disorders Program. She also worked as an intern at the Jackson Heart Study in Jackson, Mississippi, investigating African Americans with type 2 diabetes. Before beginning her graduate studies, she worked as a research assistant at the National Institutes of Health and the Uniformed Services University of the Health Sciences on a study examining the effect of interpersonal psychotherapy on the prevention of excess weight gain in adolescent girls and also coordinated a pilot study to adapt interpersonal psychotherapy to be culturally appropriate in preventing excess weight gain in racial/ethnic minority groups. Omni is interested in factors that might promote disordered eating and excessive weight gain in African American youth and how such research may be used to inform policy.

Jean Lau Chin, EdD, ABPP, is a professor at Adelphi University in New York. She is distinguished as an educator, administrator, clinician, and scholar. Jean is a former dean of Adelphi University and Alliant International University, former executive director of South Cove Community Health Center and Thom Child Guidance Center. Currently, her scholarship is on global and diverse leadership, which includes examining minority issues in regard to women and ethnicity. Jean's publications and talks are wide-ranging. She coauthored *Diversity and Leadership* (SAGE, 2015) and was one of the editors of *Women and Leadership: Transforming Visions and Diverse Voices* (Wiley-Blackwell, 2007). Jean is a Fulbright Specialist on Gender and Leadership Studies and was one of the first Asian Americans to be licensed as a psychologist both in Massachusetts and nationally. For many years, she has trained psychologists and health care professionals in the diagnosis and treatment of mental health issues. Jean has consulted widely and played a major role in developing culturally competent training and service delivery models for diverse and underserved populations. She has held leadership roles on national, state, and local boards, and is currently chair of the Council Leadership Team and on the board of directors of the American Psychological Association (APA), president-elect of the International Council of Psychologists, and council representative of the New York State Psychological Association. She is past president of several APA divisions, including International Psychology. In these roles, she has promoted policies advancing psychology, women's issues, and access to care, and has worked to reduce health disparities.

Y. Barry Chung received his PhD in counseling psychology from the University of Illinois at Urbana-Champaign. He is currently associate dean for graduate studies in the School of Education and professor of counseling psychology at Indiana University Bloomington. Barry's research interests include career development, multicultural counseling, and sexual orientation issues. He has presented and published widely on these topics. He was appointed to nine journal editorial boards internationally and was executive editor of the American Psychological Association's (APA) Division 44 Book Series. Barry was president of the National Career Development Association from 2006 to 2007 and the Society of Counseling Psychology from 2011 to 2012. He has served on APA's Board of Educational Affairs (2007–2009), the Board for the Advancement of Psychology in the Public Interest (2010–2012), and the Membership Board (2013–2015). Barry currently serves on the APA Finance Committee and Council of Representatives, and he is president-elect of the Council of Counseling Psychology Training Programs. He is a fellow of APA (Divisions 17, 44, and 45), the Asian American Psychological Association, and the National Career Development Association.

Patrick H. DeLeon is a distinguished professor at the Uniformed Services University of the Health Sciences (U.S. Department of Defense) in the School of Nursing and the School of Medicine. He was elected to the Institute of Medicine of the National Academies of Science in 2008 and served as president of the American Psychological Association (APA) in 2000. For over 38 years, Patrick was on the staff of U.S. Senator Daniel K. Inouye (D-Hawaii) and retired as chief of staff. He has received numerous national awards, including the Order of Military Medical Merit; Distinguished Service Medal, Uniformed Services University of the Health Sciences; National League for Nursing, Council for Nursing Centers, First Public Policy Award; Sigma Theta Tau, Inc., International Honor Society of

Nursing, First Public Service Award; Ruth Knee/Milton Wittman Award for Outstanding Achievement in Health/Mental Health Policy, National Association of Social Workers; Delta Omega Honor Society Award for Outstanding Alumnus from a School of Public Health; APA Outstanding Lifetime Contributions to Psychology Award; American Psychological Foundation Gold Medal for Lifetime Achievement in the Practice of Psychology; and Distinguished Alumni Award, University of Hawaii. Patrick has been awarded three honorary degrees. He is currently the editor of *Psychological Services* and associate editor of the *American Psychologist*. He has authored more than 200 publications.

Dorothy L. Espelage, PhD, is a professor of psychology at the University of Florida. She is a recipient of the American Psychological Association (APA) Lifetime Achievement Award in Prevention Science and the 2016 APA Award for Distinguished Contributions to Research in Public Policy. Dorothy is a fellow of Association for Psychological Science, APA, and American Education Research Association. She earned her PhD in counseling psychology from Indiana University in 1997. Over the last 20 years, Dorothy has authored more than 140 peer-reviewed articles, 6 edited books, and 30 chapters on bullying, homophobic teasing, sexual harassment, dating violence, and gang violence. Her research focuses on translating empirical findings into prevention and intervention programming, and she has secured $6.5 million of external funding. Dorothy advises members of Congress on legislation regarding the prevention of bullying. She conducts regular webinars for the Centers for Disease Control and Prevention (CDC), the National Institutes of Health (NIH), and the National Institute of Justice (NIJ) to disseminate research. She just completed a CDC-funded study regarding reducing aggression that included a randomized clinical trial of a social-emotional learning prevention program in 36 middle schools. The NIJ is providing funding for Dorothy to track these middle school students to examine whether the effects remain as the students navigate the challenges of high school. The CDC is funding another randomized control trial of this program in comparison to a gender-enhanced social-emotional program in 28 Illinois middle schools. Dorothy just received a large, five-year grant from the NIJ to prevent bullying and promote school safety in high schools. In addition, she is principal investigator on a CDC-funded grant to evaluate a youth suicide prevention program on sexual violence outcomes in 24 Colorado high schools. Dorothy authored a 2011 White House Brief on bullying among LGBTQ youth and attended the White House Conference in 2011. She has been a consultant on the stopbullying.gov website and for the national antibullying campaign, sponsored by the Health Resources and

Services Administration (HRSA) of the U.S. Department of Health and Human Services (HHS). Dorothy has presented multiple times at the Federal Partnership to End Bullying Summit and Conference. She is a consultant to the National Institutes of Health Pathways to Prevention initiative to address bullying and youth suicide. Dorothy has appeared on many television news and talk shows, including *The Today Show, CNN, CBS Evening News, The Oprah Winfrey Show,* and *Anderson Cooper 360,* and she has been quoted in the national print press, including *Time, USA Today, People, The Boston Globe,* and *The Wall Street Journal.*

Cheryl Holcomb-McCoy, PhD, is dean of the School of Education at American University in Washington, DC. Previously, she was vice provost of faculty affairs and professor of counseling and human development at Johns Hopkins University (JHU). Before working at JHU, Cheryl held appointments as vice dean of academic affairs at JHU's School of Education and associate professor of counselor education at the University of Maryland, College Park. She earned a PhD in counseling and educational development from the University of North Carolina at Greensboro and an MEd in school counseling and a BS in early childhood education from the University of Virginia. Her areas of research specialization include the measurement of multicultural self-efficacy in school counseling and the examination of school counselors' influence on low-income students' college and career readiness. Cheryl is the author of the best-selling book, *School Counseling to Close the Achievement Gap: A Social Justice Framework for Success* (Corwin, 2007) and is associate editor of the *Journal of Counseling & Development.* She is an ACA fellow and a founding member of the National Consortium for School Counseling and Postsecondary Success. In 2014, Cheryl was selected to speak at a White House summit titled, *College Opportunity Agenda: Strengthening School Counseling and College Advising,* held at the Harvard Graduate School of Education.

Arthur M. (Andy) Horne completed his undergraduate degree in English education and journalism in 1965 and his master's degree in counseling in 1967 at the University of Florida. He obtained his PhD at Southern Illinois University in 1971. Andy taught at Indiana State University from 1971 to 1989, during which time he served as a member of the faculty in the Department of Counseling and as director of training for the Counseling Psychology Program, which is accredited by the American Psychological Association (APA). Andy also was a member of the Marriage and Family Therapy Program, which is accredited by the American Association for Marriage and Family Therapy. In 1984, he taught with the Boston University Overseas Program in Europe. In 1989, Andy accepted a position at the

University of Georgia, where he spent four years as department head and eight years as director of training for the Counseling Psychology Program, which is accredited by the APA. He also served as coordinator of a certificate program in marriage and family therapy. Andy directed the Education Policy and Evaluation Center from 2006 to 2007 and served as dean of the College of Education from 2008 to 2012.

Andy has been active in the APA, where he is a fellow of six divisions (Counseling Psychology, Family Psychology, Group Psychology and Group Psychotherapy, Psychology of Men, Child and Adolescent Psychology, and International Psychology), and the American Counseling Association, where he is a member of the Association for Specialists in Group Work (ASGW). In ASGW, he is a fellow and past president, and he is the former editor of *The Journal for Specialists in Group Work*. In the APA, he is a past president of the Division of Group Psychology and Group Psychotherapy and a past president of the Society of Counseling Psychology. He has coauthored 11 books, coedited 14 books, served on editorial boards of seven journals, and is the former editor of the *International Journal for the Advancement of Counselling*.

Andy was a research investigator of grants and contracts for three decades, including funding by the U.S. Department of Education with a focus on at-risk children, and he was the principal investigator of the Multisite Violence Prevention Project's GREAT Schools and Families program, which was designed to reduce violence in schools and was funded by the Centers for Disease Control and Prevention. Andy retired from the University of Georgia in December 2012 and has since been active with the Safe and Welcoming Schools Program, a project developed to increase school safety and improve the quality of the school culture and climate so that schools are safe and engaging for all students (http://www.coe.uga.edu/sws/). He also serves on the boards of numerous community agencies, addressing the educational and environmental needs of disadvantaged youth and their families.

Anthony J. Marsella, PhD, is an emeritus professor of psychology at the University of Hawai'i. He received his PhD in clinical psychology, with doctoral-level minors in cultural anthropology and history/philosophy of science. He is the recipient of a Fulbright Research Scholar Award from Ateneo de Manila University, Quezon City, Philippines, and a postdoctoral Culture and Mental Health Fellowship from East-West Center/SSRI in Honolulu.

Tony was appointed to the tenured faculty of the Department of Psychology at the University of Hawai'i in 1969, a position he held until he retired in

2003. In his 33 years as a professor at the University of Hawai'i, he served as director of clinical training, director of the World Health Organization Field Psychiatric Research Center for the study of severe mental disorders, director of the Disaster Management and Humanitarian Assistance Program, and senior vice president for academic affairs. During the course of his career, Tony served as a visiting professor in Australia, China, India, South Korea, and the Philippines, and also at Johns Hopkins University and Clemson University. He also was an invited lecturer to more than 25 national and international universities. From 2005 to 2008, he served as president of Psychologists for Social Responsibility.

Tony is considered a pioneer in cultural and international studies of psychology, personality, and psychopathology. He has published 21 edited and authored books and 300 book chapters, journal articles, technical reports, book reviews, and popular national and international press/media service articles, and he is the recipient of numerous research and training grants and contracts. Much of his current writing is on peace and social justice. He continues to serve on seven journal editorial boards and scientific and professional advisory committees and is senior editor of a 37-volume cultural and international psychology book series from Springer Nature. One of his frequently cited papers, "Toward a 'Global-Community Psychology'," published in the *American Psychologist* in December 1998, called for the development of a new and innovative psychology responsive to the challenges of our global era, including the internationalization of the psychology curriculum and the reduction of ethnocentric biases. Many of Tony's graduate-degree students hold notable positions in psychology.

Tony is the recipient of numerous national and international awards, including the Medal of Highest Honor from Soka University in Tokyo, Japan, for the promotion of international peace and understanding; the American Psychological Association (APA) award for Distinguished Contributions to the International Advancement of Psychology; an honorary doctorate degree, Doctoris Honoris Causa, from the University of Copenhagen, Denmark; the Columbia University Teachers College Counselors Roundtable Award for Distinguished Contributions to Peace and Social Justice; and the International Section of the APA Division of Counseling Lifetime Achievement Award.

Tony lives in Atlanta, Georgia, where he continues to lecture and write. He enjoys reading, writing, cooking, and learning about life from people and other life forms he encounters along the way.

Isaac Prilleltensky, PhD, was born in Argentina and has lived and worked in Israel, Canada, Australia, and the United States. He is a dean of education and human development at the University of Miami, the inaugural Erwin and Barbara Mautner chair in community well-being, and the vice provost for institutional culture. He has published 8 books and more than 120 articles and chapters. Isaac's interests are in the promotion of well-being in individuals, organizations, and communities, and in the integration of wellness as fairness. He is the recipient of the 2014 Lifetime Achievement Award in Prevention by the Society for Counseling Psychology, Division 17, of the American Psychological Association (APA). He is also the recipient of the 2011 Distinguished Contribution to Theory and Research Award of the Community Psychology Division of APA. In addition, Isaac received the John Kalafat Award for the Practice of Community Psychology from the same division of APA. He is leading an interdisciplinary team developing assessments and online interventions to promote interpersonal, community, occupational, psychological, physical, and economic (I COPPE) well-being. Isaac is a fellow of the APA and the American Educational Research Association. In 2002, he was a visiting fellow of the British Psychological Society. Isaac is a vegan and fitness aficionado. He speaks several languages and has given keynote addresses in 26 countries. His humor columns have been published in the *Miami Herald* and *Miami Today*. Issac's latest book is *The Laughing Guide to Well-Being: Using Humor and Science to Become Happier and Healthier* (Rowman & Littlefield, 2016).

Edil Torres-Rivera has a PhD in counseling psychology, with a concentration in multicultural counseling, from the University of Connecticut, Storrs. He is a professor at South University, Richmond, Virginia. Edil is native Puerto Rican with a career of over 20 years in counseling. This includes 12 years in the U.S. Army. His research interests are in multicultural counseling, group work, chaos theory, liberation psychology, indigenous counseling, Puerto Rican studies, identity development, and gang/prison-related behavior. Specifically, his primary research focuses on complexity and how indigenous healing techniques are a necessary ingredient when working with ethnic minority populations in the United States. Edil has additional interests in studying the implications of social injustice and oppression in counseling and psychotherapy with ethnic minorities in the United States. His community work includes consultation services to the Pyramid Lake Paiute Tribe Council in Nevada and visiting professor to the Universidad del Valle, Guatemala. He was also the director of the Graduate School of Education's School Counseling Program in Singapore.

Melba J. T. Vasquez, PhD, ABPP, is in independent practice in Austin, Texas. One of the most exciting periods in her career was when she served as president of the American Psychological Association (APA, 2011). She is the first Latina and woman of color to serve out of 120 APA presidents. Her theme for the 2011 APA convention was social justice. Her special presidential initiatives included examination of psychology's contributions to the grand challenges in society, including immigration, discrimination, and educational disparities.

Melba has provided other leadership service, including as a member of the APA board of directors and former president of the Texas Psychological Association (TPA) and Divisions 35 (Society of Psychology of Women) and 17 (Society of Counseling Psychology) of the APA. She is a cofounder of APA Division 45, Society for the Psychological Study of Ethnic Minority Issues, and of the National Multicultural Conference and Summit. Melba is a fellow of 11 divisions of the APA and a diplomate of the American Board of Professional Psychology (ABPP). She obtained her doctorate in counseling psychology from The University of Texas at Austin in 1978. Before becoming a psychologist, Melba taught middle school.

She is coauthor of five editions of *Ethics in Psychotherapy and Counseling: A Practical Guide* (with Kenneth S. Pope; Wiley, 2016). She is also coauthor of *How to Survive and Thrive as a Therapist: Information, Ideas and Resources for Psychologists in Practice* (with Kenneth S. Pope; APA, 2005) and of the APA Ethics Code Commentary and Case Illustrations. Melba has also published more than 50 book chapters and 35 journal articles in the areas of professional ethics, ethnic minority psychology, psychology of women, counseling and psychotherapy, and supervision and training. She has been honored with over 45 awards for distinguished professional contributions, career service, leadership, advocacy, and mentorship.

Melba is married to Jim H. Miller, a big supporter of her career; she very much values the full support of her friends and extended family, including her stepdaughter, her mother, and six siblings and their families. She is grateful that despite having only elementary educations, both of her parents were politically involved at the grassroots level, engaged in civil rights activities, and articulated a strong belief in and support for education. She appreciates that they guided her into productive, social justice advocacy all her life.